'CONCEAL, CREATE, CONFUSE'

'CONCEAL, CREATE, CONFUSE'

DECEPTION AS A BRITISH BATTLEFIELD
TACTIC IN THE FIRST WORLD WAR

MARTIN DAVIES

SPELLMOUNT

To Teresa, Rachael and Hannah

First published 2009

By Spellmount, an imprint of
The History Press
The Mill, Brimscombe Port
Stroud, Gloucestershire, GL5 2QG
www.thehistorypress.co.uk

British Library Cataloguing in Publication Data.
A catalogue record for this book is available from the British Library.

ISBN 978-0-7524-5273-9

Typesetting and origination by The History Press
Printed in Great Britain

Contents

List of Maps

Preface

My interest in the use of deception arose from two disparate pieces of information. The first involved the periods of silence used by the British at Gallipoli in 1915 just prior to the evacuation. The artillery, machine gunners and riflemen were under orders not to fire or move around during those periods for the three weeks before the evacuation, but as the Turks send out patrols to investigate the unusual silence they were fired on. In this way, when the troops were evacuated and the trenches truly fell silent, the Turks were reluctant to investigate, which enabled the troops to embark in safety. The other piece of information came from F. Mitchell's book on tank warfare. As a Tank Commander in the 1st Battalion, Tank Corps near the River Selle in 1918, he had witnessed the Royal Engineers constructing dummy tanks from canvas and wood, which were then strapped to the backs of mules. The two approaches, one brilliant in its simplicity, the other bordering on the ridiculous, were effective under the prevailing circumstances. From these examples it appeared that the British Army was comfortable with the use of deception but, with a few notable exceptions, the consensus has been that the British Army failed to exploit deception as a major weapon throughout the war. However, close examination has shown that this was not the case and beginning in 1914, the imagination of various officers and men was channelled into weakening enemy defences by creating illusions of attacks and concealing the real attacks so that the enemy commanders became confused as to the best deployment of their artillery, defenders and reinforcements.

As acknowledged in the photograph captions, some of the images are reproduced with the kind permission of the Royal Engineers Museum, Gillingham and I would like to thank Miss Charlotte Hughes for her assistance. For the photographs reproduced with the kind permission of the Tank Museum, Bovington I would like to thank Mr Stuart Wheeler for his assistance.

Martin Davies
Woolaston, Gloucestershire

Introduction

Hold out baits to entice the enemy.
Sun Tzu

Military deception and ruses have formed a key part of offensive and defensive operations in conflicts throughout history, as military commanders sought to gain an advantage over their enemies by any means possible. As early as 500 BC Sun Tzu, the military strategist, stated that

> All Warfare is based on deception ... Hence, when able to attack, we must seem unable. When using our forces, we must seem inactive. When we are near, we must make the enemy believe we are far away. When far away, we must make him believe we are near. Hold out baits to entice the enemy. Feign disorder, and crush him.

Over 2,000 years later, at the beginning of the nineteenth century, the military theorist, Carl von Clausewitz, concluded that 'to take the enemy by surprise ... is more or less basic to all operations for without it superiority at the decisive point is hardly conceivable.'

Although not necessarily institutionalised, battlefield deception has been used throughout history by various armies. Instances have ranged from the mythical Trojan horse at the siege of Troy to the successful feint retreat employed by William of Normandy at the Battle of Hastings (Senlac

Hill) in 1066. The aim of these ruses was to gain even a small competitive advantage which in all great games could make the difference between victory and defeat.

Deception will never overwhelm enemy defences. However, deception can confuse those defences as to the time, the place and the troops involved in offensive operations so that defences are less prepared and reinforcements poorly deployed, both of which should increase the chances of a successful offensive operation. For these reasons, deception plans target the enemy's decision-making processes at all command levels and strive to influence the actions of all military units.

Military decisions rest on discrete activities: the gathering and evaluation of intelligence, the assessment of possible actions and finally the issuing and carrying out of orders based on the final judgment. This simplified view of decision-making applies in both offensive and defensive operations. Although these activities have always existed, they were only formally recognised, explained and documented in the early 1950s, by Colonel John Boyd (1927–1997) of the United States Air Force. Boyd, who served first in the US Army Air Corps and then in the US Air Force from 1951–1975 as a fighter pilot, only ever described his theory on decision-making in a short essay and with slide presentations.[1] Today his theory is universally accepted and is used as the basis for training programmes within the military, the police and corporate businesses.

During the Korean War (1950–53), Boyd observed that the technically inferior American F-86 Sabre Jets were more than a match for the North Korean MiG-15 aircraft with a kill ratio of at least ten-to-one. Boyd concluded that during aerial combat, decisions taken were the result of the pilots going through four distinct phases, which Boyd termed Observe (O), Orientate (O), Decide (D) and Act (A) – he coined the term OODA Loop for the whole process; later generations have also called them Boyd Cycles in recognition of his work. Boyd argued that the American pilots were successful because the bubble canopy of the Sabre Jets, compared with the semi-enclosed cockpit of the MiGs, enabled them to observe more, and more quickly, than their Communist counterparts. As a consequence, the OODA Loops of the Americans exhibited a shorter cycle time, or a higher 'operational tempo', which enabled the Americans to act on observations faster than the North Koreans and consequently achieve a higher 'kill' rate.

From the specialised environment of aerial combat, it was quickly realised that all military decisions, and probably all decisions taken in life, whether taken consciously or subconsciously, had to follow the same four phases. In military terms, if intelligence could be gathered, processed and acted upon faster than the enemy, an immediate advantage would ensue. Further, as these decision-making processes existed at every level throughout an army, from the Commander-in-Chief down to the private soldier, it was important that enhanced operational tempo was present throughout. This need was one of the driving factors behind the development and equipping of the 'fighting platoons' in 1917 and was used to great effect by the British Army in 1918 to maintain pressure on the German units during the retreat throughout the Final Hundred Days.

Although General Headquarters (GHQ) and the Army Commanders during the First World War would not have recognised the term 'OODA Loop' and the individual phases, they would have recognised the decision cycle that this represented. Intelligence would have been gathered (Observe phase) and evaluated (Orientate phase), decisions would have been made regarding the intelligence (Decide phase) and finally orders would have been issued and implemented (Act phase). These decision-making processes within any army are the DNA of its chain of command and are the key elements, along with the actual offensive actions, in the successful execution of military operations. These are also the elements that deception plans target. To disrupt these processes, belligerents have consistently employed two principal approaches.

The first approach is to shorten the time taken from receipt of intelligence to the issue of orders in response. The term 'operational tempo' has been latterly applied to this approach. The speeding up of the decision-making processes results in the enemy making decisions based on 'old' intelligence as the situation has changed from that upon which his information was originally based. Throughout history, the great commanders have always recognised a developing situation on the battlefield (Observe) and immediately acted on it (Orientate, Decide, Act). This was relatively straightforward where commanders could be present on the battlefield and where chains of command were comparatively short. However, increasing operational tempo becomes more difficult as army chains of command become longer and the nature of the interactions more complex. Intelligence has to be gathered and assessed and decisions have to be made within the command chain and then communicated and implemented often by a variety of units, each with their own unique perspective on the battlefield. In the British Army, after December 1914, there was a hierarchy of command from Army down through corps, division, brigade, battalion, company, section and platoon. At each level within the chain of command, there were separate OODA Loops. Each of these Loops derived its intelligence from information (orders) disseminated to it by the command structure above it in the chain, from battlefield reports emanating from the command structures below it and locally from its own observations regarding the situation. For success, the OODA Loops had to be synchronised, which was difficult as the margin for disruption was great. As the war progressed, the British Army introduced a command structure that to a certain extent de-synchronised the OODA Loops, with the introduction of a devolved command structure on the battlefield, especially at brigade level, and with the introduction of the 'fighting platoons', which had the ability to take battlefield decisions based on local conditions. There was of course a similar vulnerability in the German Army's chain of command and this was something that the second approach to disrupting the decision-making processes tried to exploit.

The second approach, which is arguably easier to implement and achieve, was to create false intelligence and feed it into the enemy's OODA Loops. The deception was specifically targeted at the evaluation, or Orientate, phase, which would determine subsequent military actions. Although deception at first sight seemed to be aimed specifically at the Observe phase, 'letting-them-see-what-you-want-them-to-see', it was in reality targeting, in a more subtle manner, the Orientate evaluation phase so that the enemy would interpret the false intelligence 'correctly', make the 'desired' decision and take the 'desired' action. Addressing only one of the phases would weaken the effectiveness of the deception and therefore it has to be designed to influence both the Observe and Orientate phases so that subsequent enemy actions are appropriate for the 'deception intelligence' but inappropriate for the actual situation. Boyd in 1987 recognised that the Orientate phase of the OODA Loop is *the* crucial element as it dictated the end result of the decision cycle. A plethora of false intelligence could be generated, each element of which in isolation would be credible, but when evaluated together, inconsistencies would immediately discredit all the intelligence at the Orientate phase. To address both the Observe and Orientate phases in this manner means that deception plans have to be complex affairs and not simple activities conducted in isolation by various units throughout the army. This approach does assume that the enemy Orientate phase is functioning correctly and there were examples on both sides throughout the war when the Observe phase gathered intelligence which was incorrectly evaluated during the Orientate phase and resulted in serious casualties and loss of territory.

The fact that deception must target multiple phases of an OODA Loop meant that deception intelligence had to be plausible, consistent and predictable, i.e. 'logical', for the enemy's own assessment. The complexity of deception lies in the fact that the plans must deceive the enemy commanders as well as the enemy's intelligence service. The plan should be so convincing that friendly soldiers, who are not privy to the deception, must believe it and be seen to be reacting to it rather than to the actual situation. On the Western Front where raids across No-Man's-Land were commonly undertaken as a means of gathering intelligence from captured soldiers, British troops who believed the deception often told the 'truth', which gave increased credibility to the deception activities.

Military historians have frequently been dismissive of the British Army's approach to deception during the First World War. It has often simplistically associated deception with concealment (camouflage) and the deployment of dummy artefacts (canvas tanks, dummy heads). But this is a naive approach which was not systematically adopted by the British Army during the war, as this would only have targeted the Observe phase at a local level. There is clearly evidence for the deployment of canvas tanks and dummy heads and the extensive use of camouflage, but these were just indications of something happening on a much grander scale. This was summed up in the British Army's military pamphlet SS206, published in 1918, which insightfully stated, 'deception, not concealment, is the object of camouflage'. Modern military planners base their deception plans on ten maxims or principles which were identified during a study by the United States Army in 1988.[2] These principles highlighted the complexity of deception plans far beyond the simple deployment of dummy tanks and will be discussed in detail in Chapter 10. From September 1914 until August 1918, the static nature of the warfare on the Western Front and the close proximity of the enemy required something more sophisticated to mislead the Germans and the deployment of their critical reserves necessary for the all important counterattack. Plausibility, consistency and predictability require complex strategic and tactical planning as well as a disciplined implementation.

The characteristic of plausibility was satisfied if the plan, and consequently the intelligence generated by it for the consumption of the enemy, was rational. During the build-up to the Fourth Army's attack on the Somme on 1 July 1916, the Third Army also built up men and supplies and fired bombardments in their sector. General Erich von Falkenhayn, the German commander, considered the Third Army activity to be reasonable – plausible – as he believed that an attack on the British Third Army front in July 1916 was a rational act. As a consequence, Germans reserves were held behind the Third Army sector on 1 July as Falkenhayn at first believed that the Fourth Army operation was only a feint designed to draw those reserves away. Interestingly, his army commanders, General von Below and Crown Prince Rupprecht, did not agree with his assessment.

The consistency element of the deception plan demanded that all units that were involved in the deception must be observed to be reacting to it, rather than the real plan, and in a manner that was characteristic of the British Army. Before the war, each of the major protagonists had acted as official observers at each other's annual manoeuvres. As a consequence, through this and other mechanisms, they knew the behavioural patterns of each other's armies. The consistency of deception planning can again be illustrated in the build-up to the attack on 1 July 1916 where the activities of the Fourth and Third Armies were indistinguishable from each other. There was little difference in the activities of the Third and Fourth Armies in June 1916 to indicate that either or both of the armies did not mean to attack. It is essential that the deception plan and the real plan are consistent with each other. As such, a deception plan must be almost as secure as the real plan and the enemy must be made to work hard to gather the intelligence regarding it. It is vital that there are no discernible differences between real and false intelligence and all intelligence must be seen to have been gathered either as a lapse in security or as a result of clever intervention or significant effort on the part of the enemy. At no point should any obvious facilitation be made to 'feed' the enemy with deception plan intelligence. Hence the security surrounding both the real and false intelligence must be equally secure or, more dangerously, equally lax. If the latter approach was employed, which could be the case for instance when it was impossible to hide the preparations for a real attack, the enemy OODA Loops were presented with a volume of intelligence, both real and false, that swamped the Orientate phase. This stalled the loop whilst the real and false intelligence was evaluated. The aim was to confuse the enemy so that when the real offensive began, together with the supporting demonstrations, their indecisiveness would be of sufficient duration to afford a tactical advantage. The Allied landings at Suvla Bay on the Gallipoli Peninsula in August 1915 demonstrated this admirably. The Allies were only opposed by three Turkish battalions while further north at Bulair, three Turkish divisions were held in position by a feint attack by the Royal Navy. After the feint attack was exposed for what it was, the 7th and 12th (Turkish) Divisions were transferred south to bolster the defences around Suvla Bay. This deception followed Magruder's Principle, a key element of all successful deception plans, which will be discussed later.[3] The fact that the Allies failed to seize the initiative on the ground to overwhelm the initial paltry defences and gain the high ground was a basic failure of offensive operations and not of the deception plan.

The final characteristic, predictability, means that the deception plan must create a situation that the enemy can relate to, one in which they might have adopted the same tactical approach for real, if the roles had been reversed. This was one of the key factors in the success of General Sir Edmund Allenby's deception at the Third Battle of Gaza (October 1917). Part of the plan played on the belief of General Kress von Kressenstein, the German officer in command of the Turkish forces, that the attack on Beersheba could only be a feint, as a full-scale attack did not align with his preconceived tactical assessment of the situation. At Gallipoli in both April and August 1915 the deception plans initiated against Bulair and the Asiatic coast targeted the troop deployments of Field Marshal Otto Liman von Sanders, the Turkish commander. Von Sanders considered Bulair and the Asiatic coast as strategic Allied targets and as a consequence deployed significant numbers of troops to protect these areas. The Allies targeted them with their deception plans, having no intention of attacking them. Deception plans must be placed within the same strategic and tactical context as the real plans. Both of these examples exhibit plausibility and obey Magruder's Principle, which exploits the existing beliefs of the enemy commanders. Magruder's Principle will be referred to on numerous occasions, as it was one of the elements of deception planning that the British got right from the beginning of the campaign.

It is by using the qualities of plausibility, consistency and predictability as criteria that the enemy's Orientate phase is targeted. Creativity and discipline are prerequisites. However, the deception still relies on the 'correct' interpretation of the intelligence by the enemy and this becomes the 'uncontrollable' element in all deception plans. When deception plans are executed, there are a number of potential outcomes, which range from the plan being accepted wholesale by the enemy, to their penetrating the plan and using it to their advantage. Consequently, it is important that when executing a deception plan, intelligence is gathered continually through observations and prisoner information, and the situation is continually monitored to ensure that the enemy has indeed been duped by the deception; a failure to gather real intelligence in this respect could result in significant casualties.

For real success, an army should attempt to disrupt the enemy's decision-making processes through the operational tempo *and* deception, as deception planning becomes especially effective with an enhanced operational tempo. The time available for intelligence evaluation by the enemy is decreased which diminishes the likelihood of detection. The British Army strove to achieve this throughout the war but as increased operational tempo involved a multitude of disciplines including firepower, offensive tactics, logistics and transportation, this was arguably only fully realised in the last four months of the conflict.

There have been a number of modern publications on the subject of deception in warfare but in the main these have concentrated on events from the Second World War until the present day. Those few considering the First World War have tended to concentrate on the 'headline' events where deception was famously used – at Gallipoli in December 1915, at Gaza in October 1917 (the 'Haversack Ruse') and at Amiens in August 1918. As David French pointed out in 1994 regarding the First World War:

> Little has been published about the way in which the British used deception as a way of masking their intentions from their enemies … perhaps because it runs … counter to the notion that the British Army was led by 'donkeys' who were too lacking in subtlety to devise such measures.[4]

What is apparent from a review of the information sources, including the Official Histories, is that the British Army systematically used deception to support its military operations throughout the war. It was introduced as early as December 1914, five months after the start of the war, with the first truly integrated deception plan implemented at Neuve Chapelle in March 1915. A failure to use deception to support offensive operations would have indicated that the British Army was unimaginative and naive in its approach to military operations. Further, if deception was practised but was not analysed for its effectiveness, then the army command and control structures would not be following a learning curve. This would tend to contradict the arguments of those historians who have identified the existence of distinct learning curves for various facets of the British Army during the war. It would support the notion that the war really did see lions being led by donkeys! On the contrary, there is evidence that the use of deception in support of operations originated from GHQ and the various Army Headquarters, rather the lower level units, as deception was seen as a key element in successful offensives. From Neuve Chapelle (March 1915) through to Cambrai (November 1917) and Amiens (August 1918), the Army Commander's instructions at the start of the offensive planning process were adamant that attacks must come as a complete 'surprise' to the enemy! It is important to note that the British Army rarely used the word 'deception' or its derivatives but employed von Clausewitz's favoured term, 'surprise'.

The Lessons of Three Conflicts, pre-1914

At the British Army's military training establishments at Sandhurst, Camberley and Woolwich, the young officers were routinely given case studies to analyse and appreciate based on past conflicts including the American Civil War (1861–1865), the Second Boer War (1899–1902) and the Russo-Japanese War (1904–1905). British military observers were present throughout most of the latter conflict and subsequently published their findings. In September 1909, Lord Kitchener was feted on a tour of the battlefields in Manchuria. All three conflicts provided striking examples of the military advantages that could be gained through the use of deception and the disadvantages of its neglect. For the Confederate Army at Corinth (1862) and the British at Mafeking (1899-1900), it is difficult to envisage a successful outcome to the operations without the use of deception. Hence at the start of the First World War, the British Commanders should have been aware of the potential of deception and well acquainted with previous examples, especially as a significant number of the brigade commanders had served in the Boer War.

The American Civil War, the first of the modern conflicts characterised by man-power, technology and finance, lasted from 12 April 1861 until 9 April 1865. 3,277,000 men were mobilised of whom 29.6 per cent became casualties. Whilst the United States Army outnumbered the Confederate

States Army by approximately two-to-one, the Confederacy inflicted almost twice the number of battlefield casualties on the Union in a war of attrition that the CSA could never win. In general, the Confederacy made good use of deception to redress deficiencies in materials and manpower, something that would prove to be directly applicable to the British Army in the First World War.

In September 1861, six months after the start of the war, the Confederate guns that had been trained menacingly on Washington were overrun and found to be no more than painted logs to which old wagon wheels had been fixed. The guns, subsequently termed 'Quaker Guns' set the pattern for deception which the South perpetrated to make up for their lack of men and materials. Interestingly, the ruses carried out by the Confederacy had relevance not only for the First World War but also for subsequent conflicts. The term 'Quaker Gun' would have been recognised by First World War officers.

In 1862, Major-General George B. McClellan (known as 'Little Mac'), Commander-in-Chief of the Union forces on the York-James Peninsula, was in command of 120,000 men but was unaware that he faced a much smaller Confederate force of 8,000 troops. The latter was commanded by John Bankhead Magruder, a consummate showman whose deception inventiveness was limitless. McClellan believed that the strength of the Confederate force was greater than it was, but in reality Magruder defended a thirteen-mile front with too few men and far too few guns. Magruder played upon McClellan's belief. The initial deception was simple enough in that Magruder mixed real guns with Quaker Guns; but to confuse enemy intelligence he elaborated. He continuously moved around his units, conveying the impression that his force was greater than it was, he played loud band music at night indicative of a relaxed garrison while he himself rode around conspicuously with a colourful entourage sending out the clear message that he and his troops were everywhere. To finish off the deception, Magruder had a single infantry battalion march continuously along a heavily wooded road to the side of which was a single gap in the trees, clearly visible to the Union troops. The Confederate soldiers marched in a circle all day long conveying the impression that they were an extremely large force. This latter ruse was utilised to great effect fifty years later at 'C' beach at Lala Baba on the Gallipoli peninsula in December 1915; and by General Sir Edmund Allenby, Commander-in-Chief of the Egyptian Expeditionary Force, at Gaza in October 1917 and again at Megiddo in September 1918, which played a significant role in the defeat of the Turks. A variation on this ruse was also used on the Western Front at Arras in November 1917 using six tanks in support of the preparations for the tank battle at Cambrai, thirty miles south east. By 're-cycling' the tanks, the British led the Germans to believe that a large concentration of tanks was present in the Arras area preparing for a major offensive. The Germans shelled them, failing to spot the real build-up of over 400 tanks in front of Cambrai.

In a review of deception since 1914 published by the United States Army Military Intelligence in 1988, Magruder was recognised as one of the innovators of deception and as a result one of the ten principles of a good deception plan has been attributed to him. Magruder's Principle states that if the enemy has a pre-existing belief – in the original scenario McClellan thought that Magruder's force was greater than it was – then this should be exploited by the deception plan rather than trying to change that belief.

A further useful example from the American Civil War that would find an echo in the First World War was the retreat of the Confederate Army in May 1862. Just like the British Army at Gallipoli in 1915, the CSA needed to retire under direct enemy observation with the minimum casualties. Both the Confederate Army and the British Army extracted themselves using similar techniques, although the Confederacy used trains and the British used ships.

Major-General Pierre G.T. Beauregard had to evacuate his wounded troops first and then his fighting troops from the town of Corinth in the face of a strong Union force. Corinth had a railhead and Beauregard arranged for trains as the means of extricating his troops. As the empty trains arrived, Beauregard had the band play and a regiment of troops cheer as if reinforcements were arriving. However, when the 'empty' trains left, initially full of wounded, all was silent. In this way not only did Beauregard safely evacuate the wounded but he also conveyed the impression that his garrison was growing significantly, making a Union attack less likely. Beauregard elaborated upon this by sending 'deserters' through to the Union lines to spread disinformation and confirm the build-up of troops within Corinth. A variation of this ruse was perpetrated at Anzac and Suvla Bay on the Gallipoli peninsula in December (see chapter 8).

Beauregard's real challenge came when it was time to evacuate his front line troops. The troops left the trenches silently at night leaving behind drummer boys who kept the fires going and sounded reveille in the morning. They were supported by the band which moved around. An empty train went continuously back and forth during the day and was always greeted enthusiastically on arrival. The British at Gallipoli used a variation of this.

After the Confederate Army had left, the Union soldiers, alerted by the silence, eventually moved forward, only to find Quaker Guns manned by dummy straw soldiers. At Gallipoli, the problem of 'silence' in the trenches was overcome by 'conditioning' the Turkish troops in the preceding weeks to accept the idea that silent trenches could still be full of troops.

In the last major conflict involving the British Army prior to the First World War, the Second South African War (Boer War) (October 1899-May 1902), deception was routinely practised. Due to the mobile nature of the guerrilla warfare in the latter stages, deception developed to meet needs at a local level and hence was tactical rather than strategic.

At the siege of Mafeking, Colonel Robert Baden-Powell and his small force were surrounded and outnumbered ten-to-one by over 8,000 Boer troops lead by Commandant-General Piet Cronje who besieged them from 16 October 1899 until 17 May 1900. For 217 days Mafeking was cut off from the outside world and at the mercy of the Boers. Interestingly, one of the last pieces of mail to leave Mafeking, before the siege was laid, was the final manuscript of Baden-Powell's magnum opus, *Aids to Scouting*.

Baden-Powell decided that deception and trickery could be the key to his survival. He developed an integrated deception plan whilst issuing instructions to his garrison to deceive the enemy at every possible turn. Baden-Powell's plan was aimed specifically at conveying two messages to the Boers, that the British garrison was bigger than it really was and that the British defences were more formidable than they really were.

At the outset, a series of fake outpost forts were set up around a five-and-a-half mile perimeter, a distance too large for a small garrison to man effectively thus conveying the impression that the British were a greater force than Boer intelligence had led them to believe. This also enforced the Boers' belief that the British knew what they were doing. Baden-Powell created one of the forts, a mile-and-a-half away, from a large mound of earth, buildings and trenches. The fort was adorned with two large flag poles to give the impression that this was Baden-Powell's head-quarters; this site was extensively shelled by the Boer artillery.[5] The false headquarters created the impression that Baden-Powell was in command of the fort line and not managing operations from back in Mafeking itself.

This ruse is similar to that which Sir Douglas Haig would perpetrate at Neuve Chapelle in March 1915 and Sir Henry Rawlinson on the Somme in 1916 to mislead the Germans with respect to the sectors to be attacked.

Baden-Powell also made full use of the numerous Boer spies within Mafeking itself by planting dummy minefields, laid in view of the Boers and their spies. To create these minefields, natives carried boxes (filled with sand) around the town to the sites of the minefields with strict instructions not to drop them! For authenticity, one of the minefields was tested and after all the inhabitants had been ordered indoors, 'for their own safety', a dynamite charge was set off.

Further, after Baden-Powell had observed the Boers high stepping over their barbed wire defences, he constructed fake barbed wire (string tied to wooden pickets) and ordered the British troops to simulate avoiding non-existent barbed wire by exaggeratedly stepping over it when moving between trenches. Both the 'barbed wire' and the 'minefield' presented formidable obstacles to any attackers. The type of deception was the fore-runner of the dummy trenches used throughout the First World War and which Haig instigated as early as 29 October 1914 at Gheluvelt, as part of the First Battle of Ypres (10 October–22 November 1914).

Recognising that the town was vulnerable to attack by night, one of Baden-Powell's engineers created a 'searchlight' made from an acetylene torch and a biscuit tin mounted on a pole. This was shone from one of the forts towards the Boers before moving on to the next fort. The Boers assumed that any night attack would have to be made in the full glare of searchlights which would make any attack hazardous. The use of search-lights as a means of concealing the truth was used to great effect during the Dardanelles Campaign both during the attack at Chunuk Bair in August 1915 and during the evacuation from Anzac Cove in December 1915.

Baden-Powell's engineers next developed a megaphone from a biscuit tin that could convey messages and orders up to 500 yards. Baden-Powell would issue orders to fix bayonets and prepare for attack which would result in a hail of retaliatory rifle fire from the Boers, who were subse-quently targeted by British snipers as they disclosed their positions! This tactic was a direct ancestor of the famous 'Chinese Attacks' used on hun-dreds of occasions throughout the First World War by the British Army.

Finally, to fool the Boers into thinking he had a much larger force, Baden-Powell resorted to the tried and trusted trickery that had served the Confederacy so well forty years earlier and would serve the British Army equally well fifteen years later. He moved his men and the few available cannons around from place to place and with the aid of dummy soldiers, simulated a large force.

The overall impression worked well as the Boers never tried to invade the town although they launched an eventually abortive attack on 12 May. This attack was broken up by Major (later General Sir) Alexander Godley, the officer who would be responsible for a simple but effective ruse at Gallipoli in 1915. In the main the Boers were content to shell Mafeking from a distance, for fear of the British Army's massive armaments. Given the prominence that the Siege of Mafeking held in the British consciousness, it cannot have gone unnoticed within the Army that the successful outcome was due almost entirely to bluff and deception. Both the future commanders-in-chief in the First World War, Field Marshal Sir John French, as a cavalry commander, and Field Marshal Sir Douglas Haig, as one of his staff officers, played prominent roles in the Boer War. This wealth of Boer War experience extended down the chain of command. Analysis of the 'Donkey Archive' at the Centre for First World War Studies at the University of Birmingham,[6] shows that in 1914, 62 per cent of the brigade commanders had seen active service in South Africa during the Boer War with a further 15 per cent having seen active service in other theatres.

The British Expeditionary Force (BEF) existed despite evidence from the Russo-Japanese war in Manchuria (1904–05) that industrial nations would wage 'industrial' wars and that expeditionary forces were inappropriate for these 'heavyweight' conflicts. The Manchurian War in many respects represented a blueprint for the First World War as trench warfare had developed, with the key defences of barbed wire belts and machine guns with interlocking fields of fire. The development of rifles and ammunition after the Franco-Prussian War (1870–71) increased their effectiveness with the introduction of new rifle magazines that raised the rate of fire, smokeless powder cartridges and increased ranges. This in turn forced the artillery to dig in and adopt bullet shields or deploy farther back so that they could not be targeted by the enemy infantry and to introduce new methods of indirect firing where the target could not be directly seen. Through indirect firing at the Battle of Sha-ho (11–17 October 1904), the Japanese artillery, firing from reverse slope positions, silenced the Russian artillery and machine guns. The Japanese had employed a system of artillery observers who did have line-of-sight and were in communication with their guns.

One of the other lessons that emerged from this conflict was the judicious use of deception. In general and where possible, the Japanese employed deception, while the Russians more or less expressed contempt for its use. Geoffrey Jukes has speculated that without the skilful use of cover, camouflage and deception, the enormous Japanese casualties incurred in attack would have been even higher.[7]

At the Battle of Yalu (25 April–2 May 1904), the Russian Army and the Japanese First Army faced each other on the opposite banks of the Yalu river. The Japanese carried out their preparations under the cover of darkness or through the careful use of natural features to hide their intentions from the Russians. Disguised as local fishermen they were able to determine the locations of the majority of the Russian troops, guns and positions. The Russians, on the other hand, made no attempt to conceal any of their preparations. Furthermore, the Japanese found that the water level in the river was relatively low but then implemented a deception plan to conceal this fact and to force the Russians into revealing those remaining artillery positions that the Japanese had not already detected. The Japanese, in full view of the Russians, commenced the construction of a 'decoy' bridge across the Yalu's main channel. The Russians expended a lot of ammunition and revealed all their artillery positions trying to destroy the bridge. This plan followed one of the principles of all good deception plans, Magruder's Principle, in that had the situation been reversed, this is where the Russians would also have built a bridge to get their army across the river. Meanwhile, the Japanese, hidden from Russian observers, used the premises of an abandoned timber company to build nine short portable bridges which were subsequently rushed into position across the narrower channels immediately prior to the attack.[8] At Tel el Fara in Palestine 1917, the British Army constructed a fake bridge as a decoy target for Turkish aircraft to divert their attention from the real railway bridge, which was built without interference.[9] A similar ruse was also perpetrated at Le Hamel on the Western Front in July 1918.

This pattern was reproduced throughout the Russo-Japanese war and was noted by the foreign observers. The Japanese concealed their artillery, the Russians did not. The negligence of the Russians was inexcusable; in dry weather, every time their guns fired, great tell-tale clouds of dust were thrown up, something which could have easily been remedied by dampening the soil around the gun positions with water from nearby rivers.

On rare occasions, the Russians did employ deception and fooled the Japanese because the apparent Russian moves fitted in with Japanese expectations. At the Battle of Sha-ho, believing that the Japanese would expect an attack on the flat plain, General Aleksey Kuropatkin, Commander-in-Chief of the Russian Armies, in line with Magruder's Principle, advanced on to the plains with bands and banners. This ostentatious display was believed by the Japanese, given the Russian's previous behaviour in the war and their own pre-conceptions of the situation.

Kuropatkin surprised the Japanese by launching an attack on his left flank through the mountains. With his expectations set, Field Marshal Oyama, the Japanese commander, refused to believe that the mountain attack was anything more than a feint and that the main attack would still come across the plain.

After the war, British officers studied the conflict and concluded that there were lessons to be learnt, particularly about concealment, the use of camouflage and the cover of darkness to prepare for an offensive. Barrett published an article in which he described how once the Russians guns had detected a Japanese battery and they came under fire, the latter often fell silent and moved to a new location, leaving behind remnants to simulate a burnt-out position.[10] This ruse was perpetrated on the British by the German artillery at the Battle of Loos (September 1915) while the British used a variant to target German batteries at Amiens in August 1918.

Modern Armies and Deception

Despite evidence of the advantages of deception, it does not necessarily automatically feature in the planning of modern military operations. As late as 1983, military personnel in the United States Army were advocating that deception should be incorporated into every tactical organisation and should be reflected in unit training.[11] So there was no guarantee that the British Army during the First World War would automatically employ it. Armies do not necessarily learn the lessons of history as they can often seem irrelevant in the face of significant technological advances. The United States Army conducted a series of studies of the use of deception to determine whether it was relevant to modern operations. One such study, made in 1988, examined engagements since 1914, although the overwhelming majority of examples used to support the conclusions within the document came from the Second World War, with no actual examples quoted pertaining to the First World War.

Nevertheless, the United States Army document is effective as a field guide in the use of battlefield deception. The study concluded that deception has made a significant contribution to military operations and deception enhanced the instances where surprise was achieved. The authors estimated that since 1914, warning of an imminent attack was transmitted to the enemy in about 78 per cent of all encounters but if this was accompanied by deception the warning was ignored and surprise was achieved. With the close proximity of the Germans across No-Man's-Land on the Western Front, an imminent attack would have probably been detected in almost 100 per cent of instances! Even those times when the German High Command thought that an attack was not likely, for example at Amiens in August 1918, the troops at the local level had detected the tell-tale signs. In this case the German commanders chose to ignore the evidence because the intelligence generated by the British deception plan indicated that the attack would be 100 miles farther north. It is the abundant mixture of real and false intelligence that can temporarily paralyse the enemy's OODA Loops so that countermeasures against detected attacks are not necessarily implemented in a timely manner.

The ten principles or maxims to a degree were based on the principles laid down by Sun Tzu, but were subsequently reinforced from a study of a number of conflicts including the First World War. Through deception the enemy had to be distracted, his intelligence collection and analytical capabilities had to be overloaded, illusions of strength where there was weakness and weakness where there was strength, the enemy had to be conditioned to patterns of behaviour and above all, the enemy expectations had to be confused with regard to Size, Activity, Location, Unit, Time and Equipment, known as SALUTE. Without knowing it, the British Army followed these maxims in its deception planning, as will be evident from the studies of particular battles in the following chapters.

The British Army pre-1914

In the fifty years prior to the First World War, France, Germany, Russia and the United States had fought continental-style industrial wars and France and Germany maintained a significant military presence through the use of conscription. In contrast, during the same period Britain had been engaged in colonial wars including the British–Zulu War (1879), the War in the Sudan (1881–1899) and the Second Boer War (1899–1902). These conflicts distracted command from the realities of British engagement in a continental war despite the study of the industrial conflicts at Sandhurst and Woolwich. Even as late as September 1914, military discussions mulled over flanking manoeuvres and the dominant role of infantry compared with artillery. Although machine guns were acknowledged as weapons capable of volume-fire, as a factor they were considered of no real signifi-cance, even though the British cavalry had adopted them in 1908 as a key element within its offensive arsenal. Further, despite the evidence from the Russo-Japanese War, at which the British were observers, the development of artillery tactics and trench warfare were not seriously considered.[12] This blindness can be seen in the development of the British Expeditionary Force itself, which was developed as a rapidly deployable force designed for short, frantic engagements. Major-General J.M. Grierson had iden-tified five strategic situations in which the British Army could become embroiled and it was on the basis of this analysis that Richard Burdon Haldane (later Viscount Haldane) proposed a set of reforms which resulted in a special army order issued by the War Office on 12 January 1907 for the reorganisation of the Regular Army, which included the creation of the BEF. The five strategic situations were a war with Russia in defence of India, a war against the United States in defence of Canada, a war against France, a war with France as an ally against Germany and finally a Third Boer War. In four of the five scenarios, the BEF would have had to engage a continental-style industrial army. This was likely to lead to a longer term engagement and not the short, decisive action that the BEF envisaged. In 1906, Haldane had dismissed the idea of a mass army as untenable, point-ing out that Britain had a greater expeditionary force that either France or Germany.[13] However, Haldane did propose that a Territorial Force of over one million men should be created. As a consequence, on the declaration of war on 4 August 1914, the British Army was ill-prepared for the indus-trial scale of the conflict it was about to enter.

Nevertheless, within seven months after the declaration of war, the British Army, having recognised the long-term and 'industrial' nature of the war, was actively engaged in offensive operations, against entrenched positions, which were supported by the use of deception plans that already followed the aims and maxims subsequently identified over 70 years later. This use of deception, particularly on the Western Front, has not been recognised and a number of publications have actually pointed up the Army's lack of deception planning. For instance, Michael Handel stated that the British Army almost ignored deception because the British were confident that straightforward military might would be sufficient to overwhelm the enemy.[14] Handel concluded that any deception plans were solely as a result of their implementation at a local level by local commanders and were extremely rare at a strategic level. This view was supported by Roy Godson and James Wirtz who recognised that deception was attempted but due to the close proximity of the enemy across No-Man's-Land, it was difficult to conceal the concentrated build-up of men, artillery and materials.[15] This problem was compounded by the fact that the advances in camouflage that might confuse aerial reconnaissance would not necessarily confound spies on the ground. This view is sustained by Michael Occleshaw in his book on military intelligence, which cited the 'Haversack Ruse' example at Gaza/Beersheba (October 1917) as a use of deception that could never be repeated on the Western Front. He concluded that the primary reason for this was that the armies were separated by No-Man's-Land, and as a result deception on the Western Front was not a significant factor.

The above points are valid; but all of these issues were recognised by the BEF and its commanders, probably as early as December 1914. Based on references within the British, Canadian and Australian Official Histories, there is evidence that in the realm of deception, plans were being laid after seventeen weeks and the Western Front was as active as any of the other fronts in this regard and probably led the way. Almost immediately, as the opposing trench lines formed, the British Army on the Western Front recognised the limitations imposed by No-Man's-Land and the potential for behind-the-lines spies. Straightaway the problem of how Allied offensive operations could be conducted without the Germans immediately being privy to all the preparatory activity and consequently making suitable defensive preparations that would counter any operation – whilst inflicting serious casualties – was recognised. The conundrum was not resolved in 1914 as the British Army had its attention focussed on other more pressing matters. By December 1914 however, there were signs that Sir John French had started to develop a potential solution to the problem. By March 1915 at Neuve Chapelle, the British were using dummy and camouflaged military artefacts, and providing a torrent of false intelligence that simply overwhelmed the enemy's decision-making processes. The flow of false intelligence was often achieved simply by GHQ instructing units across wide sections of the front to start preparations for an offensive. Even fake preparations would involve camouflage to conceal them from the Germans, in the knowledge that spies would detect at least some of the activities and report back. The camouflage used for fake preparations was necessary not only to conceal the false nature of the preparations but also because the German artillery would target them and casualties had to be kept to a minimum! The deception plans at Neuve Chapelle were already complex in nature. As General Sir Douglas Haig prepared a deception plan to support the offensive of the First Army against Neuve Chapelle, Field Marshal Sir John French instructed the Second Army, commanded by General Sir Horace Smith-Dorrien, to simulate preparations for an attack against the Ypres Salient and Lille. The Germans were apparently faced with imminent offensives on both the First and Second Army fronts, so where should they deploy their reserves? Unbeknown to the Germans, the British had neither the manpower nor the artillery to simultaneously conduct offensives on both fronts. Despite the successful deception, in 1915 offensive operations had yet to mature into an approach that could overrun complex trench lines and resist the predictable counterattacks.

By the end of 1915 and the Battle of Loos, the British approach to deception planning was relatively mature although it would be refined through experience and as new technological advances, particularly tanks, became significant factors. Charters and Tugnell thought that the First World War was something of a watershed for the British Army as it used deception on the battlefield to support military operations.[16]

The use of deception plans throughout the First World War can be attributed to the approach of both Sir John French and Sir Douglas Haig at the start of 1915. The solution which resolved the No-Man's-Land conundrum consisted of the three basic elements of *Conceal, Create* and *Confuse* (deception's 3C). The *Conceal* element followed the lead of the French Army who had begun their work on camouflage by setting up a school in September 1914. Throughout 1915 the British Army relied on French expertise and manpower to develop camouflage techniques. The British themselves introduced the all-important second element of *Create* by the time of the Battle of Neuve Chapelle. It was evident that camouflage alone was not the answer as it could be easily penetrated. Therefore the British Army introduced the second element to create a wealth of false intelligence. This intelligence coupled with that which the Germans gathered by penetrating camouflaged artefacts gave them a problem – the separation of the real from the false. This it was hoped would 'paralyse' the decision-making processes long enough to *Confuse* them when the attack came. It was anticipated that the indecision, if only for a brief period, would be sufficient to enable the attackers to cross No-Man's-Land and capture the first line of trenches. Subsequent trench lines would not benefit from this type of deception although at Bazentin Ridge on 14 July 1916, British pilots transmitted fake wireless messages which indicated that the second line had been captured, in the hope the Germans would not reinforce this line and would fall back to their third line. In the event, the Germans failed to pick up the messages and subsequent reinforcements forced the British to retire.[17]

As No-Man's-Land allowed the Germans to observe British Army activity, so deception was employed to enable the Germans to 'see' activities that were false and misleading. These activities were usually aimed at concealing the time and place of the attacks and the units involved, as it was not possible to conceal the preparations altogether. As the war progressed however, even preparations could be concealed especially when the Royal Flying Corps (RFC) was in command of the air space over the front and the forward areas were restricted to authorised personnel.

The main sources on deception are the official histories, a distillation of a huge volume of documents including war diaries, operational orders and after-action reports. Consequently references to deception were comparatively few, owing in part to the condensation of the available information and in part to the official historians' perspectives. As a consequence, multiple sources need to be consulted to determine whether deception was used in a particular operation. This applies particularly to personal memoirs and unit histories written in the post-war period. For example, the diary entry of Private Edward Roe (6/East Lancashire) at Gallipoli for 16–17 December 1915 described a 'sacrifice duty', which involved parading along 'C' beach at Lala Baba in full view of the Turks to convince them that the British Army was at full strength and maintaining normal duties.[18] Clearly a deception activity, straight from Magruder's bag of tricks. The 6th Battalion war diary written for the same period by adjutant A.C. Bailey stated that the 'whole four companies were then engaged in digging and rebuilding trenches'.[19] The latter was a somewhat less hazardous task than deliberately exposing oneself to Turkish fire. But this also was in fact a deception, designed to create the impression that the situation was normal and not the prelude to an evacuation. The War Diary shows that the regiment was evacuated on 18 December 1918, two days after the trench building entry in the diary. Roe lived until 1952.

Through the examination of instructions and orders issued by GHQ and the Army Headquarters it appears that Sir John French and latterly Field Marshal Sir Douglas Haig and the Army Commanders were keen to employ deception where possible. On the Western Front, the desire that an attack should come as a 'complete surprise' to the enemy was almost desperately reiterated.

The British and the French Armies frequently engaged units of each other's armies in their deception plans. The Germans, primarily because of their defensive stance, were possibly less adept at deception, although there were notable instances when the British Army was fooled by German ruses.

Although started on the Western Front, the use of deception was extended to other theatres, notably at Gallipoli in 1915 and in Palestine in 1917–18. In the latter theatre, where No-Man's-Land did not impose the same constraints, the British Army, primarily under General Sir Edmund Allenby, employed deception that became possible because of the more fluid nature of the warfare. At the Third Battle of Gaza in October 1917 and at the Battle of Megiddo in September 1918, some of the most spectacular deceptions of the First World War were carried out.

Any analysis of the role of deception in British Army military operations from 1914 to 1918 must be investigated with the same rigour that has been applied to offensive operations. Three key questions must be addressed – did deception play a central role in the planning and execution of military operations; was the use of deception in military operations attributable to central direction from GHQ and other senior headquarters; and did deception actually influence the outcome of these military operations? The first two questions are relatively easy to address while the third, in most instances, must be the subject of considerable speculation. Some of the demonstrations and feint attacks have often been scornfully described as 'sideshows' which gave the impression that they were irrelevant and the casualties they caused were unnecessary. This study will aim to show that these 'sideshows' were usually part of a grander scheme aimed at deceiving the enemy, although the troops involved with their limited horizons would never have understood this.

1

The No-Man's-Land Conundrum

One who is skilful at keeping the enemy on the move, maintains deceitful appearances, according to which the enemy will act.
Sun Tzu

The first units of the BEF landed at Boulogne on 12 August 1914 and advanced through France and Belgium towards Mons where they fought their first engagement on 23 August 1914. Throughout the remainder of August and the first days of September, 'mobile' warfare was the norm and although the numbers of enemy troops far exceeded British expectations, the BEF fought very much in the manner that had been instilled into it during training over the previous seven years since its inception following the Haldane reforms in 1907. After Mons, the Battle of Le Cateau (26 August 1914) being the exception, the BEF were in a fighting retreat. However, as the German Army assumed that victory was theirs, they deviated from the long-prepared Schlieffen Plan. The German First Army under General Alexander von Kluck was ordered to advance south-east in front of Paris to join with Field Marshal Karl Bülow's Second Army in an attack on the failing French armies. The now over-extended German First Army presented the Allies with an opportunity to attack its vulnerable right flank and the BEF was ordered by Lord Kitchener to halt its retreat and attack, along with the French Sixth Army on its left and the French Fifth Army on its right. Between 7 and 10 September, the French armies and the BEF counter-attacked along the River Marne and as the German First Army turned to meet the attack, a gap opened up with the German Second Army. With a potential military disaster facing the German Armies, they withdrew northwards followed cautiously by the exhausted BEF and French Armies. By 11 September, the Germans, under intense pressure from the Allied Armies, had retreated behind the River Aisne and occupied the defensive positions which they had identified as suitable during their execution of the ultimately abortive Schlieffen Plan. As the German Armies retreated away from Paris, the Allies, no longer capable of continually harassing the enemy, allowed them sufficient time to dig in and establish a fully manned defensive line. The retreat by the Germans to these positions changed the nature of the warfare into the form that would forever define the First World War.

The German defensive line of trenches and strong points was not placed randomly across the countryside but was carefully chosen for its lines of communication and supply and more importantly for the geographical advantages it offered. This usually simply meant that the Germans occupied the high ground with its beneficial fields of observation and fire, especially in the flat lands of northern France where even the smallest rise conferred a military advantage. The Germans initially chose the Chemin des Dames ridge just north of the Aisne, which even without trenches and strong points would have provided a natural defensive 'fortress'.

As the pursuing Allies came up against the German defensive positions (Battle of Aisne, 12–15 September 1914) there was a realisation that straightforward frontal infantry assaults were futile and wasteful against entrenched defences. In an attempt to consolidate their position and shorten their lines of communication, the British Army disengaged itself from the Aisne and moved across General Michel-Joseph Maunoury's French Sixth Army's lines of communication. Until now the BEF had been on the right flank of the French Sixth Army but now the British lined up on the French left flank with the French XXI Corps on their immediate right between Béthune and Fruges.

As the trench lines at the time still retained a flank, the British and the Germans now attempted a series of movements north in an effort to outflank each other. This simply resulted in the trench lines extending in the direction of the North Sea. These outflanking manoeuvres are now known as 'The Race to the Sea', but both sides were not attempting to reach the coast *per se* but were attempting to outflank each other's defences in a game of military leapfrog. As the outflanking operations moved north, they resulted in a number of engagements, particularly at La Bassée (12 October–2 November), Messines (12 October–2 November), Armentières (13 October–2 November) and Ypres (First Battle, 19 October–22 November) which defined the front lines and resulted in British casualties of approximately 60,000 men killed, wounded or taken prisoner.

Each side nullified the other as the coast was reached. In a final act on 29 October 1914, the Belgians had flooded the land north of Diksmuide so completing the Allied defensive line in the north. The German defensive line now stretched from the Chemin des Dames behind the Aisne continuously to the Belgian coast. With the defensive systems now similarly extending southwards, the net result was that the German defensive system stretched uninterrupted from the coast of Belgium to the Swiss border.

In response to the German defences and the realisation that ill-prepared infantry frontal assaults were futile, the Allies now also dug in and developed their own trench systems. These were some distance away from the German line, in the best positions that remained available to them. As the Allied lines had to be 'in contact' with the enemy, the positioning of their trench systems was often a compromise and they were invariably dominated by the German defensive line. Further, because the Allies had no intention of allowing the Germans to occupy France (and were not an occupying force themselves!) their trench systems did not have the same 'air of permanence' as those of the Germans.

The BEF had been specifically designed to cope with the five strategic scenarios mentioned previously, but it soon became clear that the nature of the 'planned' warfare had drastically changed. For the foreseeable future, there would be no decisive battle. The advantage now lay with the Germans. An attacking force would have to be at least three to five times greater in number than the defenders to prevail. The defences would have to be sufficiently nullified through artillery bombardments before the infantry could advance with any expectation of success. Elaborate schemes would have to be developed to co-ordinate infantry and artillery fire plans. This was not really achieved until 1917 and even then, the German defences had become more sophisticated, thereby partially negating the mature effectiveness in attack.

In order to assault the trenches and strong points successfully, novel infantry tactics, creative artillery fireplans and new weapons systems would have to be developed. Complex preparations would always be required: stockpiling of ample quantities of munitions and supplies close to the front; the concentration of first-line attack troops and their reinforcements; the erection of casualty clearing stations (CCS) and hospitals; the creation of command headquarters; the assembly of horse lines and fodder (not only if the plans involved cavalry, for that ever elusive breakthrough, but also for transport); the accumulation of sufficient food and water to feed the troops and the development of suitable transport links (roads, light railways) into the attack sector to bring forward all of this war material. These preparations would inevitably generate vast numbers of busy personnel, huge volumes of dust in dry weather, large tracts of mud in wet weather and would be visible from the German front and behind the Allied lines to any remaining inhabitants and German spies alike! For an offensive operation, none of these preparations could be made away from the front line and then brought forward, they would, because of the static nature of the trench systems, have to be assembled within striking distance of the front line.

As the British could observe the Germans, it was obvious that the Germans, from their advantageous location and as world leaders in optical equipment, could see into the British lines with an even greater degree of clarity. Once alerted to an impending assault, it was a relatively straightforward matter to bolster the defences through the redeployment of front line troops, the positioning of the reinforcements, the location of artillery pieces and machine gun teams and the closure of all passages through the barbed wire entanglements.

All these glaringly visible signs of an impending attack would in fact be the very things that the British would use so often throughout the war to convince the Germans that the next offensive would be at a sector distant from the real one. These preparatory activities would form the basis of the deception plans of the British Army during the First World War and would be copied during the Second World War and beyond.

Not only did the Germans hold and exploit the advantage of hills for observation, they also utilised the reverse slopes to hide their men, artillery and preparations from everything except aerial observation. For the British and the French, the situation was reversed as the Germans were able to observe everything from the build-up of supplies and materials to the movement of troops. Not only could these Allied activities be observed, but they could also be effectively targeted by the German artillery with the use of line-of-sight observers and spotters. For the Allies, targeting the German dispositions required the development of more sophisticated techniques including map shooting, flash spotting and sound ranging, which would eventually force the Germans to move their guns farther back into hidden locations.

By the end of 1914 the 'No-Man's-Land conundrum' was fact. How could Allied offensive operations be planned and prepared without the Germans immediately being privy to them and making suitable defensive preparations that would counter any operation, whilst inflicting serious casualties on the attacking force? During the final few months of the year, both sides engaged in the battles that had raged at the northern end of the trench systems had concealed their activities from each other by making best use of the natural foliage, particularly the woods that were scattered throughout the countryside. These woods had remained relatively intact. Although the artillery had started to 'prune' the trees and bushes, a comparative lack of shells had prevented their total devastation. Soon this would change as the great artillery bombardments would turn the front lines and beyond into featureless landscapes.

Camouflage

The initial attempt to solve the conundrum was straightforward: concealment of the offensive preparatory activities. This actually was very much the domain of the French Army as it led the way in the development of camouflage, which was primarily used to hide artillery installations, munitions and stores from the German observers. The use of the term 'camouflage' became universally accepted and was derived from the French *camoufler*, meaning to hide or conceal.

The art of camouflage on the Western Front developed rapidly, initiated as early as September 1914 by the French who developed a school at Toul utilising the skills of renowned artists. The earliest experiments were conducted by Lucien-Victor Guirand de Scévola, a French artist serving in the ranks of the artillery, and Eugène Corbin. The results were sufficiently encouraging and the first French workshop was set up at Amiens on 12 February 1915, dedicated to the production of artillery camouflage and disguised observation posts. The output of these workshops was significant. The camouflage of the artillery was believed to be vital. Any build-up of ordnance would send a clear signal of intent and alert defences. The guns were camouflaged with painted canvas sheets, designed by de Scévola, which replaced the branches and foliage previously used, materials that would soon be scarce on the Western Front. This approach was subsequently superseded by more effective measures developed by the British in the summer of 1917, as the painted canvas was particularly vulnerable to detection by the rapidly developing science of aerial observation.

The other major output from the French workshop were camouflaged or disguised observation posts, used for detecting preparations taking place within the German zone of attack, in order to make the necessary defensive preparations. The favoured, and most iconic, device was a tree, the first of which was erected 25 miles east of Amiens, near Lihors in May 1915. There were plenty of trees at the front back then. The tree, as an object, was particularly suitable as it gave gave height to an observer. The original French design for this type of observation post replaced real trees. This meant that the work to erect them including the removal of the real tree was usually done over two nights. Later, the British developed a 'tree' that could be erected in a single night. British officers made coloured drawings of the real trees and the surroundings from which small plaster models were made. The models acted as guides not only for recreating the tree but also for determining the amount of preparatory work that was required prior to the night when the two were swapped. It is believed that this type of work was never detected even though two of the observation posts, a tree and a telegraph pole, were within 50 yards of the Germans. From this it should be obvious that the observers who crawled inside them, had to be small, brave, and at ease in confined spaces! The first British tree was erected on 11 March 1916 and of the 45 erected, six were destroyed by shell fire. Although the number of these types of observation posts erected seems relatively low, it must be remembered that the opportunities were scant, not least because of the lack of suitable real trees to replace. Although the observation posts were armoured to the front which gave the observers some degree of protection from small arms and machine gun fire, they were vulnerable to artillery fire. Real trees were targeted anyway, as they still presented an opportunity to gain height for observation. The majority of the trees were erected north of the Béthune-La Bassée road where the country was flat and even a small increase in height yielded significant observational advantages. An example can be seen at the Imperial War Museum in London.

The French developed even more imaginative observation posts, which were placed out in No-Man's-Land near the German lines to act as listening posts. Dead soldiers and horses were sketched and were replaced with painted canvas representations, below which pits were dug to conceal the observers. These posts were put in place in a single night but were of limited value as real bodies decayed while the fake canvas ones did not and hence were detectable within a matter of days. It has been suggested that these types of observation posts led to the practice of shooting wounded soldiers lying out in No-Man's-Land.

The success of the first workshop encouraged the French Army to create additional establishments at Chalons and Nancy in August and September 1915 respectively. Subsequently an official unit within the French Army, the *Section de Camouflage,* was set up under the command of de Scévola.

Having seen the advantages offered by the French approach, the British Army followed their example in the area of camouflage, although initially it was entirely reliant on French personnel and expertise. Camouflage was not a new art to the British who had preferred to use the term 'concealment'. The khaki uniform was of course camouflage. Natural and specially planted vegetation was used to conceal more permanent structures. The British, as described in the 1905 *Manual of Military Engineering*, were familiar with the creation of dummy trenches, 'Quaker' guns and the use of natural foliage and waterproof sheets to conceal guns. The idea of an independent British Camouflage Service was first suggested in the winter of 1915, after a fact-finding visit by a group of officers to the French workshop at Amiens. Like their Allies, the British subsequently employed artists to develop the techniques, in particular Solomon Joseph Solomon (1860–1927), a Pre-Raphaelite painter and member of the Royal Academy. A call for volunteers amongst the troops with experience of theatrical work, carpentry and skills in cardboard-work lead to the setting up in January 1916 of a small workshop in Amiens, close to the French facility. The staff were later transferred to a permanent larger workshop in an old factory at Wimereux, close to the port of Boulogne.

On 22 March 1916, the British established the Special Works Park (the British Camouflage Section) under the command of Captain F.J.C. Wyatt, with Lieutenant-Colonel S.J. Solomon as the technical adviser. The establishment at Wimereux supported the northern area British First and Second Armies while similar work was carried out from the French workshop at Amiens to support the southern area British Third and Fourth

Armies. It was soon realised that Wimereux was far too distant from the front to react to the immediate demands of the Army Commanders and as a result additional British establishments were set up at Amiens and Aire, the latter twelve miles south-east of St. Omer. By November 1916, the factory at Amiens was known as the Southern Special Works Park, servicing the Third and Fourth Armies, while the establishment at Aire was termed the Northern Special Works Park, supporting the First and Second Armies. The factory at Wimereux remained as the parent factory and dealt with special or large scale orders, which were soon requested as the Army Commanders came to fully appreciate the use of camouflage in supporting their ambitious deception plans.

The British factories initially followed the French example and concentrated on the production of camouflaged observation posts and camouflage netting. Their work gradually evolved to support the concealment of all military artefacts, including machine-gun emplacements, ammunition dumps and troops. After the war, two manuals were produced which detailed the techniques required to achieve effective levels of concealment.[1,2]

Camouflage had to be quick to develop because of the technical progress in the design of binoculars, telescopic sights and cameras, combined with improvements in aerial observation. Although the French were the acknowledged masters of camouflage, their artists relied upon the idea that nature (leafy branches and, very soon, mud) could be imitated sufficiently well on painted canvas. This faith persisted until the summer of 1917 when the British established an Experimental Section at an aerodrome at St. Omer and showed that aerial reconnaissance could easily detect military installations covered in painted canvas. Unless there was direct bright overhead sunlight, the canvas, because if its lack of texture, 'shone out' on aerial photographs, making detection easy. The British experimented with different systems, using aerial reconnaissance and photography to test them, and found that raffia and canvas strips tied onto wire or fish netting gave better results. This is similar to the camouflage netting now used by the modern British Army. However, the artillery teams soon found that raffia easily caught alight during artillery bombardments so it was replaced with canvas strips. This coincided with the observation that the green raffia strips faded in sunlight and a shortage of raffia from Mozambique. Although the canvas strips were better, the issue of the inflammable nature of the camouflage materials was never satisfactorily resolved during the war.

To develop the science of camouflage the British established a Camouflage School in Kensington Gardens in London where new techniques were developed based on requirements defined by the Special Works Parks in France. The school, along with the Wimereux establishment, also educated officers in the art of camouflage.

A particular product that came from the camouflage units were lifelike dummy heads designed by sculptor Henry Bouchard. These were popped up above trenches with the express aim of inducing an enemy sniper to open fire and disclose his position which was subsequently targeted. By the use of a periscope to sight down the hole made by the bullet in the dummy head, the sniper could be located. Obviously a poor sniper who missed his target, unless unlucky, would remain undetected! Some of the heads were particularly elaborate and could have a cigarette placed in their mouths and 'smoked' through a tube by a soldier safely on the floor of the trench. The same types of heads were used by the snipers themselves to lure unsuspecting soldiers to expose themselves and take a last pot-shot at the enemy.

From a deception perspective, the art of camouflage was only part of the solution. Simply concealing activities as the only component of a deception plan made it vulnerable and when discovered the information could be easily turned into an advantage by the enemy. All camouflaged artefacts would be scrutinised intensely from the enemy across No-Man's-Land, from the air and from behind the lines by German spies and other agents. The location of camouflaged supplies, ordnance and troops in numbers that were not consistent with the levels expected on a 'quiet' front would immediately disclose Allied intentions. The Germans could choose to react discreetly and strengthen and alert their defences in readiness for the imminent attack. The combination of artillery camouflage and disguised observation posts was a far too simplistic approach. The truth that rapidly dawned on the British High Command, as early as December 1914, was that deception activities had to be extended in a much more creative manner to present 'illusions' to the enemy across No-Man's-Land. The real deception solution lay in letting the enemy 'see-and-hear' what you wanted them to 'see-and-hear' – and more importantly what they expected to 'see-and-hear'! On this basis complex integrated deception plans were required of which camouflaged artefacts would only form one of the elements. As will be discussed in more detail, the British Army in general, and Field Marshal Sir John French and

General Sir Douglas Haig in particular, quickly recognised this reality and within seven months of the outbreak of war, were actively engaged in solving the No-Man's-Land conundrum in a methodical manner. The plans required preparations for attacks to be made at different sectors across the front. These preparations, both real and fake, had to be camouflaged from the enemy. Any lapse in concealment would alert the enemy with regard to the veracity of the preparations.

By March 1915, during the preparations for their first major engagement at Neuve Chapelle, there was evidence that the British Army was beginning to turn the constraints imposed by No-Man's-Land into an operational advantage. As No-Man's-Land allowed the Germans to observe British Army activity, so deception plans were employed to hide the real preparations whilst enabling the Germans to 'see' activities that were false and misleading but displayed as if for real. The false intelligence created attempted to mislead the German decision making processes, but in the event of security lapses it could be mixed with real intelligence to 'blind' these processes. To be effective and believable, the fake intelligence could not be 'fed' to the Germans but had to be gathered by them in exactly the same way that real intelligence was gathered. Throughout 1915, the British Army perfected its deception planning primarily at the Battles of Neuve Chapelle (March 1915), Hooge (August 1915) and Loos (September 1915) and developed a template or checklist of techniques that could be employed to deceive the enemy.

In order to keep pace with the demands of the British commanders who made industrial-sized requests for camouflage material across multiple sectors, the Special Works Parks extended their output. The returns from the Parks after the war showed that 6,000 miles of six-foot-wide hessian, 6.2 million square yards of wire netting and 3,022 tons of dry paint were used. At the Battle of Cambrai alone in November 1917, General Sir Julian Byng, commanding the British Third Army, had ordered half a million square yards of camouflage netting to conceal 476 tanks, 1,000 guns and howitzers, their supplies and munitions and for the first time, troop concentrations. Across a five-and-half mile wide front, the Germans failed to detect the build-up of 500 tanks, proof of the effectiveness of camouflage. The British had also supplemented this with the creation of a fake tank build-up north of Arras which had been detected and targeted by the Germans. As a consequence of this 'discovery' of camouflage, three further factories were created in the summer 1917, at Wormhoudt to service the Fifth Army, at Godewaerswelde to support the Second Army and at Duisans for the Third Army.

The other camouflage material demanded of the factories was screens used to conceal the movement of traffic. The screens, made of both natural and camouflaged material, were erected on the enemy-side of a road and were made to resemble the surrounding location. They were constructed in independent sections to minimise the effects of shell damage and facilitate repairs, and were intended to conceal traffic from ground observation. The screens 'blended' into their backgrounds and allowed the daylight movement of traffic which would not have been possible in full view of the enemy. They were fabricated to resemble natural foliage and local ground conditions as well as man-made structures such as brick and stone walls. They were used all along the Western Front including the Ypres Salient but were most effective with high ground behind them when breaking the sky line was minimised.

There was also considerable demand throughout the war for dummy soldiers to simulate a false attack, known as a 'Chinese Attack'. There is some speculation regarding the first use of dummy soldiers but it is thought that the first use of *factory-made* dummies was at the Battle of Loos on 25 September 1915, operated by the 142 Brigade (Brigadier-General F.G. Lewis) of the 47th (London) Division (Major-General C. St L. Barter).[3] However, a document issued by the Royal Engineers after the war indicated that they were first used in May 1917,[4] while a published memoir puts the first use of *home-made* dummy soldiers as early as September 1914. At Loos the dummy figures were designed to draw off fire from the real attack, but in time their use became more sophisticated: to test enemy barrages, to make the enemy disclose undetected machine gun posts and other defensive arrangements and to make the enemy man his front line trenches and expose himself to an anti-personnel shrapnel barrage.

The factory-made dummy soldiers were manufactured initially from plywood, and later stout millboard, and came to represent soldiers in a number of positions – standing, crouching and kneeling. The 'flat' soldiers were attached to a frame which was placed level to the ground out in No-Man's-Land during the night and was covered with soil or other debris to prevent detection. The dummy soldiers were laid in groups and formations to simulate a real attack and each group was attached to wires that led back to shell holes or other suitable cover. Soldiers subsequently raised and lowered the dummies at the appropriate time.

The 'Chinese Attack' was usually accompanied by smoke and supported by machine gun and artillery fire, which meant that the defenders did not get a proper sight of the 'attackers', numbering anything up to 300 figures. The defenders often concluded that they were under attack and retaliated with artillery, mortar and machine gun fire, fire power that was drawn away from a simultaneous real attack. The retaliatory fire meant that there were often casualties amongst soldiers who operated the dummies.

The problem for defenders was that it was impossible under battlefield conditions to properly determine whether an attack was real or fake, so they had to react as if all attacks were real. On one occasion the British tried a double bluff with the dummy soldiers. On 28 July 1917, three days before the Fifth Army attack at Ypres, a 'Chinese Attack' was launched with several hundred dummy soldiers with the specific aim of locating enemy machine guns. The 'attack' also showed that the Germans were manning their front line in anticipation of an offensive. This meant that they would be vulnerable to an artillery barrage, which was initiated immediately. After the barrage had ceased the dummy soldiers were left standing to show the Germans that they had been fooled, in the hope that when the real attack was launched, they would delay their artillery barrage and the manning of their trenches.

The effectiveness of the dummy soldiers in deceiving the Germans was highlighted in Field Marshal Haig's Fourth Despatch dated 25 December 1917:

> These measures [feint attacks] would seem to have had considerable success, if any weight may be attached to the enemy's reports concerning them. They involved, however, the disadvantage that I frequently found myself unable to deny German accounts of the bloody repulse of extensive British attacks which in fact never took place.

In the latter stages of the war in 1918 dummy tanks were used to great effect to support infantry attacks. At that stage the tank had a devastating effect on the morale of the Germans soldiers, particularly the Mark V tank launched in July 1918 and first seen by the Germans in August at Amiens, although a few had been used at Le Hamel, a few weeks previously. The Germans had underestimated the value of tanks, based on observations of the previously unreliable British models, but after Amiens the appearance of tanks would affect the outcome of engagements, particularly as the

British infantry and the tanks operated as units. Consequently the appearance of dummy tanks had an effect that more than compensated for the effort required to 'knock up' the canvas and wooden structures. In preparation for the major offensives throughout 1917, mock-up tank 'factories' had created lifelike wooden structures towed by the infantry but with the return to more mobile warfare at the end of 1918, the engineers displayed ingenuity in creating mock-ups overnight using whatever materials were at hand.

After the first deployment of tanks on 15 September 1916, the mass build-up of tanks was indicative of an impending infantry offensive. The British deployed masses of dummy canvas and wooden tanks to indicate an offensive operation distant from the real attack sector in order to ensure that German reserves where deployed ineffectively. These fake preparatory activities were especially effective when the Royal Flying Corps were in command of the air space over the front, denying enemy planes the use of aerial reconnaissance and a close look at the 'tanks'.

The Western Front deception model was reproduced in other theatres of war, notably in Palestine where No-Man's-Land was not such a constraint and there the British Army (The Egyptian Expeditionary Force, EEF), primarily under General Sir Edmund Allenby, employed deception that made use of the more fluid nature of the warfare. The deception planners were able to 'contact' the enemy patrols and plant false intelligence in a manner that was not possible on the Western Front. This was utilised by Allenby's intelligence officer, Colonel Richard Meinertzhagen, in the perpetration of the 'Haversack Ruse' at Gaza/Beersheba in October 1917.

Despite the regular references in the Official Histories, few instruction pamphlets (SS manuals) were published during the war concerning deception. The notable exceptions were 'Notes No.4 Artillery in Offensive Operations' (SS 139/4, February 1917), 'The Use of Smoke' (SS 175 August 1917) and 'The Principles and Practice of Camouflage' (SS 206, March 1918). How the information in these manuals was to be used in an integrated deception plan was left entirely to the imagination and creativity of the individual officers charged with the task.

The most significant deception measure arising from the manuals was the use of camouflage but its real value was only gradually appreciated by higher command. The French pioneered the use of camouflage but for a significant period, they continued to dress their soldiers in blue coats and red trousers! As well as wearing khaki, British soldiers were taught field craft which included a large element of personal concealment using natural foliage and their waterproof sheets. Within the first few weeks, while the war was still above ground, the British soldiers exercised their concealment skills to great effect. At Mons on 23 August, the German First Army had difficulty locating the troops until three to four hours before the action, while at Le Cateau on 26 August, the Germans thought that they were fighting the whole of the BEF rather than just three divisions!

The post-war manuals which dealt with camouflage were instructional texts for the construction of camouflage for objects such as machine gun emplacements, observation posts and gun pits, rather than suggestions in the abstract for its employment in an attacking or defensive role. 'The Manual of Field Works (All Arms)' published in 1921 addressed the issue of camouflage with a detailed approach to its implementation.[5] The post-war publication of the *Camouflage Service of the RE*, although primarily an instructional text, did adopt a broader view of camouflage than simple concealment. It addressed the use of dummy soldiers in the 'Chinese attacks' and evaluated their effectiveness. However, other than the specific use of dummy soldiers, the manuals did not detail how the concealment of objects could be used to influence the outcome of battles.

The value of these manuals lay in the fact that they illustrated that the creation of relatively inexpensive constructions could support complex deception plans. *The Manual of Field Works* demonstrated that for dummy trenches to be convincing to German aerial reconnaissance, they needed only be dug to a depth of six inches and provided that the sides were vertical or preferably undercut, they would create shadows sufficiently realistic to convince the German aviators, whose time over the 'trenches' would be kept to a minimum by ground fire.[6] At Meteren in July 1918 the 9th (Scottish) Division took coconut matting with a large black line painted down the middle, to represent a shadow, and laid it over the trenches containing soldiers to create the impression of empty, abandoned trenches prior to an attack.[7]

By the end of 1914 the development of parallel trench systems separated by No-Man's-Land posed a conundrum for the attacking armies. By 10 March 1915 the British were well on their way to solving the problem.

2

The Tools of the Trade

All men can see the tactics whereby I conquer, but none can see the strategy out of which victory is evolved.
Sun Tzu

To truly deceive an enemy an array of techniques and skills are required. There are techniques, some of which can be described and written down, some of which cannot and remain intuitive. There are skills, some of which can be learnt and acquired, some of which cannot and rely on natural ability. Effective deception plans are not prescriptive and require a degree of creativity on the part of the officers and men developing them.

Between 1915 and 1918, the British Army developed a template or framework of deception techniques, a proportion of which were captured in a variety of manuals and pamphlets published during and after the war; 'how to camouflage a machine gun emplacement' for example, or 'how to operate dummy soldiers in a "Chinese Attack"'. Whilst not exhaustive, these manuals explained what to do and how to do it but failed to explain why, when and, on the Western Front in particular, the all important where. The failure to address the why, when and where was not surprising as these elements required creativity and intuitiveness, by definition difficult to capture in any publication, let alone a military manual. By the end of 1915, GHQ, the army commanders and the majority of senior officers had a good appreciation of the why, when and where, which they ably demonstrated throughout the rest of the war.

For truly effective deception plans, the right blend of all five elements was required. Although not exclusive, the 'what' and 'how' were the domain of the lower units while the 'why', 'when' and 'where' belonged to GHQ and the army commanders; but there were occasions when initial instructions issued by the army commanders also contained the 'what' and 'how' elements. For example, prior to Cambrai (1917) and Amiens (1918), Generals Sir Julian Byng and Sir Henry Rawlinson issued instructions through officers of their General Staff that specifically referenced some of the techniques that should be employed.

The publication of the various manuals highlighted the fact that deception was in the consciousness of the British Army throughout the war and was seen as a tool that should be taken forward into the post-war period. However, these manuals did not capture the entire range of techniques practised as their emphasis was firmly on camouflage. Systematically examining British Army operations throughout the war reveals at least 30 different deception techniques employed to assist with the offensive operations. These ranged from dummy soldiers and tanks, to bogus wireless messages, the spread of false rumours, feint attacks and artillery 'back' barrages. These techniques could be selected and combined into a deception plan once the assigned officer understood the plan's objective ('why'), its timing with respect to the real operation ('when') and its location ('where'). Generally these deception plans were aimed at concealing the time, the place and the units involved in an attack, with Gallipoli being a notable exception, as this was essentially a defensive operation.

Over the five years of war on the Western Front, not only did British and French offensive operations evolve but so too did the Germans' approach to defence. From the beginning of 1915 offensive operations were primarily the domain of the Entente and evolved as hard lessons were learnt regarding attacks on trench systems with well dug-in defenders. From early in the war, the British were able to regularly capture, at a cost, the German front line positions but their retention proved difficult as German counter-attacks found it easy to storm the entrenched positions that now faced the 'wrong' way. Through the implementation of a deception plan that concealed the real time and place of an attack and presented intelligence for an imminent attack somewhere else, it was hoped that the trenches would either not be fully manned or, more beneficially, that the reinforcements needed for the counter-attack would be concentrated behind those sectors targeted by the deception plan. It was hoped that the delay in the transference of the reserves to the correct sector would be sufficient to enable the British to consolidate and 'turn' the trenches to form positions which were now defensible against the counter-attacks. The major problem with this tactical approach was that although deception planning matured relatively rapidly, the offensive operations which were actually required to capture the enemy positions developed at a slower pace and were based on painful, but not necessarily always obvious, lessons! As a result, the benefits of the deception plans were not fully exploited until later in the war, as the British Army moved along the offensive learning curve.

German artillery had often pre-registered on their own front-line trenches, which when occupied by the attacking British troops turned them into extremely dangerous places. Hence the deception plans had to be targeted at the redeployment of the German artillery, and not just the German reserve troops, away from the actual attack sector. As the fake preparations progressed in parallel with the real preparations, the response of the German artillery was often a tangible measure of the effectiveness of the deception plan. Further, as British artillery methods became more sophisticated, local deceptions were practised to reveal the enemy gun emplacements, which were then targeted through counter-battery bombardments to diminish their effectiveness against the British-occupied enemy trenches.

The basic aims of the deception plans were therefore four-fold. They were to target the enemy troops manning the trenches (defenders), to coax the enemy into deploying troop reinforcements in the wrong sector as well as his artillery, and to locate the position of all the remaining artillery batteries. A deception plan worked on the fundamental premise that the German Army could not mount a credible defence over the entire 450 miles of the Western Front because of the constraints on men and materials, even allowing for those sectors where, geographically, attacks were not feasible. Conversely, and for exactly the same reasons, the Allies could not mount a credible attack along the whole of the Western Front; if so, the war would indeed have been 'over by Christmas'. Deception therefore had the potential of tying down defenders to particular sectors for considerable periods of time to repulse fake operations and as a consequence the Germans were unable to move them to the real attack sectors until the nature of the feint attacks had been established. The greater the length of the front line targeted by the deception plan, the bigger the problem, with respect to the deployment of the reserves and the artillery, that it posed for the Germans; the greater the length of the front the bigger the task for the British, as it required a significant investment in men and materials. Deception, combined with progress in offensive operations – in particular, advances in artillery barrages, counter-battery work with more reliable guns and shells and the development of infantry firepower within the fighting platoons, resulted in an efficient fighting machine by the time of the Final Hundred Days in 1918. In the period 1915–1917, the deception plans were relatively ahead of offensive operations and as a result the full benefits of the deceptions were not taken advantage of and the Allies suffered numerous setbacks.

As the war progressed, the fighting reputations of certain units, in particular the Canadians and the Australians, supplemented the deception template. The appearance of these units in a particular sector in 1918 could signify an impending attack. In August 1918, the Canadian Corps were relatively fresh and were withdrawn from the First Army front and secretly moved south to the Fourth Army front, although the intelligence generated by the deception plan indicated that they had gone north to join the Second Army. The suspected presence of the Canadians in the British Second Army sector, 100 miles from their real positions, seriously stalled the movement of German reinforcements southwards to Amiens. Similarly, at Hooge in August 1915, concealing the units involved in the attack was a key factor. The 14th (Light) Division, which had previously made an unsuccessful attack towards the Hooge Chateau, was exhausted and while the men remained in the front line the Germans would not expect another attack. A deception plan was implemented which in the Ypres Salient created false intelligence concerning the time and point of attack, while the 14th (Light) Division was secretly replaced with the fresh 6th Division immediately prior to the successful 9 August attack.

As deception planning reached a high level of maturity and expertise relatively early in the war, it remained basically unaltered from March 1915 until November 1918. It was possible to classify deception activities into seven categories: *Concealment, Illusion, Location, Confusion, Behaviour Modification, Unusual Practices and Inadvertent*. Within each category, the different techniques were combined to create the desired result and at a high level the seven categories combined into a deception plan to *conceal* the real military artefacts, *create* false military artefacts and to *confuse* the enemy's OODA Loops.

Concealment, Illusion and *Location* were variations on a theme. *Concealment* was of course primarily achieved as previously discussed through the use of camouflage. Systematic camouflaging of artillery, infantry units, stores and command centres began early in 1915, following the example set by the French Army: 'weakness where there was strength'.

The converse of camouflage was *Illusion,* the creation of 'something that was not there' and hence complemented *Concealment* by creating 'strength where there was weakness'. The British Army was particularly adept at this creative activity and crafted dummy assaults and formations, tanks, ordnance, trenches, headquarters and amphibious landings. Whatever the deception planners required, the British Army developed. Perversely – and this needs to be stressed – all dummy artefacts had to be hidden from the enemy through the use of camouflage in exactly the same way as the real thing.

Dummy artefacts were designed for specific observers. For instance, if dummy assembly trenches were dug to simulate an imminent attack, then piles of earth to give the appearance of a parapet were all that was needed to convince the enemy troops in the opposing trenches. But if the dummy assembly trenches had to convince German aerial reconnaissance, then something else was needed. To fool enemy aircraft, as mentioned, dummy trenches needed only to be dug to a depth of six inches but with undercut sides to create the requisite shadow. Obviously the earth from such a shallow trench could still be piled up to be convincing at ground level. Similarly dummy soldiers came in a variety of forms for different audiences. There were the three-dimensional versions with uniforms and sandbag 'heads' stuffed with straw and earth, convincing at ground level and creating the right kind of shadows to fool aerial reconnaissance. The other main version were the regimented two-dimensional 'cardboard' cut-outs, raised and lowered on frames to simulate an infantry attack where smoke shells and machine gun and artillery barrages prevented opposing defenders from gaining a proper look at the 'attackers'. The dummy soldiers came in a variety of poses. The front-line soldiers were also issued with head-and-shoulder painted silhouettes which could be moved and poked over the parapet from the relative safety of a trench. But dummy artefacts of all kinds relied on aggressive action to conceal the truth by denying the enemy any prolonged view. In this respect, throughout the war there was a great reliance on the aggressive stance of the Royal Flying Corps and latterly the Royal Air Force. The first official reported use of a 'Chinese Attack' was at Loos on 25 September 1915 (as previously mentioned), although the first use of 'dummy' soldiers could have been as early as 13 September 1914 when the 1/East Lancashire Regiment left dummy soldiers and guns in gun pits abandoned by the British and French artillery during the Battle of the Aisne (12-15 September 1914), to convince the Germans that the gun pits were still in use.

The feint attacks involving the dummy soldiers were not without risk for the troops involved. If they were successful in creating the illusion, they could expect to be subjected to intense artillery bombardments. These activities resulted in casualties without the soldiers ever leaving their trenches. As a cruel measurement of effectiveness, the levels of real casualties amongst the soldiers was a good indication of how seriously the enemy had been deceived. A less dramatic but equally valid measure was the state of the dummy soldiers, which after a 'Chinese Attack' were examined under the cover of darkness for bullet damage. There were instances throughout the war when a 'Chinese Attack', for whatever reason, was found not to have attracted enemy fire. The 4th Division (Major-General L.J. Lipsett) and the 51st (Highland) Division (Major-General G. Carter-Campbell) operated dummy soldiers for over an hour in support of the First Army at the Battle of the Canal du Nord on 27 September 1918. However, the Germans paid scant regard, although the British blamed this failure on the poor visibility that morning rather than any failing on their part.

The 'Chinese Attack' was not simply designed to distract the enemy's attention away from the real attack but was additionally used to seek out undetected machine gun emplacements which often opened fire on the dummies. It was also used as a method of ensuring that the Germans were less eager to man their front line trenches in the face of the real attack. A reaction of German front line troops to the dummies with rifle and machine gun fire would attract the attention of the British artillery firing shrapnel. The British adopted the practice of initiating 'Chinese Attacks' on successive days before the real attack to condition the enemy troops to remain in their dugouts for longer than necessary; these actions could also be classified under the *Behaviour Modification* deception category. Simple actions over a period of only two or three days could change the behaviour of defenders in the face of a real attack.

The third variant, *Location,* followed the *Illusion* theme and was the employment of deception in order to make something appear to be located on another sector of the front. Dummy wireless traffic and the use of uniforms and emblems by the 'wrong' troops were both employed to great effect at Amiens 1918.[1] The deception plan was implemented with the specific aim of making the Canadian Corps, which was withdrawn from the line on 30 July, appear to move northwards to join the Second Army, where the dummy wireless traffic was emanating from around the Mount Kemmel area. In reality, the Canadians secretly moved south to join the Fourth Army sector around Amiens. Various deceptive measures were combined into an integrated plan which indicated that the Canadians were further north than their actual position. The *Location* type of deception was also used to make units disappear. This applied particularly to the Tank Corps where the officers on reconnaissance in the front line removed their distinctive skull-and-crossbones emblem, denying the information to any enemy spies.

The fourth deception category, *Confusion,* was employed when it was difficult to conceal the real preparations. Recognising the fact that real intelligence would be gathered by the Germans, the approach was to mix false information and events in with the real information, so that the enemy OODA Loops were slowed down during the Orientation phase as they evaluated the weight of intelligence. The enemy could often distinguish the real from the false intelligence but in a timeframe which it was hoped would be too slow for the developing operation. At Neuve Chapelle in March 1915 the British, unable to conceal the assault preparations, confused the German defences by creating dummy breastworks, with an equal lack of concealment, in adjacent sectors, thereby disguising the point of the attack. When the real attack happened the German defences were not initially supported by redeployed reserves as the issue of the dummy breastworks had still not been resolved. At Neuve Chapelle, as with a lot of the British deception plans, no single method was relied on and other measures were also used to tie down the German reserves to other sectors of the front. The *Confusion* type of deception was regularly employed by the British during the build-up to their major offensives as it became increasingly difficult to conceal the massive preparations required for the major offensives. When the Fourth Army preparations for the Somme offensive in 1916 were impossible to conceal, Haig ordered the Third, First and Second Armies to engage in similar activities. As it was recognised that the British did not have sufficient men and materials to mount offensives on all these army fronts, the preparations were simulated, for instance, through the build-up of camouflaged empty 'boxes' on the Third, First and Second Army fronts and camouflaged full ammunition boxes on the Fourth Army front. To the opposing troops and airmen, there was no difference. The behind-the-lines spies posed a difference problem and command relied on the military police and sentries aggressively obeying orders.

The next category, *Behaviour Modification,* was employed to locally 'condition' the enemy to expect and to react to certain events created specifically for the deception. The first, and possibly best known, example of *Behaviour Modification* was instigated by General Godley on the Gallipoli Peninsula in December 1915, as previously referred to.[2] The deception, both simple and effective, was initiated to prevent the Turks immediately discovering that the British trenches had been evacuated at the end of December 1915. On 24 November 1915, Godley ordered that, during designated periods, all sniping and artillery should cease, unless an exceptional target presented itself, and all troops were to remain silent. The periods of silence were introduced from 7 December and initially the Turks sent out patrols to investigate. At a given signal, these were fired on causing casualties. By this ruse, the Turks '…were successfully taught……that complete silence in a trench did not mean that the garrison had withdrawn'.[3] This ruse was a contributory factor in the successful evacuation of the Gallipoli Peninsula. There were circumstances throughout the war when out of necessity the implementation of a local deception plan was needed which did not extend the apparent frontage of an attack. The British Army would regularly initiate successive feint attacks which would gradually de-sensitise the enemy defenders and as a result when the real attack was launched, the defenders were less alert. Under these circumstances, the employment of *Behaviour Modification* proved to be remarkably effective as it enabled the attacking troops to cross No-Man's-Land before the defenders had fully manned their parapets and machine guns.

The *Behaviour Modification* category complemented the *Unusual Practices* category. The latter is best described as a deviation from standard procedure. For instance, it was customary for the artillery barrage to lift from trench line to trench line and under these circumstances the Germans would often withdraw their troops or hide them in deep dugouts, only manning their trenches once the barrage had been lifted. On 25 September 1915, the British changed this standard practice. At Loos, after the 18-pounder shrapnel barrage had been lifted, seemingly to target the next trench line, unusually it returned for a second pass to catch the Germans in the open manning their trenches.[4, 5]

The final category, *Inadvertent* deception, was an inappropriate reaction to events that were genuine but which were misinterpreted by the enemy and subsequently acted as a deceptive measure. Under these circumstances, the Observe phase of the OODA Loop worked perfectly well, but the Orientate phase simply misread the intelligence presented. For example, the Germans misconstrued the weak artillery bombardment at Loos in 1915 by the British as a poor attempt to distract their attention from the real attack further south by the French. In reality, the British were short of shells.[6] This cannot really be claimed to be a method of deception in the same way as the other categories, in that it was, quite simply, a happy accident, though it could be exploited. The misinterpretation of intelligence was not confined to the Germans. On 5 April 1918, General Erich von Ludendorff abandoned his attack on Amiens and as the momentum slowed he switched his troops northwards where he intended to launch an attack on the plain of the Lys between Armentières and La Bassée. This was a strategic move which could have had the benefit of dragging British troops southwards from around Ypres to deplete and weaken the Flanders front for a later German offensive. The BEF and the French Army interpreted the movement northwards as a feint designed to weaken the Amiens front and consequently Foch refused to alter either the Flanders or the Amiens troop dispositions.

The *Inadvertent* category is the result of a wrong conclusion at the Orientate phase. Real intelligence is inadvertently interpreted as false intelligence by the enemy, which can be advantageous or disadvantageous, depending on the action taken by the enemy. The provision of intelligence by the deception plan which is misinterpreted, however advantageous, must ultimately be classed as a failure of the deception plan and lessons should be learnt.

The seven categories proposed here are based on operational activity. Other authors have categorised deception differently. Field Marshal Archibald P. Wavell, who was assigned to Sir Edmund Allenby's staff in Palestine in 1918 and who became Commander of the British Army forces in the Middle East during the Second World War, recognised that all deceptions were variations on the few basic themes of counter-surveillance, displays, feint operations, demonstrations and ruses.[7]

Most of the seven deception categories identified had been employed by the time of Neuve Chapelle, 10–13 March 1915. The first uses were seen of *Illusion* on the Aisne, September 1914, *Concealment, Location, Confusion,* and *Unusual Practices* at Neuve Chapelle, *Behaviour Modification* at Gallipoli, December 1915 and *Inadvertent* at Loos, September 1915. So the deception learning curve was relatively mature by the end of 1915 and was in advance of the offensive learning curve; arguably the two learning curves only coincided during the latter half of 1918.

The concealment of real military artefacts or the creation of false ones will not influence the behaviour of the enemy unless these are placed within the context of a wider deception plan. Local deception plans will address specific problems but to change the course of a war, more far reaching, integrated deception plans needed to be developed. This truth was grasped by French and Haig by March 1915 when the first true integrated deception plan was instigated at Neuve Chapelle. Deception plans had to be implemented across multi-unit fronts and where possible across multi-army fronts. The plans had to involve units not involved with the attack, who were to generate false intelligence to be picked up by the enemy intelligence organisations and fed into their decision-making processes. This approach could be high risk if the criteria of plausibility, consistency and predictability were not rigidly adhered to; the more complex the plan, the higher the risk that it would be penetrated. To protect the plans, they had to be developed from the top down and on a need-to-know basis, so that allied troops were also deceived. Lapses in security, inept implementation, units 'doing their own thing' – or bad luck – could penetrate multi-sector deception plans.

The multi-sector approach was the key to a successful deception plan although there were a few exceptions to this, notably at Gallipoli in December 1915 and Gaza in October 1917 where the deception plans were implemented in a single sector but where the plans were so well constructed and 'tangled' that their brilliance became their shield against penetration. Throughout the war there was still scope for restricted plans, especially in the latter half of 1918, to address a local situation.

In 1982, Daniel and Herbig concluded that there were two varieties of deception, namely the 'ambiguity-increasing' variety (A-type) and the 'misleading-variety' (M-type).[8] The A-type was designed to conceal the true aim of activities while the M-type was aimed at reducing ambiguity by suggesting that only one action was plausible. These varieties were based on functional classifications and were achieved through the implementation of the categories described in this work. For example, the offensive preparations by all four British armies prior to the Battle of the Somme (1916) followed the *Confusion* category, in that as the Fourth Army preparations were massive and could not be effectively concealed, similar preparations were conducted, to varying degrees, on the Third, First and Second Army fronts. This would be classed as an A-type deception. The complex deception plan initiated at Gaza/Beersheba (1917) by Sir Edmund Allenby and his intelligence officer, Lieutenant-Colonel Richard Meinertzhagen, simply misled the Turkish Army and their German commander by creating an *illusion* with respect to the objectives and targets of the real and feint attacks, an example of an M-type deception.

Throughout the war, whereas the objectives of the plans remained fairly constant, the template of techniques gradually evolved to reflect changes in offensive operations. As the deception plans became more ambitious through 1916, the need-to-know principle emerged. The majority of the troops had to be kept in ignorance. The usefulness of the need-to-know principle was proven when prisoners were captured after a raid, who would inadvertently give credence to the deception. Even the build-up of dummy artefacts was concealed from the troops in the same sector. In 1918, Mitchell was amazed to find a wooden tank under a camouflage net after he sneaked a look during the build-up to the Battle of Amiens.

Perhaps the most important implementation principle to emerge from 1916 was the selection of the target of deception. Haig had instructed that all four armies should engage in preparations for a major attack in their sector. This resulted in a deception plan which was implemented across 100 miles of the Western Front and generated intelligence which could be gathered by three separate German armies. Although each German army commander had to be convinced that the preparations in front of him were real, the deception plans were actually targeting General Erich von Falkenhayn (Chief of the German General Staff), his staff and intelligence organisation at the German Supreme Army Command (*Oberste Heeresleitung,* or OHL). Falkenhayn was the only commander in a position to be able to evaluate the intelligence gathered from all four British armies. If intelligence could be gained regarding the mindset of the commander, then the deception would target this on the premise that once the commander held a particular belief, he would not change his mind even if intelligence were obtained to the contrary. The British used this to target Field Marshal Otto Liman von Sanders during the April and August 1915 landings on the Gallipoli peninsula and General Kress von Kressenstein at Gaza in October 1917. This was Magruder's Principle in action.

Although there does not seem to have been any official policy adopted with respect to deception planning, the Commander-in-Chief and the various army commanders on the Western Front promoted its use for the majority of offensive operations. The ideas of deception were promoted by Sir Edmund Allenby in 1916 at the Third Army School where the attending officers were encouraged to share their experiences in the use of ruses and to refine these techniques so that consistency could be achieved across all units involved.

The implementation of the multi-front deception plans revealed inherent weaknesses. The plans could only target the initial phase of the battle. This weakened the effect of deception until the final Hundred Days of the war, when, after the first day of each battle, as the engagements became mobile, local deception activities could be instigated. Once the battle commenced, the threat posed by fake attacks could not be maintained and the enemy could quickly re-deploy his reserves. The British tried to mitigate this by staggering the zero hours of the real and fake attacks, thereby holding German reinforcements for a little longer. At the Battle of the Somme Haig instructed the Third, First and Second Armies to maintain pressure on the Germans from July to November by initiating minor real and fake operations of sufficient threat to hold the German troops in their sectors. Haig created sufficient doubt within the German higher command to influence their re-deployment of reserves.

Despite the relatively sparse references to deception planning in the Official Histories and postwar literature, it is apparent that the British Army, GHQ and its army commanders did give it a high priority, as it is difficult to find a significant engagement from March 1915 onwards where deception plans were not implemented, often across multi-army fronts. The high cost in the expenditure of men and materials and the considerable effort involved was obviously considered justifiable by the Army High Command.

3

The Western Front 1914:
Local Necessities

The clever combatant imposes his will on the enemy, but does not allow the enemy's will to be imposed on him.
Sun Tzu

For the British Army, the war in 1914 came as a shock. The Haldane reforms had created the British Expeditionary Force, designed to be rapidly transported to the area of conflict, fight a decisive battle and return home having vanquished the enemy and installed an army of occupation. Even today, an expeditionary force is defined as an armed force designed to accomplish specific objectives in a foreign land, which is agile, flexible, and rapidly deployed. The expeditionary force of 1914 fitted this definition and because of its mobile nature, it was assumed that the few crucial battles that it would have to fight would be dominated by the rifle and the bayonet. Haldane had argued that Britain required a greater expeditionary force than either France or Germany to support the needs of a global empire.[1] What it had not been designed for was a continental, 'industrial' style war which required a mass army sustainable only through the politically unacceptable introduction of conscription. Haldane had, in 1906, dismissed the idea of a mass army as untenable. As a consequence, the BEF of 1914 consisted of six infantry divisions and a cavalry division and totalled about 160,000 men. Besides this force there were about 120,000 British troops on garrison duty across the globe, about 230,000 reservists and 268,000 members of the Territorial Force, the latter formed in 1908 based on Haldane's recommendation. To put this into perspective, in January 1914 the French Army consisted of 47 divisions, some 820,000 French and colonial troops; that summer another 2.9 million Frenchmen would be mobilized.

Immediately after the declaration of war on 4 August, Lord Kitchener, as the newly appointed Secretary of State for War, addressed the British Cabinet on 5-6 August and announced that only four of the promised six divisions of the BEF should be sent to France and that the BEF should concentrate at Amiens, instead of Maubeuge, to prevent its destruction – a suggestion that was overruled. Further, he urged that Britain should immediately raise a volunteer army of over one million men to fight a war that would last at least three years. The remaining two divisions of the BEF would be retained within mainland Britain not only to assist in the training of the 'New Armies' but also to meet any invasion threat posed by the Germans.

On 12 August, only eight days after the declaration of war, the first units of the BEF arrived in Boulogne en route to the French battlefields. In the middle of August 1914 the BEF in France, commanded by Field Marshal Sir John French, consisted of four divisions of about 100,000 men. It was divided into the I Corps (GOC, Lieutenant-General Sir Douglas Haig) (1st and 2nd Divisions), II Corps (GOC, Lieutenant-General Sir J.M. Grierson) (3rd and 5th Divisions) and the cavalry division (GOC, Major-General Sir E.H.H. Allenby). On 17 August Grierson suffered a heart attack and was replaced by General Sir Horace Smith-Dorrien. The III Corps (GOC, Lieutenant-General Sir William Pulteney) (4th and 6th Divisions) was retained in mainland Britain.

The BEF advanced towards the German Army but the French Fifth Army (GOC, General Charles Lanrezac), covering its right flank, was already suffering under an onslaught from the German Third Army and was pulling out and retreating in the direction of Paris in order to stay in contact with the French Fourth Army on its right. However, the BEF continued its forward march, even though its flank was now exposed, and set up their defensive lines along the Mons canal. On the morning of 23 August 1914 at 06:30, the BEF engaged the German First Army (GOC, General Alexander von Kluck) at Mons. Although the British inflicted significant casualties on the German Army, it was still a one-sided fight that the British could not win and by the evening the British Army was retreating back towards Paris in the same direction as the French Army. As it retreated, it aggressively engaged the pursuing enemy but despite these rearguard actions, which undoubtedly made the German Army more cautious in its approach, the British Army was now vulnerable to destruction. There were notable engagements which were subsequently recognised by the Battles Nomenclature Committee, at Elouges (24 August), Solesmes (25 August), at Le Cateau, Le Grand Fayt and Etreux (26 August), at Cerizy (28 August) and Nery, Crepy en Valois and Villers-Cotterets (1 September).

With Paris at its back and the German armies manoeuvring east of the capital, the BEF finally halted, following the intervention of Lord Kitchener and along with the French armies went on the offensive. Fighting battles around the Marne and the Aisne, the Germans retreated to their defensive alignments which they would occupy for some time. As the trench lines became established and gathered an air of permanence, in the north the 'Race for the Sea' began, characterised by a series of operations as the British and the Germans tried to outflank each other and destroy the rapidly stabilising defences. All of these battles still possessed the characteristics of battles that the now decimated BEF was designed to fight, although the decisive battle that the British had envisaged pre-war remained elusive. For both the British and the Germans, each battle failed in its primary objective of outflanking the enemy.

From 23 August until 29 October both sides had launched a multitude of attacks and in the absence of the well defined No-Man's-Land, the opportunity for deception had been limited. The use of deception in 1914 was rare and generally confined to the lower units at a local level, possibly as a legacy of the lessons learnt from the South African War (1899-1902).

The 1914 volumes of the British Official History make no mention of deception activities, however the first volume from 1915, which actually covers the end of 1914 from 23 November, showed that the British Army started to implement deception plans, although the majority were haphazard.

During the initial engagements the fighting was fairly straightforward in both attack and defence with both the Allies and Germans making full use of the natural foliage that still existed across the Western Front to conceal their activities. The trenches did not stretch from the Swiss border to the North Sea in a continuous line, they were shallow affairs which were often separated from the next section by 200, 300 or even 400 yards.

As a consequence the troops were often fighting in small scattered groups, taking advantage of the natural surroundings.

On 26 October 1914, German troops from the XXVII Reserve Corps easily passed through the fragmented British line between the Scots Guards and the South Staffordshire Regiment at Kruiseecke during the First Battle of Ypres. Although other British troops farther back had spotted the insurgents, they refrained from firing on them for fear of hitting their own men. At 10:00 the German's main body of troops advanced and as they did so the German troops behind the British line shouted out 'Retire!'[2] A few soldiers of the 1/South Staffordshire Regiment withdrew, which enabled the attacking troops to capture the village of Kruiseecke.

During these last few months of 1914, there were a couple of examples of deception being practised by the British, which would be used on numerous other occasions throughout the war. Disinformation was first used at the Battle of the Marne (7–10 September 1914). The British Government and the British Army used rumours that were sweeping throughout Britain, France and Germany to their advantage, simply by not denying them; there is no evidence to suggest that the British had deliberately started the rumours. The retreat from Mons was a period when rumours were rife. The British and the French had variously been saved from destruction by St George, Joan of Arc, the Angel of Mons and English longbowmen. By 28 August, first in Britain and then elsewhere, rumours spread that Russians 'with snow on their boots' had landed at Aberdeen and had been secretly transported by rail through Britain en route to the south coast and the Western Front. These rumours were widely reported in the British press and British intelligence encouraged Carl Lody, a German spy, to feed them back to Berlin. On 6 November 1914, Carl Lody was shot at the Tower of London. Clearly, in the desperate days prior to the Battle of the Marne, it was worth encouraging a rumour that indicated the badly mauled BEF and French Armies were being bolstered by units of the Russian Army. As the Germans retreated across the Marne, their front line troops could no longer assume that their level of fatigue and war weariness was matched by that of their attackers.

Seven weeks later at the Battle of Gheluvelt (29–31 October 1914), part of First Ypres (10 October–22 November 1914), General Haig, commanding I Corps, was alert to the potential for deception. On the morning of 29 October, Haig inspected the trenches dug by the 7th Division (GOC, Major-General Sir Thomas Capper). However he was dissatisfied with them as they left his men in an exposed position. He immediately instructed General Capper and Brigadier-General Royal Engineers Spring R. Rice to walk the area to find more suitable locations. However, he expressly instructed them to leave the original trenches to act as dummies to distract the Germans. Although these plans were forestalled by German artillery action, it is interesting to note that Haig thought that there was merit in the use of dummy trenches so early in the conflict. Several weeks later, the editor of the magazine *Berliner Tageblatt* who was serving as a reserve lieutenant in Flanders wrote 'The shelter trenches [of the British] were so well constructed that they could not be discovered with the naked eye.'[3] At this time, the natural landscape, relatively unscarred, could still be effectively used to conceal.

On 13 October 1914, the British III Corps attacked from the Mont de Cats towards Outtersteene and Meteren, capturing the two villages. They found that the Germans had an appreciation of natural camouflage and had sited their trenches immediately in front of houses, walls and hedges, which meant that the defenders' heads were invisible against the backgrounds. Further, instead of using the excavated soil to form a parapet, the soil had been scattered, which had rendered the trenches virtually invisible to the attackers. Isolated groups of soldiers concealed their positions using techniques that had been taught in basic training. Although the 1914 Official Histories made no further reference to any deception being used by the BEF at this time, individual soldiers' memoirs from the same period make it clear that at battalion level at least, ruses were being employed in an attempt to modify German military behaviour. The testimonies were from soldiers who were either privy to the act of deception or often, for reasons of security, were ignorant of these acts and simply 'stumbled' across them as part of their daily activities. The methods described were similar to those employed during the South African War and probably owed much to the experiences gained by the young officers who campaigned there and who now commanded in France.

The 1/East Lancashire Regiment, who had used dummy soldiers at the Battle of the Aisnes on 13 September 1914, used the same ruse on 4 May 1915 at Ypres, but in more grisly fashion. A 'sacrifice platoon' of the 1st battalion had been left behind to cover the retreat of the remainder of the regiment. When the sacrifice platoon subsequently retired, they propped up their dead comrades on the parapet to create the impression that the trench was still manned to deter the Germans from immediate attack.

Premeditated deception plans perpetrated by the higher command seem at first sight to have been practised as early as December 1914. The British and French armies launched a series of co-ordinated attacks supported by demonstrations and feints. These were initiated by various British units and used to support the French attacks near Arras and Ypres. However, these demonstrations were not necessarily always deceptions – things were more complex!

After discussions between Sir John French and General Joseph Joffre, Commander-in-Chief of the French Army, it was agreed that the German line would be assaulted on 14 December 1914 by a series of co-ordi-nated British and French Army attacks from the area around the Yser in the north to the Champagne region in the south. On 12 December Lieutenant-General A.J. Murray, French's Chief of the General Staff at GHQ, issued 'Instructions for Operations Commencing 14 December 1914'. The instructions clearly indicated that the French Army offen-sive would be supported by a co-ordinated series of corps attacks by the British II, III, IV and Indian Corps.[4] In conjunction with the French Eighth Army (General d'Urbal) the BEF would attack in the Yser district and around Ypres, while the French Second (General de Castelnau) and Tenth (General de Maud'huy) Armies would attack between the Oise and La Bassée Canal with the French Fourth Army (General de Langle de Cary) striking northwards through the Champagne region.

In detail the British II Corps (GOC, Lieutenant-General Sir C. Fergusson) would attack on the right flank of the French Eighth Army along the Wytschaete Ridge-Messines line, while the III Corps (GOC, Lieutenant-General W.P. Pulteney) would attack on the right of II Corps, astride the Ploegsteert-Messines Road. The II Corps objective was the capture of Messines while the III Corps objective was Warneton. The IV Corps (GOC, Lieutenant-General Sir Henry S. Rawlinson) and the Indian Corps (GOC, Lieutenant-General Sir James Willcocks) were simply to carry out local operations to engage the enemy and prevent them from transferring troops south to defend the sectors being attacked by the French and the British II and III Corps.

Despite Sir John French's confirmation that real offensive operations were being initiated, his detailed plans ordered the attacks to be scaled back or 'diluted' to demonstrations unless a real opportunity presented itself. The emphasis of the attacks was switched from corps attacks to divisional attacks, with the divisions ordered not to get ahead of the neighbouring division on their left flank. French ordered the 3rd Division (II Corps), adjacent to the French Eighth Army operation, to attack with determination. The 5th Division, also from II Corps, was ordered simply to engage in a lot of activity as if *about* to attack and III Corps was ordered to make demonstrations that would hold the attention of the enemy on its front. As a consequence the feint attacks and demonstrations, characteristic of future deception plans, were carried out, but their intention was less deception and more the preservation of troops and munitions.

A similar situation arose on 18 December 1914. The French XVI Corps was to launch an attack south of the British and Joffre requested British support. French agreed and issued instructions that the II, III, IV and Indian Corps were to attack vigorously. However during the detailed planning stage, French's orders indicated that the II Corps should attack in conjunction with the French XVI Corps but the III, IV and Indian Corps were directed to initiate demonstrations to tie-down the German reserves on their respective fronts. The demonstrations consisted of attacks ranging from a few companies to two battalions. Although the demonstrations meant that troops left their trenches and casualties resulted, the attack involved between 5 per cent and 10 per cent of the Corps' fighting strength, which was unlikely to seriously tie down German reserves.

So these demonstrations were not really part of a deception plan but were the result of French's assessment of potential casualties and the lack of sufficient ammunition to support the proposed offensive actions. True deception planning, with activities designed from the outset to deceive the enemy, did not happen for at least another three months, until March 1915, although it could be argued that the order given to IV Corps and the Indian Corps for 14 December represented an embryonic deception plan.

Although the British Army was yet to engage in the kind of deception that would bring significant military advantages, it is interesting to note that by December 1914 the Royal Navy had executed a significant naval deception. By 1 November 1914, Vice-Admiral Graf von Spee's German East Asia Squadron had already engaged and defeated a small British force at the Battle of Coronel. British Naval Intelligence soon deciphered the simple coded messages between Vice-Admiral Graf von Spee's German East Asia Squadron anchored at Valparaiso in Chile. Using the same

cipher, British Naval Intelligence ordered von Spee's force of five cruisers (SMS *Scharnhorst, Gneisenau, Leipzig, Nurnburg* and *Dresden*) to attack
the Falkland Islands. Waiting for them at Port Stanley was Vice-Admiral
Sir Doveton Sturdee's force of two battlecruisers and three cruisers. At
the Battle of the Falklands on 8 December 1914 the British battlecruisers
HMS *Invincible* and *Inflexible,* sank the *Scharnhorst* and the *Gneisenau* while
the cruisers HMS *Glasgow* and *Cornwall* sank the *Leipzig.* HMS *Kent* sank
the *Nurnburg.* SMS *Dresden* escaped, only to be sunk in March 1915.[5]

It is significant that the mighty Royal Navy was prepared to use trickery to ambush the enemy. This act alone send a clear signal that the British
were prepared to use any means possible to defeat an enemy that was gar-
gantuan compared with British forces, especially the army. Within seven
months of the start of the war, the British Army would become engaged
in its first real offensive action at Neuve Chapelle in March 1915 and
would employ a deception plan that displayed a high degree of maturity.

4

The Western Front 1915: Laying the Foundations

Numerical weakness comes from having to prepare against possible attacks; numerical strength, from compelling our adversary to make these preparations against us.
Sun Tzu

By December 1914 the Western Front had 'stabilised' with a marked trench system existing from the Swiss border to the North Sea. In response to the war that would not be over by Christmas, the British Army had reorganised itself into a number of distinct armies. The First and Second Armies came into existence on 26 December 1914, the former commanded by General Sir Douglas Haig and the latter by General Sir Horace Smith-Dorrien. The remaining armies were formed on 13 July 1915 (Third Army, General Sir Charles Monro), 5 February 1916 (Fourth Army, General Sir Henry Rawlinson), while the Fifth Army (General Sir Hubert Gough) was formed out of the Reserve Army in October 1916. For the moment Field Marshal Sir John French retained the role of British Commander-in-Chief of the British Army on the Western Front.

In that year it became clear to all that the methods of the colonial wars were inappropriate for this massive conflagration and that new techniques and new weapons systems had to be developed. Within the area of deception also, 1915 would prove to be a watershed and would challenge the imagination of army commanders and their staffs.

The British Army became engaged in a number of major offensive operations throughout the year, primarily at Neuve Chapelle, Aubers Ridge, Festubert, Hooge and Loos on the Western Front. It would also be forced to extricate itself from the Gallipoli peninsula.

Battle of Neuve Chapelle, 10–13 March 1915

Early in 1915 the French Commander-in-Chief, General Joseph Joffre, decided that the British and French Armies should mount an offensive on the Western Front, primarily to relieve pressure on the Russians on the Eastern Front, but also to effect a breakthrough of the static German defences and to show the commitment of the British to the war. General Sir John French agreed that the BEF in conjunction with the French Army should attack relatively close to each other in the Artois and Champagne regions. The double attack would have the strategic aim of capturing the railway network which ran north-south across the Plain of Douai and directly supported the German trench systems. Driving the Germans behind this rail network would force them to retreat from large areas, both north and south. The preoccupation with Douai would return again in 1918 as the British simulated threats against the railhead to distract German attention from offensives at Ypres in the north and the Hindenburg Line in the south.

In 1915, the BEF decided to attack at Neuve Chapelle, north-west of the plain, while simultaneously the French Tenth Army would deliver the main blow twenty miles further south in the Champagne region between Arras and Lens towards the heights of Vimy Ridge, from which they could dominate the whole of the Douai region. For the British, the area around Neuve Chapelle presented a salient that protruded into their line, making the positions either side vulnerable. French decided that the reduction of the salient would represent a tactical objective whilst maintaining the plain of Douai as the strategic goal.

The First Army under Haig's command was chosen for the task which would involve the 7th and 8th Divisions from IV Corps (Lieutenant-General Sir Henry Rawlinson) and the Lahore and Meerut Divisions from the Indian Corps (Lieutenant-General Sir James Willcocks). Haig initially instructed Rawlinson to devise a plan for the forthcoming offensive. When produced, it simply involved the capture of Neuve Chapelle, thereby pinching out the salient. Haig, dismayed by its lack of ambition, modified it so that after the capture of Neuve Chapelle, the army would press on and take the heights of Aubers Ridge almost three miles behind the village. The 'heights' were a mere 25 feet higher than the surrounding area but as was becoming evident, the army that held the high ground, any high ground, held a distinct advantage. It was from positions on Aubers Ridge prior to the start of the offensive that the German Army could observe Haig's preparations for the forthcoming attack.

On 12 February, Haig submitted a plan to GHQ for an offensive towards the Aubers Ridge that would begin with the capture of Neuve Chapelle, a fortified village at the centre of the First Army front. On 15 February, Sir John French approved the plan.

For the first time, the proposed offensive operation by the BEF would be an all-British affair as the French declared that until they were relieved by extra British divisions at Ypres, they had insufficient troops to support. The main attack on the First Army front, which stretched thirteen miles from La Bassée canal to Bois Grenier, would involve a sudden and heavy bombardment of the German front line trenches, in front of Neuve Chapelle, from 500 guns firing for only 35 minutes prior to zero hour. Beside high explosives, shrapnel shells would be fired to clear passages through the enemy barbed wire.

On 10 March 1915, after those 35 minutes, the bombardment lifted to its second objective, the village of Neuve Chapelle and its various strong points. The change signalled the start of the offensive by three infantry brigades – the Garhwal Brigade from the Meerut Division (Lieutenant-General C.A. Anderson) on the right, the 25 Brigade from the 8th Division (Major-General F. Davies) in the centre and the 23 Brigade from the 7th Division (Major-General T. Capper) on the right. The infantry advance began at 08:05 along a 2,000-yard front and after a relatively easy capture of the first objective of the German front line trenches, the infantry dug in and waited for 30 minutes until the bombardment of the artillery's second objective, the village, lifted. The attack resumed with the remainder of the Indian Corps and IV Corps, focusing on Neuve Chapelle but expanding the front to five miles wide. After the capture of this second objective, the offensive faltered through a basic lack of communication, as each of the Corps commanders halted and waited for the other to act. Haig eventually was made aware of the cessation of the advance and after a period of five hours, ordered its resumption. This fatal delay enabled the Germans to strengthen their positions with machine gun emplacements and to bring down reinforcements. At 10:00 when it became apparent that Neuve Chapelle had fallen, General von Claer at VII (German) Corps HQ ordered the 14th Infantry Division to recapture the village. But a counter-attack became impractical as all the new troops were required simply to hold the line. This enabled the British to dig in to the south-east of Neuve Chapelle in front of the Bois de Biez, close to the Germans' second line. Despite the subsequent arrival in the evening of additional German reinforcements from XIX Corps, who had been holding the line between Bois Grenier, Armentières and the base of the Ypres hills, the British position remained secure. In total at the Battle of Neuve Chapelle, the British suffered 572 officers and 12,239 other ranks, killed, wounded or missing, while it was deemed that the Germans sustained comparable casualties.

An initially successful attack that ended in a communications farce highlighted problems that would beset the BEF over the next few years, with a failure to suppress the enemy trenches beyond the initial objectives, a lack of reliable communications and a vulnerability to German counter-attacks through their rapid movement of reinforcements. However, Sir John French in his Seventh Despatch to the Secretary of State for War on 5 April 1915, still reported that a victory had been achieved and that '… the wire entanglements had been almost entirely swept away by our shrapnel fire'. Although the continued bombardment initially prevented the Germans bringing up reinforcements, the bombardment in the end proved fragile owing to darkness, weather conditions, lack of aerial observation, and a breakdown of communications between the artillery batteries and forward artillery observers.

The attack marked the passage of the British Army from an expeditionary force into a continental army although some of the engagements towards the end of 1914 had begun that transition. The BEF at Neuve Chapelle had sent out the clear message that the British on the Western Front had to be taken seriously by the Germans – and the French. The Official Historians commented that all subsequent attacks until the end of the war were based on methods developed and lessons learnt by the First Army at Neuve Chapelle. However, it was evident that the British, in common with the French and German Armies, still had a lot to learn about fighting on the Western Front and that they had only just started the long journey along what is now termed the 'learning curve'. At Neuve

Chapelle, the British Army truly set off on the deception learning curve, and the climb was rapid.

The Battle of Neuve Chapelle was the first test of the army commanders to determine whether they truly understood the No-Man's-Land conundrum. The attack had to come as a surprise to the enemy, despite the fact that the Aubers Ridge provided the Germans with a natural viewing platform. Haig in his instructions to his corps commanders stressed this need for surprise. In the '1st Army Operation Order No.9' issued by Brigadier-General H. Butler on 8 March, it was made clear that the attack by the IV and Indian Corps would be supported by fire attacks from the I and Canadian Corps. The orders to the latter two corps stressed that they should be prepared to take the offensive and occupy the enemy trenches opposite them, if the Germans withdrew either under their their fire or through the actions of the IV and Indian Corps.

The main focus of this first deception plan was the concealment of the point of attack. It was to be conducted by elements of Indian Corps and IV Corps but the deception plan extended the attack 'frontage' to include the I Corps, the 1st Canadian Division, and vitally, the III, II and V Corps of the Second Army. In all of these sectors, preparations were made for attacks to confuse the German defences. This type of deception required the participation of both First and Second Army commanders, Haig and Smith-Dorrien, as well as the Commander-in-Chief Sir John French to co-ordinate the whole affair.

The British I Corps were on the right of the Indian Corps and threatened an attack (demonstration only) towards Violaines, while the 1st Canadian Division on the left of IV Corps targeted Fromelles, again with only a demonstration.[1] Both the I Corps and the Canadian Division were well placed to threaten the high ground of the Aubers Ridge in a pincer movement (see Map 1). Both of these attacks were logical operations from a German perspective and therefore had to be defended, especially as the capture of Aubers Ridge would have subsequently threatened Lille. Two months later on 9-10 May, the British Army would launch an offensive against the Aubers Ridge for this very reason. The 1st Division (Major-General H.S. Horne), I Corps, supported the Indian Corps on their left with a bombardment and sporadic bouts of rifle fire. The 2nd Division (Major-General R.C.B. Haking) fired a bombardment at 07:30 on 10 March synchronised with that of the main attack and then the 6 Brigade (Brigadier-General R. Fanshawe) feigned an attack towards Violaines, only

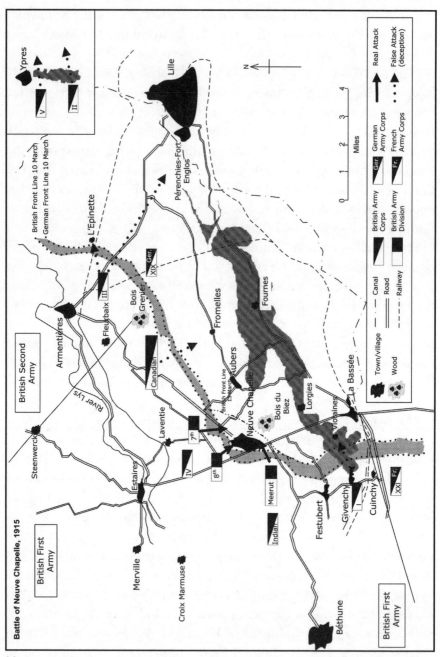

Map 1

to be decimated by machine gun fire. At 14:15 Horne decided to attack again and after a further, inadequate 30-minute bombardment, the resulting infantry attack met a similar fate. Throughout the war, demonstrations could be just as deadly as real attacks if the deception plan called for troops to leave their trenches to authenticate the feint.

Throughout the initial attack on 10 March, on the right of the line, the British were supported by French artillery from the 58th Division, XXI Corps firing from south of La Bassée canal. This bombardment had the double benefit of limiting German enfilade fire from sectors adjacent to the main attack and also extending the apparent attack frontage; any French involvement would have been a concern to the German commanders who would assume that they were facing Anglo-French co-ordinated attacks.

On the left of the line, the 1st Canadian Division had shelled German positions opposite them, a bombardment that, again, was synchronised with the main assault. As the main infantry attack began 35 minutes later at 08:05, so the Canadian riflemen and machine gunners opened up with fifteen-minute bursts of fire accompanied by bouts of cheering, which they continued throughout the day. The US Army in 1988 termed this 'Cry wolf', where repeated false alarms could eventually lead to surprise. But with the British activities further south, the enemy defenders would have to assume that one of these displays could lead to a real attack. By the simple expedient of the expenditure of fifteen minutes-worth of ammunition and cheering troops, the Germans would have to remain alert. This was the short-term effect of this approach, but over a longer period of a number of days, this type of tactic would desensitize the enemy and lull them into a false sense of security and was the basis of the *Behaviour Modification* deception category.

On 11 March the Canadians repeated their previous day's activities but the artillery had limited amounts of ammunition and was ordered to fire only on German batteries that disclosed themselves. As a result, the deception plan was revealed as just that, which enabled von Claer to transfer all available troops from the German XIX Corps south to meet the main threat against Neuve Chapelle.

The Second Army to the north of the line had been planning an independent offensive in the Ypres salient but this was cancelled to enable sufficient guns and ammunition to be transferred and concentrated in the Neuve Chapelle sector. Sir John French ordered the simulated continuation of the assault preparations, with demonstrations to be made to co-ordinate with the main offensive. On the left of the Second Army, the II Corps with the V Corps, in the centre, were to undertake feints against the high ground east of Ypres, while the III Corps on its right, east of Armentières, was to make demonstrations towards Pérenchies-Fort Englos, part of the outer defences of Lille. On 12 March, the 17 Brigade (Infantry), 4th Division of the III Corps actually launched an attack, with support fire from the 18 Brigade, which captured the village of L'Epinette, just behind the German front line, thereby making the threat against Pérenchies-Fort Englos seem more real. Although these demonstrations extended the actual frontage of the attack, from a German perception they also shifted the Allied focus. All of the British and French attacks had an apparent strategic aim to take Lille – from the north, west and south.

To German Sixth Army (Prince Rupprecht of Bavaria), it became obvious that an attack was imminent from the observable preparations visible across No-Man's-Land. However, the preparations involved units scattered across a 30-mile front, garrisoned by seven British Army Infantry Corps, sufficient to disguise the actual place of attack and the units involved, provided that there were no discernible differences between the units engaged in real and the fake preparations. It was these deception activities that prevented von Clear from transferring reinforcements from the XIX Corps directly to support the Neuve Chapelle defenders until the evening of 10 March. This delay enabled the British to consolidate the captured trenches in front of the Bois de Biez.

Prior to the attack on the front in the proximity of Neuve Chapelle, both sides had created breastworks, mounds of sandbags and earth four feet high and five feet wide, as the main protection for shallower trenches rather than the more developed, deeper trench systems. For the attack, the British had to create additional trenches and breastworks ('forming up trenches') to provide cover immediately prior to the attack for an influx of the Indian and IV Corps assault troops. As the British were unable to conceal these extensive assault preparations, they confused the German defences by creating dummy breastworks in adjacent sectors manned by the I Corps and 1st Canadian Division troops. Although the preparations in the I Corps and the 1st Canadian Division fronts were meant as diversionary tactics, Haig instructed both units to be ready to exploit any breakthrough achieved by the Indian and IV Corps. Whether this was an unintentional or a deliberate ploy by Haig is unclear, but this instruction alone, which would have been endorsed by French, ensured a perfect consistency in approach across these sectors as the troop preparations were real. Throughout the war there examples of these 'have your cake and eat it' instructions issued on behalf of Haig with regard to the fake preparations. With a view to the geography and in deference to Haig, the GOC of the Canadian Division, Lieutenant-General E.A.H. Anderson, could not afford to ignore this instruction. If the attacking divisions had captured Neuve Chapelle and advanced to Aubers Ridge, an attack by the Canadian Division could have surrounded a significant number of German troops. Besides the obvious preparations and development of dummy trenches, additional troops were needed for the assault and Haig disguised their arrival. The attacking infantry brigades had been billeted six miles behind the lines and were only brought up when required at night, after an arduous route march.

All the additional guns were moved up gradually at night into pre-prepared camouflaged positions. There was surreptitious, piece-meal artillery registration, utilising map references and aerial observations from spotter planes equipped with wireless, with the rate of fire no greater than that generally expected of any front, so that there was no indication that any additional ordnance had been brought up. The piecemeal build-up in artillery concentration was an example of what the United States Army in 1988 called 'Susceptibility to Conditioning', whereby accumulative small changes would not register with the enemy even if the overall result was significant.

To counteract German spies behind British lines, Haig deployed another deception stratagem reminiscent of Baden-Powell at Mafeking in 1899. Rawlinson's IV Corps advanced HQ was situated four miles behind the front at Estaires while the equivalent establishment for the Indian Corps was located at Croix Marmuse and as a result Haig established the First Army HQ at Merville, some three-and-a-half miles away, where he was ideally placed to maintain contact with both HQs. However, Haig established a false HQ at Béthune, marked with his own flag, which, although not ideal, was better situated to cover a wider front that the sector where the attack would occur. From Béthune it would be possible to control all the corps which the deception plan had identified as attackers.

As a final touch, Major-General G.M.W. Macdonough, the Head of Intelligence, I(b), at First Army Headquarters, spread rumours that an amphibious landing would take place on the Belgian coast to support Second Army. This was specifically intended to divert German reserves away from the area around Neuve Chapelle. Macdonough and Colonel Walter Kirke spread this disinformation via uncoded wireless transmissions, by planting bogus information on returning refugees and by persuading Belgian refugees to include spurious but not too obvious references to it in their letters to relatives in the occupied territories, which were routinely censored by the German authorities. Whether the Germans believed the ruse was unproven, as they had insufficient available troops to transfer north because the French Army were simultaneously launching an offensive towards Vimy Ridge.

British intelligence reports had already indicated that there was a relative lack of defenders in the Neuve Chapelle sector and the deception maintained this state, as the Germans, uncertain of the actual attack zone, were unable to concentrate their forces to meet the onslaught. In the event the British were to learn that the greater number of attackers than defenders was nowhere near enough.

The effectiveness of deception plans was always difficult to assess after the event, especially when the state of readiness of defences and the effectiveness of offensive operations were so difficult to know. However, Sir John French in his Seventh Despatch to the then Secretary of State for War, Lord Kitchener, seemed in no doubt that the deception plan had been effective. He reported that the deception activities, especially those of the 1st Canadian Division and the Second Army, were 'instrumental' in keeping the Germans occupied and delayed their sending reinforcements to the point of the main attack. Once the deception activities were revealed, von Claer ordered the transfer of reinforcements from the XIX Corps who were holding the line in front of III Corps. Their location would also have made them available for supporting the front opposed by the 1st Canadian Division but the perceived threat had diminished by the morning of 11 March. In view of Haig's orders that they should assist in the event of a British breakthrough, the Germans had made themselves vulnerable, although their support of their second line at Neuve Chapelle prevented any disastrous breakthrough onto the Aubers Ridge.

The effect of the diversionary actions did not last long and by mid-afternoon on 10 March the main zone of operations was obvious and this enabled von Claer to redeploy his reinforcements. Throughout the war and in all theatres, this was an inherent weakness in the deception plans.

Deception plans were good at supporting attacks on 'day one' but the latent threat could not be sustained after that.

Types of Attack

The feint, or 'Chinese Attack'[2] utilised artillery bombardments, dummy soldiers, smoke and machine gun barrages while the troops often cheered and showed their bayonets above the parapet.[3] The infantry never left their trenches, although they were still often subjected to artillery bombardments.

The false attack involved all the elements of a real attack and the troops left their trenches with the sole objective of ensuring that German reserves were tied down in their sector. Once it was perceived that this had happened and the real attack had had time to make an impact, the false attack was broken off. The timing of the latter was crucial so that the main attack was not disadvantaged. False attacks did not have physical objectives to capture. 'Demonstrations', a term frequently used by military commanders were a mixture of feint and false attacks. The problem with feint and false attacks was that their threat could be exposed as impotent relatively quickly, which enabled the Germans commanders to redeploy their reserves. But relatively few resources could, for a while, pose a threat above and beyond the investment of men and materials.

The final type of attack, the subsidiary attack, was a real attack with real objectives, which was timed to coincide with the main attack but in an adjacent or nearby sector of the front. This type of attack made a significant contribution to the concealment of the actual point of attack and the German commanders were faced with the difficult decision of determining which attack represented the main strength of the Allies. This type of attack was a better option for a deception plan but could result in a significant number of apparently pointless casualties. Throughout the war there was a tendency by commanders, particularly Haig, to order a false attack but with the caveat that if the opportunity arose, enemy trenches and objectives should be captured, thereby turning it into a subsidiary attack. As false attacks lacked the resources given to real attacks, changing the type of attack once out in No-Man's-Land could prove disastrous! The innocuous phrase 'breaking off' the attack is stained with blood and sacrifice.

Battle of Aubers Ridge, 9–10 May 1915

Within two months of Neuve Chapelle, the British launched a second attack against Aubers Ridge (9-10 May 1915) as part of Joffre's grand plan to capture the Plain of Douai and cut off German communications. The British Army's objectives were to capture of the village of Aubers and to establish a presence on the Aubers Ridge. The attack would be based on the lessons learnt at Neuve Chapelle. However, from a deception perspective, it will be seen that the lessons of Neuve Chapelle had not been thoroughly assimilated by the whole of the Army.

The attack was again conducted by the First Army and was designed to simultaneously breach the German line in two places, approximately 6,000 yards apart. The offensive was planned in two phases, first a combined attack by the I Corps and Indian Corps from the south along a 2,400-yard front from Chocolat Menier corner to Neuve Chapelle. Simultaneously, the IV Corps was to attack on a 1,500-yard front astride the Sailly-Fromelles road. Once the German front line was breached, the two attacks would converge on each other in a pincer movement surrounding and outnumbering an estimated six to seven German battalions and twelve to twenty guns. Only after these were dealt with could the second phase begin; an advance eastwards from the Aubers Ridge to Herlies and Illies to link up with the French Tenth Army, which would be attacking towards Notre Dame de Lorette and Vimy Ridge.

The Battle of Aubers Ridge was disastrous for the British in casualties, lack of ground gained and lack of assistance to the French, fifteen miles to the south. The two-pronged attack should have put the Germans in a dilemma regarding the disposition of their reinforcements. However, the attacks were relatively easily dealt with because of the different approaches adopted by I Corps and the Indian Corps in the south and the IV Corps in the north, which has to be blamed on Haig's lack of control and communication.

The British were confident after their success at Neuve Chapelle, attributed to the careful registration of the artillery on the German trenches. But the Germans had learnt their lesson from Neuve Chapelle and had strengthened their front line defences. No longer were they the 'light field defences' encountered at Neuve Chapelle, the breastworks were strengthened and were now fifteen to twenty feet across and six to seven feet high, semi-permanent defences with wide barbed-wire fields and machine gun emplacements every twenty yards along the front. These were placed at ground level, designed to sweep No-Man's-Land at knee height, which made them difficult to spot owing to the flatness of the countryside. Further aerial reconnaissance was hampered by existing natural foliage cover. Where the natural cover was lacking the Germans had used camouflaged blinds and had covered the trenches, 'blinded' them, with hurdles and other natural materials. The German Army was also improving its deception techniques.

The German defences were at their most developed on the I Corps and Indian Corps front, as the preparations for the British attack had taken place with very little effort made at concealment. The German observers saw old trenches being reclaimed, the digging of assembly trenches and improvement in communications trenches. All these activities had also been evident at Neuve Chapelle but along multiple corps fronts and not confined to a single area!

The 40-minute British preliminary bombardment from 625 artillery pieces made very little impact, in part because of worn out, inaccurate guns with insufficient and faulty shells. The bombardment was considered adequate, despite contrary evidence gathered by intelligence officers, to deal with defences that were still thought to be the flimsier variety as seen at Neuve Chapelle. The geography of the ground was such that the barbed wire defences, still intact, could not be seen from the British trenches. When the I Corps and Indian Corps infantry attacked, they were challenged by intact defences which had been alerted, as observed on the British side immediately prior to the attack: German bayonets were clearly visible above the parapet. Further, despite pre-war tactical instructions, the infantry attack was not given any covering rifle fire from the support trenches, which meant that the German infantry could stick their head above the parapet almost with impunity, observe what was happening and choose any targets that the machine guns had missed.

On the IV Corps front the situation was completely different. During the weeks prior to the attack, two mine galleries, 285 and 330 feet long, had been dug in secret by the 173rd Tunnelling Company RE (Major G. C. Williams). Although there was a discolouration of the ground as the spoil was extracted and disposed of, this was not spotted by the Germans. Similarly, the Germans failed to spot any of the other preparatory activities by IV Corps that Rawlinson had sought to conceal. The British Official History quoted an account from the Bavarian Reserve Regiment No. 17:

'The British Offensive [IV Corps attack] came as a surprise on our front. No special preparations had been noticed, and even the presence of the mines driven under the front trenches of the regiment next to us had not been perceived [and that the enemy had] thereby prepared a way for his initial success.'[4] The attack by the IV Corps troops, who had secretly assembled at night and were in place undetected by 02:30, was initially a success and the German front line was breached, although in three separate areas. Though a serious lack of communication and a failure to link up, permanent residence in the German trenches proved untenable! The lack of adequate communications was such that German prisoners sent back to the British lines were mistaken for a German counterattack. With inadequate artillery support and the arrival of German reinforcements, this attack subsequently fared no better than that in the south and the isolated troops were withdrawn.

Seeing the preparations on the I Corps and Indian Corps front and apparent lack of any similar preparations on the IV Corps front, the Germans concentrated their efforts in strengthening their defences to meet the 'only' threat in the Aubers region. So the German defences, strengthened on the basis of inadequate, but fortuitous, intelligence, were strong enough to withstand the southern attack. The failure of the British to co-ordinate their attack preparations destroyed any advantage that could be gained from the pincer attack, which had been the basis of Haig's offensive at Aubers Ridge.

Nevertheless, the multi-front principle of deception plans implemented at Neuve Chapelle was not abandoned. While Haig's Army made its preparations for Aubers Ridge, the British Second Army was preparing an attack on Hill 60. The attack, assisted by three mines dug by the 3/Monmouths and 171st Tunnelling Company RE, was conducted by the 13 Brigade (Brigadier-General R. Wanless O'Gowan) (5th Division, II Corps). The brigade, after special training, had been inserted into the line at night without attracting the attention of the enemy. At 07:05 on 17 April 1915, the mines were exploded and the infantry went in and captured the hill with few casualties, within two minutes. Holding on to the hill was a different matter! Hence on 21 April, in an attempt to divert German attention away from Hill 60 and away from the First Army preparations on the Aubers Ridge front, the 3rd and 46th Divisions (II Corps), south of Hill 60, near Wystchaete, and the V Corps, slightly north of Hill 60, in front of Zillebeke, simulated preparations for an attack on their front.

Assembly trenches were dug, wire was cut, enemy parapets were shelled, roads bombarded and enemy batteries engaged. Despite these activities, which were probably too late and unconvincing, Hill 60 was lost on 5 May 1915, just prior to the attack on Aubers Ridge.

There was no doubt in the minds of the army commanders and the Commander-in-Chief at Neuve Chapelle that their relatively sophisticated deception plan had tied down the German reinforcements and contributed to the success of the operation. However, the lack of substantial German defences, which arguably could probably have been overcome without any deception plans, led to over-confidence. The British advance at Neuve Chapelle was finally stopped by the arrival of German reinforcements which had been deployed elsewhere on the front to counter the simulated activities.

At Aubers Ridge, there were no simulated offensive preparations. The British signalled their intent to capture Aubers Ridge. Despite the fact that the real points of attack were 6,000 yards apart, it would have been evident that their ultimate objective was the ridge, even though there was significant activity near Hill 60. The 'pincer' attack should have posed a dilemma for the Germans but the fact that IV Corps effectively concealed its preparations actually reduced the value of the two-pronged attack. This has to be attributed to a communication failure at GHQ and at Haig's corps commanders conferences.

Battle of Festubert, 15–27 May 1915

Within a week of the Battle of Aubers Ridge, the British Army had the opportunity to rectify its mistakes as an offensive was launched at Festubert on 15-27 May 1915, although this left very little time for analysis and lessons to be learnt. The attack, again planned by Haig, was to be conducted at night by the 2nd and Meerut Divisions followed three-and-a-half hours later by a 7th Division attack to the south.

The British decided that prolonged bombardments, which of course sacrificed the element of surprise, were necessary to nullify German defences. In this they followed the example of the French. A two-day bombardment, which again lacked real effectiveness as it suffered from the same problems as at Aubers Ridge, supported a two-pronged infantry night attack. The northern prong, just below Port Arthur (La Bombe) was made up of the Garhwal Brigade, Meerut Division, with 5 and 6 Brigades of the 2nd Division (Major-General H.S. Horne) on their right. This attack at 23.30 had the objective of capturing the first two lines of defences and was followed at 03:15, a mile and a half to the south, by an attack by the 7th Division (Major-General H de la Poer Gough) with the aim of striking at the rear of the Germans. The initial attack met with mixed fortunes. The 6 Brigade was not fired on until the line was almost reached and as a consequence its first objective was quickly taken. But the 5 and Garhwal Brigades were spotted as soon as they left their trenches and came under intense machine gun fire. The attack by the 7th Division made some progress with 20 Brigade, for example, taking the first line. On successive days the 2nd and 7th Divisions made further advances as the Germans withdrew to a new defensive line; but progress was limited even after the 47th and Canadian Divisions were thrown into the attack. With the realisation at First Army HQ that further progress was unlikely, the attack was broken off after some gains and substantial casualties. The remaining stores and ammunition were transferred northwards where they were required to stem the German attacks at Ypres.

Were there any lessons here about deception? Obviously the use of a night attack, in strict silence, did introduce an element of surprise and night attacks would be used again on the Western Front. The lengthy artillery bombardment, which forfeited the element of surprise, incorporated some quite imaginative elements to counter-balance this. Throughout the fire programme, stops and starts were introduced. During a cessation the infantry would cheer, something normally done as they left their trenches. The British infantry remained hidden while the artillery resumed its bombardment in the hope of catching the Germans in the open making ready to meet the expected attack. This also had the additional benefit that when the real attack came, the Germans would be slow to man their parapets. In deception terms, this is an example of *Behaviour Modification*. The overall deception fire-plan of the artillery was quite complex. On 14 May, there were three bombardments of three minutes from the howitzers, followed by two minutes of silence and then two minutes of heavy fire from the 18 and 13 pounder batteries accompanied by rapid rifle fire into the German first and second lines. On 15 May at 10.00 and 15.00 the bombardment intensified for five minutes, standard practice immediately prior to the infantry going over the top. The firing suddenly stopped and as the front line infantry cheered, the German lines were immediately subjected to shrapnel bursts in the hope of catching the enemy troops in the open, manning their parapets to repulse the expected attack, an example of *Unusual Practices*.

Instructions issued to the 2nd Division contained explicit references to the element of surprise and ensuring that the advance was conducted in strict silence. But problems arose when independent activities were initiated to mislead the Germans. By order of Corps Command (Indian Corps, Lieutenant-General Sir J. Willcocks), the Lahore Division, north of the attack, was to assist with rifle and machine gun fire at designated intervals throughout the bombardment, to coincide with the time expected by the Germans for an infantry attack. The Jullundur Brigade was ordered to open fire with five-minute bursts on 15 May at 20:45, 21:30, 22:00 and 22:30 but, as this was not synchronised with the other activities, it only served to put the Germans on the alert! At 23:30, when the Germans detected movement, they sent up light balls and disrupted the attack with machine gun fire. The artillery fire-plan was imaginative but the main problems with the overall deception fire plan were that it was performed too close to the real attack and that the infantry brigades involved were exhibiting unusual behaviour patterns, contrary to the principles of a good deception plan. In contrast, the artillery had established a pattern over a number of days and as a consequence had 'conditioned' the Germans, with the result that 6 Brigade walked over almost undetected.

The strengths and frailties of the deception plans implemented at Neuve Chapelle, Aubers Ridge and Festubert were only evident with hindsight. In 1915, the British Army on the Western Front still had two significant opportunities to apply the wisdom of that hindsight, at Hooge in August and at Loos in September.

Action at Hooge, 9 August 1915

By August 1915, the plans reassumed a multi-unit nature, as at Neuve Chapelle, rather than being confined to single formations. In the development of the 'Deception Template' the army learnt that the different techniques were relatively easy to implement but to be effective they had to be applied over a multi-unit front whilst remaining plausible, consistent and logical; characteristics in evidence at Neuve Chapelle but lacking at Aubers Ridge and Festubert. In the attack at Hooge, the Second Army

(General Sir H. Plumer) planned a co-ordinated attempt at deception that widened the apparent front, disguised the time of the attack and generally caused confusion.

Hooge, in the Ypres Salient, had been the scene of fairly continuous heavy fighting, beginning on 2 June 1915, when the 9 Brigade (3rd Division), holding the area around the Chateau and stables, was attacked and overwhelmed, although a subsequent counterattack had regained the stables. The British retaliated with the 175th Tunnelling Company, RE (Major S.H. Cowan) which exploded a mine under the new German positions at 19:00 on 19 July 1915. This is the Hooge Crater which is still visible today. The following series of operations resulted in a salient projecting into the British line, which it was decided had to be pinched out.

The preparations for the attack were difficult to conceal as the army had already launched similar attacks on 19 July (3rd Division), 22 and 31 July (14th (Light) Division) in an attempt to regain ground lost and to remove the salient, which threatened to enfilade the British positions. All of the British attacks were ineffective. For the next attempt, on 9 August, several divisions were involved in an elaborate deception plan against targets which were well chosen (see Map 2).

The 49th (West Riding) Division (Major-General E.M. Perceval) in conjunction with the French XXXVI Corps, which held the left of the line, feigned preparations against the 25 to 30 metres high Pilckem Ridge, while the 46th (North Midland) Division (Major-General E.J. Montagu-Stuart-Wortley) on their right attacked Hill 60 to deny the Germans an observation post from which the deception might have been detected. The 17th (Northern) Division (Major-General T.D. Pilcher) dug jumping off trenches and assembly trenches that attracted considerable artillery fire while the 28th Division (Major-General K.S. Bulfin), to their right, simulated assault preparations and were severely bombarded by the Germans. The real attack came from the 6th Division (Major-General W.N. Congreve) which had quietly entered the line and replaced the 14th (Light) Division who had been in the previous attacks and were not ready to launch another offensive. These infantry preparations over a wide front confused the Germans with regard to the point of attack and the artillery tried to add to the obfuscation. From 2 to 9 August the artillery subjected the German line to a nightly bombardment with the timing and duration varying from night to night, for example between 03:00 and 04:00 on one night and between 02:00 and 03:30 the next. When the 'real' bom-

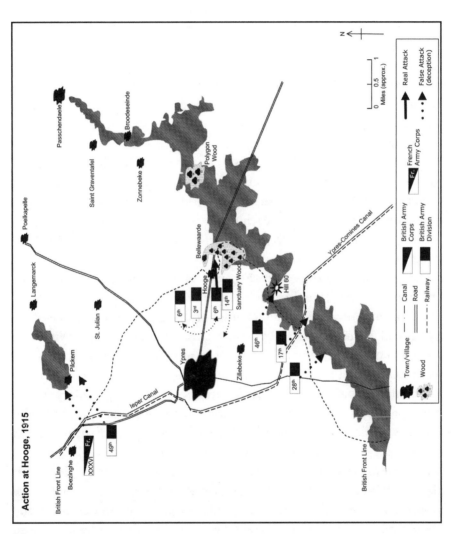

Map 2

bardment came, it was hoped that the Germans would assume that it was just the normal nightly barrage and would shelter in their dugouts rather than man their parapets.

The actual night attack, which took place at 03:15 on 9 August after a short bombardment between 02:45 and 03:15, took the Germans completely by surprise and all of the ground previously lost was regained, including the ruins of the Hooge Chateau. The infantry of 18 Brigade (Lieutenant-Colonel F.W. Towsey) and 16 Brigade (Brigadier-General C.L. Nicholson) had crept out into No-Man's-Land on the limit of the bombardment with the bombers in advance of the riflemen. As the bombardment lifted the British troops were in the German trenches before they could react and the whole of the front of 700 yards that had been lost was recaptured.

This co-ordinated deception plan, comprised only of dummy preparations and feint bombardments, displayed the characteristics of plausibility, consistency and predictability across a wide section of the front. The deception was plausible because at each of the sectors that the British targeted there were strategic gains to be made. The high ground of the Pilckem Ridge, 49th Division 'objective', that south of Ypres 17th (Northern) and 28th Division 'objectives', together with Hill 60, 46th (North Midland) Division 'objective', would all have been plausible targets in the flat lands of the salient. After the mixed fortunes of the actions at Hooge between 2 June and 30 July, it was also plausible that the British would switch the actual point of attack and all the divisions showed an approach consistent with this, making it impossible to detect the feint preparations. As feint preparations always attracted the attention of the enemy artillery if they were convincing, the preparations dictated by the deception plan had to be as real as possible to withstand the expected bombardment. Even though the infantry often did not leave their trenches, they were invariably subjected to artillery bombardments, an excellent indicator that the deception plan had worked. The feints were predictable as the Germans would have probably attempted the same attacks had the roles been reversed, especially at the northern end of the Western Front, as the side that held the high ground enjoyed a distinct advantage.

The quiet insertion of the 6th Division into the line also contributed to the deception as the Germans still thought that in the area around Hooge they faced the 14th (Light) Division, a unit badly affected by an attack using flamethrowers on 30 July. It would not have expected another attack from this division. However effective a deception plan was, the actual capture of objectives was of course still solely in the hands of the infantry and their supporting artillery fire plan.

The three primary aims of deception, to conceal the point and time of attack and the units involved, were all achieved at Hooge on 9 September. The techniques employed consisted of dummy preparations, feint bombardments and an attack against Hill 60. The key to success was that these activities were spread out across multi-unit sectors. This multi-unit approach would become a common denominator in deception plans throughout the remainder of the war and would be employed by both sides.

Battle of Loos, 25 September–8 October 1915

At the Battle of Loos, the British Army faced an essentially flat mining area with the few high places (such as Hill 70, numerous spoil heaps) held by the Germans. The assault plan, developed by Haig called for I Corps (Lieutenant-General H. Gough) and IV Corps (Lieutenant-General Sir H. Rawlinson) to attack at 06:30 on 25 September between the La Bassée Canal in the north and the Grenay-Lens line in the south. The assault was to be preceded by a four-day bombardment commencing on 21 September followed by a gas attack immediately prior to the infantry assault by the 2nd, 9th (Scottish), 7th and 28th Divisions from I Corps and the 1st, 15th (Scottish) , 47th (London) Divisions from IV Corps together with the 3rd Cavalry Division.

The build-up of troops, artillery and materials necessary was unsurprisingly incredibly difficult to conceal. This problem was further exacerbated by the now favoured artillery bombardment over days, which removed the element of surprise. Consequently, Haig and Sir John French instigated a number of measures aimed at merging real with false intelligence.

The assault on 25 September was accompanied by simultaneous feint attacks and demonstrations. The preparations for these operations widened the apparent front and disguised the actual sectors to be attacked. These deception activities were outlined in Sir John French's 'General Instructions for the Army Commanders and GHQ Reserve' dated 18 September 1915 and issued by Lieutenant-General W.R. Robertson, Chief of the General Staff, GHQ. These involved units of the

III, Indian and I Corps units, not involved in the real operation, attacking north of La Bassée Canal. Further north, at sectors around the Ypres Salient, the II, Canadian, V and VI Corps of the British Second Army were engaged in actions that were part of the overall deception plan. In the south, the XII, X and VII Corps from Monro's Third Army situated between Curlu on the Somme to Monchy au Bois, were ordered to support attacks by the French Tenth Army timed to coincide with the British Attack at Loos.[5] The British Third Army was initially limited to providing artillery support but in the event of a German retirement, nine divisions of the Third Army would be ordered to take the offensive to assist the French. The very fact that the Third Army infantry had to be offensive-ready on 25 September meant that their preparations acted as part of the overall deception plan and blurred the intelligence gathered by the Germans. It is difficult to determine whether GHQ deliberately intended this to be a benefit but the British would not have been oblivious to such an obvious advantage.

Defending the front between the British First and Third Armies was the French Tenth Army, which scheduled a series of attacks for 25 September. These were initially successful but eventually stalled as the Germans gradually determined the real from the fake and reinforcements were moved around appropriately to meet the real French and British operations.

Finally, in the far northern sector of the Western Front, the Belgian Army, when informed about the pending Allied attacks and in conjunction with the French XXXVI Corps, engaged in simulated preparations for a general advance threatening the German lines. The Belgian 1st Division simulated a crossing of the Yser Canal while a number of raids by the 2nd, 3rd and 6th Belgian Divisions were conducted throughout their front supported by ineffectual artillery bombardments. This meant that there were preparations for an attack in progress from Curlu on the Somme to the North Sea coast, a distance of over 100 miles (see Map 3).

Although the multi-unit deception activities initiated by Sir John French were in place across a wide area of the front, Haig instigated an additional series on the operational front at Loos to convince the Germans that the army activity was not to be taken any more seriously than the activities in the other sectors.

On each day of the four-day bombardment, at varying hours and on different divisional fronts, demonstrations and feint attacks were initiated. In support of the artillery, the infantry initiated two minutes of rapid rifle

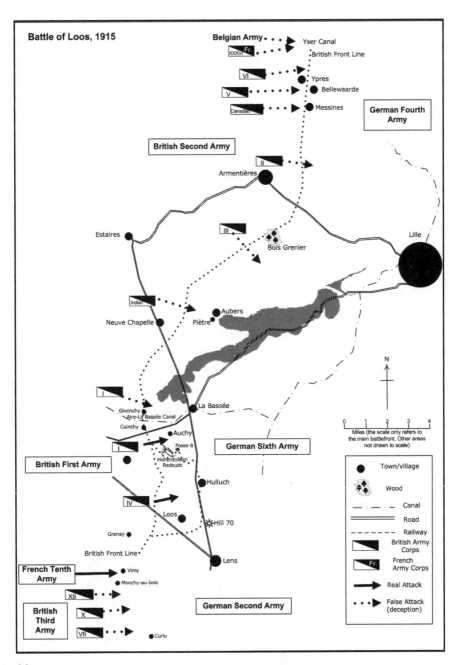

Battle of Loos, 1915

Belgian Army

Yser Canal

British Front Line

XXXVI Fr.

VI — Ypres

V — Bellewaarde

Canadian — Messines

German Fourth Army

British Second Army

II

Armentières

Lille

Estaires

III

Bois Grenier

Indian

Aubers

Neuve Chapelle — Piètre

I

Givenchy

Aire-La Bassée Canal

Cuinchy

La Bassée

German Sixth Army

I

Auchy

Fosse 8

Hohenzollern Redoubt

British First Army

Hulluch

IV

Loos

Hill 70

Grenay

British Front Line

Lens

French Tenth Army — Vimy

Monchy-au-bois

XII

British Third Army

X

German Second Army

VII

Curlu

N

0 1 2 3 4

Miles (the scale only refers to the main battlefront. Other areas not drawn to scale)

Town/village

Wood

Canal

Road

Railway

British Army Corps

Fr. French Army Corps

Real Attack

False Attack (deception)

Map 3

and machine gun fire, moved dummy soldiers around, raised their bayonets above the parapets and shouted while the Scottish divisions played
their bagpipes. The show of bayonets above the parapet was often the first
signal of an immediate attack. These measures would force the Germans,
who would be sheltering in their dugouts, to man their trenches ready
to repel the anticipated attack. They were then subjected to a shrapnel
bombardment, which was lethal to troops in the open. The repeated use
of these measures not only resulted in confusion over the time and actual
point of the attack but it also made the Germans reluctant to man their
front line trenches. This deception was further enhanced by the digging
of various dummy trenches in the midst of the real assembly and jumping off trenches. All of this would have de-sensitised the Germans to the
British activity.

There were some practices initiated at Loos which were to become
commonplace throughout the war. For instance, the actual assault units
were only moved into the front line under cover of darkness at 22:00
on 24 September, zero hour minus eight-and-a-half while the reserves
(XI Corps) were held at least six-and-a-half miles behind the line, making
their detection difficult. The holding of the reserve so far back was on the
orders of General Sir John French and although as a deceptive measure
it was effective, it would have been entirely *inadvertent*. In the event, the
reserves, especially the 21st and 24th Divisions were held too far back to
make their intended impact on the battle and this was one of the factors
that led to French's subsequent dismissal as Commander-in-Chief.

On the morning of the attack demonstrations were initiated.
Amidst gas, smoke and with poor visibility, the 1/21 London (First
Surrey Rifles) and 1/22 London Regiments, 142 Brigade (Brigadier-
General F.G. Lewis), 47th (London) Division (Major-General C. St.L.
Barter), IV Corps operated a large array of head-and-shoulder dummy
soldiers which had been placed out in No-Man's-Land during the night
and which now drew rifle and artillery fire. This was the first recorded
instance of a Chinese Attack using dummies. Meanwhile the Canadian
Corps in the Second Army sector, 35 miles to the north, launched their
Chinese Attack with a simulated gas attack. Just before 06:00, at a time
similar to that of the real gas attack further south, from dummy assembly
trenches, sacks filled with damp straw and sulphur were set alight over
a 10,000-yard front. However the straw did not light properly in the
wind and although the Germans sounded the gas alarm, Nicholson, the

Canadian Official Historian, considered that the deception was not sufficiently persuasive to affect the battle's outcome.

From a German perspective, British attacks were seemingly initiated
from north to south at Bellewaarde at 04:20 (V Corps), 06:00 at Messines
(Canadian Corps), 04:30 at Bois Grenier (III Corps), 06:00 at Piètre
(Indian Corps) and at 06:30 at Loos (I and IV Corps). The two-hour
spread would have been insufficient time for the Germans to determine
the real attack and as a consequence reserve troops would have been
retained in their sectors. The French Tenth Army, which was engaged in
the joint offensive, did not plan to launch their attack until 13:00 although
this was brought forward to 12:25 as news of the initial British successes
filtered through to the French Army Headquarters. The vigorous nature
of the British attack, as requested of the troops by Lord Kitchener, would
have provided the French Army with the ideal offensive opportunity, as
the British attack could be interpreted by the Germans as part of the
French Army deception plan.

The British artillery barrage swept over the German trench lines, and
lifted from one trench line to the next. The troops were supposed to follow
in closely behind the barrage to deny the enemy the opportunity of manning their parapets and machine gun emplacements. At Loos, the German
trenches were so close together that it resembled a creeping barrage, an
approach which was effective later in the war. In the I Corps sector the
closeness of the trenches enabled the artillery to mount an 18-pounder
back barrage firing shrapnel. The usual practice was for the barrage to
lift from trench to trench with the infantry attacking as soon as it was
'safe' to do so. As soon as a barrage lifted it became a race between the
British infantry charging across No-Man's-Land and the German defenders emerging from their protective dugouts. On 25 September at Loos,
the barrage lifted but the infantry did not attack immediately and waited
until the guns returned to the front trench line for a second devastating
shrapnel burst, hoping to catch the Germans when they were vulnerable.

As a final touch to the deception plan, Major-General C.E. Callwell
(Intelligence Section of the Directorate of Military Operations, First Army)
spread rumours that there would be an amphibious landing on the Belgian
coast on 25–26 September, which would threaten to outflank the German
defences. This plan was supported by a bombardment by the Royal Navy
under the command of Vice-Admiral Bacon, of the coastal towns of
Knocke, Blankenberghe, Westende, Middelkerke and Raversyde and was

consistent with the preparations observed amongst the Belgian Army and the French XXXVI Corps. Bad weather delayed additional attacks until 2 October, but the Germans still moved troops to Ostend to counter the pending invasion but in insufficient numbers to influence the outcome of the Battle of Loos. The amphibious element of the deception plan became a favourite of the British and was used on several occasions, although the plans and activities generally lacked conviction. The most convincing plan was that used during the 1916 Battle of the Somme, which not only fooled the Germans but also caused panic within the British Government. As the Germans sent two divisions northwards to counter the threat, the British Government, ignorant of the real situation, interpreted the German deployments as the prelude to an invasion!

Whilst the British were busily engaged in concealing their true intentions, the Germans perpetrated their own ruse with a nod to the Russo-Japanese War. During the initial four-day bombardment, if a shell landed near one of the German batteries, the guns immediately fell silent, 'destroyed' by counter-battery fire. The British artillery consequently targeted other gun positions only to find that the 'destroyed' guns came to life again during the assault. In the Russo-Japanese War, the Japanese artillery would fall silent if they came under fire, move to a new location and leave old remnants behind to simulate a burnt out position.[6]

The Germans also misinterpreted the weakness of the British bombardment, on the first day, as a poor attempt to distract them from the obvious preparations of the French Tenth Army further south. However, this interpretation was based on a lack of intelligence, for in reality the British were simply short of shells. This is another example of *inadvertent* deception.

As everyone knows, the command of the British Army in the Great War has been seriously criticised, particularly in the literature throughout the 1970s and 1980s and the phrase 'Lions led by Donkeys' is the memorable summary. There has been some serious research to refute this accusation and analysis of deception planning showed that if they were 'donkeys', they were intelligent ones. The small amount of research on deception-planning todate has erroneously concluded that it was only conducted at a local level or used sporadically. In the detailed planning, the deception techniques were indeed local. A brigade Chinese Attack was planned and perpetuated locally but this was often just one element in a divisional, corps, army or multi-army deception plan. The target and timing of the Chinese Attack were *not* decided locally. The complex co-ordinated deception plans seen in the majority of engagements in 1915 on the Western Front required the 'donkeys' to not only co-operate with each other but also to expend a significant amount of effort in developing their plans. The success of these plans was witnessed by the expenditure of German artillery shells aimed at stopping them and the deployment and retention of the German reserves. The fact that the battles, in the main, were considered failures, by using casualty numbers and yards gained as criteria, has overshadowed any of the attempts at deception and has clouded judgment on the abilities of the High Command in this respect. The BEF had to follow numerous learning curves to convert itself into an efficient continental army. Deception was one of those learning curves, offensive operations was another, and until the latter was sorted out, the former would never be appreciated by the historical observer.

In 1915, there was another theatre of war where the simple deception techniques were combined into a complex plan whose success cannot be denied by even the harshest critic. This elaborate deception plan was associated with the Dardanelles expedition to the Gallipoli peninsula which is discussed in detail in Chapter 9.

In deception planning the British Army had learned fast and the deception template was mostly complete by the end of 1915 and, more importantly, was being utilised and actively encouraged. The final element of the template, the use of tanks in deception plans, was only incorporated after September 1916 with their arrival. However, at the end of 1915 there was still a disconnect between deception activities and offensive activities and this was a reflection of the different rate of progress along the two learning curves.

In 1915 British experience showed that all offensive operations should be supported by a deception plan. Even if the results on the Western Front were disappointing, the effectiveness of a well planned and co-ordinated deception plan would be amply demonstrated at Gallipoli both in offence and defence. The 'golden rule' to emerge from all British operations in 1915 was that any deception plan should involve multiple units across multiple sectors, which were sufficiently geographically distant from each other that the enemy reserves could not be deployed to cover those multiple sectors.

As 1915 came to an end with the successful evacuation of the MEF from Gallipoli, the focus that had temporarily switched to the Gallipoli peninsula returned to the Western Front and the battle which would see the highest casualty rate for a single day in British military history.

5

The Western Front 1916: The Reality of Deception

The spot where we intend to fight must not be made known; for then the enemy will have to prepare against a possible attack at several different points; and his forces being thus distributed in many directions, the numbers we shall have to face at any given point will be proportionately few.
Sun Tzu

From the British perspective, there were changes at the end of 1915 that had a profound effect on the conduct of the war as a whole and on 1916 in particular. There was an appraisal of the handling of the war to date and as a result Field Marshal Sir John French was removed as the Commander-in-Chief of the British Armies in France and moved to the command of the British Home Forces. French had shouldered the blame for the disastrously bloody Battle of Loos. On 19 December 1915 General Sir Douglas Haig was appointed as the Commander-in-Chief of the British Armies on the Western Front. The politicians in London hoped that this would be the longed for 'new dawn' and that the British Army and its allies would now triumph over the Germans in battles where casualties would be kept to an 'acceptable' level.

Before settling comfortably into his new role, Haig was invited by the French Commander-in-Chief, General Joseph Joffre, to a conference at Chantilly on 29 December 1915 to discuss the execution of the war through 1916. Following the conference, Joffre wrote to Haig and proposed a joint Franco-British offensive astride the Somme with additional units engaged in fake preparations and offensives. Joffre's proposal called for the BEF to fight a number of attritional attacks in preparation for the main French offensive between the River Somme and Lassigny. Haig had immediate reservations, not only from a logistical stand point but also from a political perspective; as he rightly surmised, the British attacks would always be viewed as costly defeats rather than as part of an elaborate deception plan and the seemingly futile resulting casualties would be viewed with anger and dismay. Haig counter-proposed that then to fourteen days before the main French attack, the BEF would conduct a series of large-scale raids along the British front with real, but restricted, objectives and limited resources specifically aimed at drawing off the German reinforcements but without incurring major casualties. The raids would have the specific aim of convincing the Germans that they were intended to probe their defences and they were the prelude to a forthcoming major offensive by the British Army. This, it was hoped, would distract the Germans from the offensive activities within the French sectors.

Haig had his own view of the situation on the Western Front and how the war should be waged. In January he independently instructed General Sir Edmund Allenby to study the British Third Army sector, north of the River Somme, to determine the feasibility of an offensive operation with fifteen divisions attacking over a 24,000-yard front. In January, the Third Army sector ran from Maricourt in the south to Hébuterne in the north; three months later this sector would be largely taken over by the newly formed Fourth Army and the Third Army would move northwards to take over the front from the French Tenth Army. Before assuming command of the newly formed British Fourth Army, Haig subsequently instructed General Sir Henry Rawlinson to continue Allenby's feasibility study for an attack in the current Third Army sector together with an assessment for an offensive north of Ypres towards the Forest of Houthulst and Roulers.

From the start of 1916 it was apparent that both the French and British Armies appreciated the problems caused by No-Man's-Land and that for a successful offensive, distant sectors had to be targeted to blur the focus of the enemy. This was the intention behind Joffre's plan, Haig's proposal to Joffre, and Haig's initiation of the feasibility studies by Allenby and Rawlinson. However, the plan proposed by Joffre lacked the basic elements of a real deception plan, from a British perspective, as it was merely a device to draw the German reinforcements north-wards, not through deceit but through a series of British attacks with no real aims other than to engage the Germans and cause as many casual-ties as possible – the standard war of attrition. The 'raiding' approach suggested by Haig could still involve significant casualties but if the enemy intelligence organisations evaluated them as preludes to a mas-sive attack, then the German defences could potentially be bolstered with troops drawn from other sectors including the one where the real attack was planned. Although the British plans appeared to be similar to the French as they were also designed to draw off reinforcements, the British approach relied more on trickery. This British tactic, built on the work started by Sir John French and Sir Douglas Haig, promoted the use of deception in all the major engagements as a means to resolve the No-Man's-Land conundrum. The main lesson that had emerged from 1915 was that deception plans had to result in confusion with respect to the sectors that the enemy needed to strengthen to withstand an impending attack '... to create the illusion of strength where weakness exists ... and weakness where strength exists.'[1]

Haig, the new Commander-in-Chief, with his new army command structure, had the opportunity to instil the culture of deception through-out all army planning and operations. The chance to put the newly acquired lessons into practice would arise early in the year but the real test would come in July, as the British launched their Somme offensive. Haig and his army commanders had made serious attempts to employ decep-tion and invested significant effort in terms of men and materials but at the sticking point the implementation lacked the verisimilitude required to be truly effective.

A Change of German Policy

The need for deception was apparent to all the armies engaged on the Western Front and the German Army was the first to employ it in 1916, in support of their major offensive at Verdun. At the start of 1916, the German Army held more or less the same defensive positions on the Western Front that they had seized at the end of 1914, having successfully repulsed a number of attacks throughout the previous twelve months. Although there had been Allied gains, these were not significant in advancing the ejection of the Germans from French soil and had resulted in significant Allied casualties.

In 1916, the German High Command changed its defensive approach to the war and decided that it would bleed the French Army to death in a battle of attrition at Verdun, which it predicted they would attempt to defend to the last man. The attack by the German Fifth Army (GOC, Crown Prince Friedrich Wilhelm) was initially planned for 10 February but the Germans were forced to delay the commencement first to 12 February and finally to 21 February, but the battle once started would last until 18 December. This engagement would require a major commitment of men and materials in a build-up that would be difficult to disguise. The German Army decided on a series of demonstrations throughout different sectors of the front to engage both the French and British Armies and to distract them from the German Fifth Army build-up in front of Verdun. The demonstrations were planned to be a mixture of real and feint attacks, involving artillery bombardments and infantry attacks, and all accompanied by activities which were indicative of a build-up of German forces at the northern end of the trench lines. Their objective was to create the illusion that they were the precursors to major offensives against the British in the area around Ypres and the French near Vimy. These attacks were initiated from 9 to 20 February and are shown in Map 4.

These minor attacks were supported by measures including the use of tethered balloons, spurious troop movements and artillery fire plans, to convey the impression of the arrival of large numbers of reinforcements throughout the Ypres salient and around Vimy.[2] The attacks were initiated to create the impression that the Germans were attempting to 'understand' the British and French defences, prior to an offensive. However in terms of pure deception, these attacks, although designed to focus attention away from Verdun, were real and involved a significant commitment of men and ordnance. Since the German attacks had clearly limited objectives, their real purpose, according to the Official Historian, was not fully understood by the British Army who had difficulty interpreting the strategic or tactical significance of these operations. There was a certain lack of predictability regarding the actions, although the demonstrations were aligned to Magruder's Principle as the British believed that the German Army would attempt a breakthrough in the Ypres Salient, which had huge strategic implications as the key to the channel ports. The British believed that the Germans would attempt to create a flank to threaten

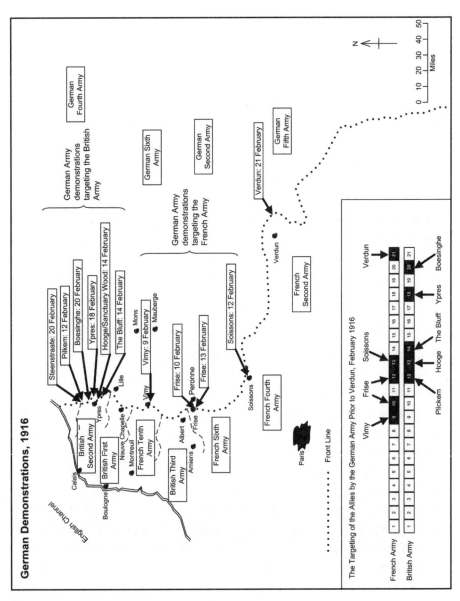

Map 4

the communications and supply routes; four significant battles through-out the war would bear testimony to this belief. As a consequence, the apparent build-up of troops around Ypres completely misled the British with regard to German intentions in front of Verdun. The French Army was similarly confused.

Throughout the weeks preceding the attack at Verdun, there were significant attacks in the British sectors targeted at Pilkem-Boesinghe on 12 February, Hooge and Sanctuary Wood on 14 February, The Bluff, also on 14 February, an artillery duel focussed on Ypres on 18 February, and Steenstraate, Het Sast and Boesinghe on 20 February. These attacks enveloped Ypres and, as intended, challenged and threatened the British presence. Between the start of Verdun and the start of the Somme, the Germans forced the British to launch a series of attacks at The Bluff, St. Eloi and Mount Sorrel to deny the Germans observation platforms which would have provided them with a significant advantage in their threat to the Ypres salient. All of the British attacks were characterised by being only able to instigate local deception plans and while two of the engagements employed *Behaviour Modification* and were successful, the third relied on zero-hour deception activities and suffered as a consequence.

Action at The Bluff, 1–2 March 1916

Although the British failed to understand the overall purpose of the German attacks, one of their targets was the area known as The Bluff, whose strategic value was readily appreciated by the British. The Bluff, known to the Germans as the Kanal Bastion, was a bank of earth, 30–40 feet high, on the northern side of the Ypres-Comines canal, formed by spoil from the digging of the canal in 1863 as it cut through ground three miles south of Ypres. The Bluff, held by the British, presented the army with a unique observation platform. Although the attack on The Bluff was part of the German demonstrations, it also represented a valuable strate-gic prize and would be an area that the Germans would want to capture prior to their seemingly imminent offensive within the Ypres Salient. At 17:45 on 14 February, the Germans exploded three small mines under The Bluff, rapidly followed by an infantry attack which drove out the British, who hit back with disastrous, badly planned and hastily implemented local counterattacks. As a result by 07:30 on 15 February, the Germans were in total possession of The Bluff. It was apparent that the British would have to make an attempt to recapture the lost ground and the Germans consolidated their defensive system, an activity significantly aided by the 24-hour delay in any British retaliation.

The recapture of The Bluff represented a sizeable challenge. Any attempt to divert German attention to other sectors through the implementation of a multi-sector deception plan would prove futile as the real target was obvious. Further, as the British assumed that Ypres was the focus of the next German offensive and with the apparent build-up the enemy forces in the region, any attack against these 'large' troop concentrations would lack credibility, although in reality it might have enjoyed some success.

The British concluded that a frontal assault against The Bluff, using experienced troops, was the only course open to them. On the night of the 16/17 February, the 76 Brigade (Brigadier-General Ernest St. G. Pratt), 17th (Northern) Division, V Corps (Lieutenant-General H. Fanshawe) which had been recently relieved but was familiar with the terrain, now returned to the line to replace the 51 Brigade. The 76 Brigade had trained on an exact model of the German defences in the British back area using shallow trenches constructed on the basis of recent aerial photographs, prior to their return to the line.

A plan was formulated which did not rely on a preliminary bombardment to ensure that the attack timing came as a surprise, as demanded by General Sir Herbert Plumer (GOC, British Second Army). As it was impossible to disguise British intentions and the attack would be conducted on a narrow front, the artillery produced a fire programme aimed at modifying the behaviour of the defenders. Brigadier-General Herbert Uniacke (GOC, V Corps Artillery) offered to 'drill the enemy' and make them 'obey' his commands, using none of the deception categories, *Behaviour Modification*. Over a period of several days prior to the attack, the artillery fired a 60-pounder salvo at The Bluff trenches, followed by two minutes of inactivity and then a second salvo. The aim was to condition the Germans locally to expect the second salvo and to remain in the protection of their dugouts. At 17:00 on 1 March an artillery bombardment destroyed the wire defences and whilst the British infantry fixed bayonets, cheered and blew whistles, they remained in their trenches as machine gun and mortar barrages targeted the German trenches for exposed defenders. Throughout the night the mortars and machine guns

kept up a low level of activity, insufficient to alert the German defenders
but of sufficient ferocity to ensure that the damaged defences could not
be easily repaired. At 02:00, after inspection of the trenches for repairs or
lack thereof, the attack was ordered to go ahead and by 03:45 the assault
troops had moved silently into position, lying out in No–Man's–Land. At
04:30 the attack began, preceded immediately by another 60-pounder
salvo which drove the defenders into their dugouts, to remain there, it
was hoped, in anticipation of the second salvo. At 04:32 as the first British
troops entered the German trenches, an artillery barrage targeted the
back areas and isolated the German reinforcements. The attack came as
a complete surprise to the Germans and many of the prisoners surrendered unarmed although some carried rifles but without fixed bayonets,
such was the lack of readiness. The recapture of The Bluff cost the British
1,622 casualties, officers and men. *Behaviour Modification*, as at Gallipoli
in 1915, had shown itself to be an extremely potent weapon when used
properly at a local level. With imagination, a degree of coordination and
only requiring a few days to implement, it was possible to affect the
readiness of local defences. This tool would be used frequently by the
British throughout the war.

Action of St. Eloi Craters, 27 March–16 April 1916

Whilst the plans for the recovery of The Bluff were still under discussion,
Plumer decided that a scheme should be advanced for the capture of the
area around St. Eloi. A year prior, on 14 March 1915 the Germans had created a 600-yard wide salient into the British lines in the middle of which
was 'the Mound' an artificial hill, originally 30 feet high, which provided
the Germans with a view over of the British front. Once again Plumer
decided that the attack should come as a surprise with the preparations
completely hidden and an infantry assault coordinated with the artillery
in a deviation from normal practices.

A series of five mines were dug under the German front lines and
the Mound by the 172nd Tunnelling Company Royal Engineers, which
was nothing new – throughout 1915 it had already been subjected to
the firing of 42 British and 22 German mines and camouflets. There
was a lack of obvious infantry preparation, no assembly or jumping off
trenches dug and no attempt to destroy the wire through preliminary

bombardments. The troops were to carry wire cutters and planks to lay across the wire to force a passage. At 04:15 on 27 March, twenty seconds before zero hour, the heavy howitzers opened fire, followed ten seconds later by the heavy guns. The flight time of the shells was carefully calculated so that as the shells fell, the mines were synchronously detonated with the infantry assault, consisting of 2nd Canadian Division, Canadian Corps and 3rd Division, V Corps, commencing 30 seconds later. The 1/ Northumberland Fusiliers, having lain out in No-Man's-Land, reached the wire, having suffered only one casualty, and captured shaken German prisoners, but the 4/Royal Fusiliers suffered badly from flanking machine gun fire as they left their trenches. The presence of so many craters in the area however caused confusion on the ground and the establishment of a continuous line proved a problem. Significantly, 40 seconds after the infantry left their trenches, the German artillery laid down a defensive barrage in No-Man's-Land to prevent reinforcements reaching the British troops. Despite the lack of immediate reinforcements, the British were able to consolidate their positions and resist the early German counterattacks. However by 15 April the Germans had reorganised their forces sufficiently and a series of counterattacks forced the British back to their starting line of 27 March.

Whereas activity had taken place to conceal their offensive preparations, none of the available deception techniques were applied at zero hour. Although the co-ordinated artillery programme was imaginative, it was clear that the preparations had been spotted, hence the rapid response of the German artillery. Zero hour deception, such as *Behaviour Modification*, could have been used to target the defenders and hamper their defensive barrage as had already been successfully done at The Bluff three weeks earlier. There was an important lesson to be re-learnt. Local deceptions required a great deal of luck and if penetrated could prove disastrous. In the period prior to the assault there had been no attempt to mislead the Germans who were able to isolate the British troops. A local deception, whilst lacking a multi-front element, had still to generate enough false intelligence to confuse the enemy if only for a short period. At St. Eloi the Germans had picked up the real intelligence associated with the attack, despite the lack of trench digging, and had acted on it. The British for their part relied mainly on an imaginative fire programme, perpetrated at zero hour, and there was no effort to target the adjacent enemy sectors to prevent devastating enfilade fire.

Battle of Mount Sorrel and Tor Top (Hill 62), 9–13 June 1916

On 2 June, the Germans attacked the Canadian positions at Mount Sorrel, Tor Top (Hill 62) and Hill 61 as they tried to gain another prominence at the southern end of the Ypres Salient. Following a massive artillery bombardment and the explosion of four mines, the Canadian positions were overrun. The attack was seen by some observers as another attempt to shift the Allied focus from the ongoing Battle of Verdun as the limited front and resources showed a lack of real commitment.

The observational value afforded by these hills left the British with no choice but to re-capture the positions. With the German defences alerted, the Canadian Corps instigated their version of *Behaviour Modification*. Between 9 and 12 June, the British artillery carried out four intense bombardments of 20–30 minutes. Each time the enemy expected that an infantry assault would follow as the Canadian troops engaged in bayonet displays, cheering and rapid rifle fire. Any Germans who reacted to these demonstrations were subjected to rifle and machine gun fire. The objective was to persuade the Germans that a 20- to 30-minute bombardment was not necessarily the prelude to an infantry attack.

On 12 June for ten hours the British shelled the German front line between Hill 60 and Sanctuary Wood, isolating the Mount Sorrel sector from flanking fire. At 01:30 on 13 June the infantry, under the cover of smoke, went in behind the now customary 30-minute bombardment. The majority of the Germans were taken by surprise and the only real resistance came from isolated pockets. The British suffered a total of 8,430 casualties compared with 5,765 Germans.

The targeting of The Bluff and Mount Sorrel and the continued presence of the Germans at St. Eloi were all consistent with an impending attack throughout the Salient. British attention had been firmly focused around Ypres and the Battle of Verdun had thwarted the grandiose 1916 plans of the Allies for a series of co-ordinated attacks. The battle of attrition instigated by the Germans took a great toll on the French Army and Joffre called on the British to implement an offensive primarily designed to relieve the pressure on the French Armies. Although Haig would have preferred to launch an offensive to resolve the problem in the Ypres Salient, French pressure demanded that the offensive was further south, closer to Verdun. The British initiated the now infamous Battle of the Somme (1 July–18 November 1916), which would be regarded as a series of discrete engagements as defined by the British Battles Nomenclature Committee.

The Battle of Albert, 1–13 July 1916

The first day of the Battle of the Somme has been characterised in the memory by failure, by high casualties and by the naïve and sometimes callous approach of the British High Command. However, it is essential that the offensive operations are placed in context and that it is recognised that rather than simply sending the assaulting troops across No-Man's-Land against largely intact defences there was an attempt, before the artillery intervened in the period leading up to 1 July, to weaken those defences through a resource-intensive deception programme.

The preparations for the Somme offensive of 1916 suffered from the same constraints as previous battles, in that long bombardments and frontal infantry assaults were still believed to be the keys to unlock the German defences. The build-up of men and materials and the preparatory work of trench construction and the installation of transport links could not be totally hidden across No-Man's-Land or from spies behind the lines, despite the extensive use of camouflage. Within the Fourth Army area, for instance, vast amounts of material were required, primarily for 'umbrella camouflage' to thwart aerial detection and to make terrestrial discovery more difficult. For example, on 25 June 1916 an order was placed for 3,500 square yards of wire-netting with painted canvas strips for concealing a mere 24 guns in the Arras area in support of the 1 July attack. With the everyone working at full speed the order was completed in fourteen hours by the factory at Wimereux. To camouflage the 1,500 guns in the Fourth Army sector would have required an estimated 220,000 square yards of material! With the scale of the attack, unprecedented in British military history, the simple concealment of the preparations would not be feasible.

Field Marshal Sir Douglas Haig had planned the battle to be a Fourth Army (General Sir H. Rawlinson) offensive against the German Second Army (General Fritz von Below) centred along the axis of the Albert-Bapaume road. It would involve thirteen infantry divisions on the first day alone supplemented by huge quantities of ordnance, munitions, supplies and backup support. South of the River Somme, eleven French divisions would also attack. The activities involved in the preparation for an offensive on this magnitude removed any possibility of taking the Germans by surprise. So the only option available to the British Army for deception was to cause *Confusion* in the German command structure by flooding the OODA Loops with fake intelligence.

To create this confusion, Haig instigated an ambitious deception plan with the aim of disguising the point of attack. He immediately ordered that offensive preparations, similar to those of the Fourth Army, should simultaneously commence in the Third (General Sir E.H.H. Allenby), First (General Sir Charles Monro) and Second (General Sir H. Plumer) Army sectors.[3,4] See Map 5. The size of this deception plan across such a vast area and the commitment of so many resources was testament to the importance Haig placed on these activities.

The British Third Army, on the left of the Fourth Army, had been ordered to capture the Gommecourt salient with a subsidiary attack. Haig also ordered Allenby to make fake preparations for attacks against the Monchy Salient (VII Corps), against the sector 1,500 yards north of Ficheux (VI Corps) and the salient north of Roclincourt (XVII Corps).

Monro's First Army was ordered to make fake preparations for an attack on a three-mile sector near Hulluch (I Corps) and another in the sector around Neuve Chapelle (XI Corps). Similarly, the five corps (I and II ANZAC, V, Canadian and XIV Corps) of Plumer's Second Army, despite limited resources, began preparations for an attack around Ypres, between Laventie and Boesinghe.

The preparations by the Third Army for the fake attack against the Monchy salient were typical of the activities of the various armies during the period leading up to 1 July. In line with Haig's specific instructions, all preparations were made ostentatiously and were as obvious as those of the Fourth Army. The 37th Division (GOC, Major-General Lord Edward Wilfred Gleichen) on the left of VII Corps was holding a four-and-a-half mile sector as far as Ransart and undertook the same preparations as the other divisions in VII Corps, the 56th (1/1 London) (GOC, Major-General C. P. A. Hull) and 46th (North Midland) (GOC, Major-General Hon. E. J. Montagu-Stuart-Wortley) who were detailed to mount the subsidiary attack against Gommecourt. In early June, the 37th Division dug advanced trenches, embarked on a wire cutting programme, made occasional releases of gas and smoke and during the five days prior to Zero day concentrated machine gun and mortar fire on the sectors either side of the Monchy salient. There would also be the build-up of stores

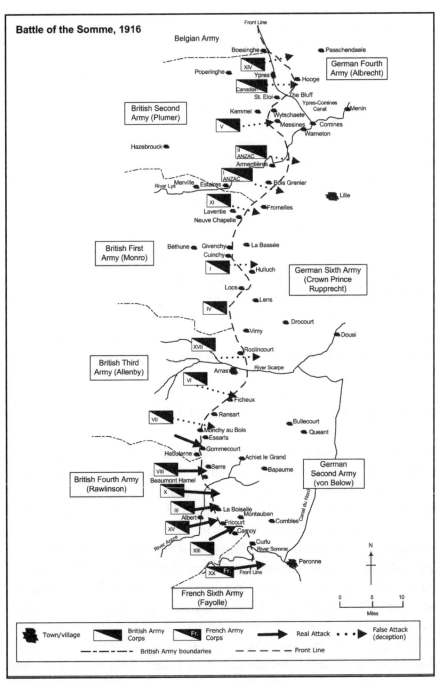

Map 5

and materials, all camouflaged to be as detectable as those in the Fourth Army sector. The boxes would be empty. Through the fire programme north and south of Monchy, the British indicated that they were isolating the salient from flanking fire prior to the infantry attack. This illusion was further enhanced by artillery targeting the roads and approaches to Essarts behind the salient.

The value of these activities would disappear very soon after zero hour on 1 July when despite the artillery, rifle and machine gun fire, the smoke discharge and the noise, the infantry remained in their trenches. However, depending on the quality of the false intelligence generated, there would be an initial reluctance by the Germans to re-deploy their troops in case the attack at Monchy had a later zero hour. This reluctance can be seen in Falkenhayn's reaction to the whole deception plan, which will be discussed later.

The real value of Haig's use of the deception category of *Confusion* can be seen from the fact that in mid-June the Germans inserted the 2nd Guards Reserve Division between the 52nd and 111th (German) Divisions to hold Gommecourt and the Monchy Salient. Without any attack, the VII Corps had managed to divert a division and six supporting heavy batteries, which could have been deployed against the Fourth Army.

Subsidiary Attack at Gommecourt, 1 July 1916

The attack at Gommecourt was designed as a subsidiary attack and, despite the fact that it had the physical objective of the capture of Gommecourt, its primary aim was to divert German attention northwards from the Fourth Army attack across the Ancre. The task was assigned to the Third Army by General Sir Edmund Allenby, to the VII Corps, the 56th and 46th Divisions in particular. Between the right of the VII Corps and the left of the VIII Corps (GOC, Lieutenant-General Sir A. G. Hunter-Weston) at Beaumont Hamel-Serre was a two-mile gap in which there were to be no attacks. The aim of the attack was to ensure that German artillery and infantry that could harass the left flank of VIII Corps would focus on the VII Corps at Gommecourt. The Germans strengthened their line, with disastrous consequences for the attackers. Prior to the attack Haig had asked Lieutenant-General Sir Thomas D'Oyly Snow (GOC VII Corps) how the preparations were progressing and he replied 'They know we are coming all right.'[5] The 46th Division suffered 2,455 casualties and the 56th Division 4,314 casualties. As a deception, the attack was a success!

After the Gommecourt attack, General D'Oyly Snow felt the need to pen a message which was read to all surviving troops and explained that although Gommecourt had not been taken, the main aim of the attack had been as a subsidiary action to ensure that the Germans could not transfer troops to the Fourth Army sector.[6] The reaction to this revelation can only be guessed at. On the basis of D'Oyly Snow's comments, it can be argued that there was still a certain level of naivety in the planning of these operations. They should have been implemented to cause confusion within the German defences, certainly not in a manner which could only result in high casualties.

The nature of the subsidiary attack at Gommecourt was different to the demonstrations within the rest of the deception plan. In the sectors north of Gommecourt to the Ypres Salient, the demonstrations would be exposed as fakes within hours of the attack. Haig gambled on the fact that the Fourth Army would achieve its objectives and consolidate its new positions before troops could be transferred to bolster the German Second Army defences. As the movement of vast numbers of troops was not something that was readily achieved this was not a great gamble on Haig's part, provided that the German troops were held in their own sectors prior and up to 1 July for fear of a British attack.

The attack at Gommecourt was different in that it had a real physical objective and the infantry left the relative safety of their trenches. The main aim of this operation was to protect the Fourth Army's left flank; the right flank of the Fourth Army was protected by attacks by the French XX and XXX Corps south of the River Somme. As it became apparent that the German defenders were committed to the Gommecourt sector, the attack was finally broken off at midnight. As the attack had been real, the withdrawal of the British troops back to their own trenches was not the signal for the Germans to denude this sector of troops to assist against the main attack further south; the troops had to remain in position until the British threat was judged to be over.

All the preparations of the Fourth, Third, First and Second Armies had been similar in nature. All the armies had dug advanced trenches, saps, assembly trenches and gun emplacements. These features, apart from those in the Fourth Army sector, were dummies, and the Fourth Army also dug dummy trenches simply to add to the confusion and to align themselves with the other armies and satisfy the desired attribute of 'consistency'. A large number of raids were conducted creating the impression that the British were testing the German defences. For several nights before zero day, the Third Army conducted 12 raids, the First Army 14 raids and the Second Army 14 raids. In total the Germans conducted only six raids against these three armies during the same period. British air superiority ensured that the Germans to a large extent were denied aerial intelligence and had to rely on direct observation and intelligence gathered by spies.

When the bombardment proper began in the Fourth Army sector on 24 July, the other armies instigated an artillery programme aimed at wire cutting, the destruction of front line defences and the discharge of gas. Behind the lines German communications targets were hit while at night the rest billets were shelled. Although the artillery programmes varied between the armies, the Third Army initiated a systematic bombardment which was as similar as possible in all respects to that in the Fourth Army sector and of course represented a huge investment in munitions. The Third Army targeted the Gommecourt salient, the Monchy salient and north of Roclincourt, while the First Army bombarded Hulluch and north of Neuve Chapelle. However, the Second Army preparations, focused around the Salient, were curtailed due to labour and material shortages.

All of this activity presented the Germans with possible impending major offensives along a 100-mile sector of the front from Albert to Boesinghe. Even though German Intelligence estimated British strength quite accurately and understood that all the preparations could not possibly be real, it was difficult to determine where the real blow would fall. The potential for major problems with the implementation of this extremely ambitious deception was great considering the multi-army nature and the length of the targeted front. These preparations required GHQ involvement not only to initiate them but also to co-ordinate them and to ensure adherence to the three criteria. It would have been easy to lose the consistency requirement if each Army had independently planned their own deceptions.

As a result, the Germans were confused but not entirely deceived, which is evident from Map 6 showing the situation prior to 1 July from a German perspective. The German view of the developing front showed that they were confused regarding the actual point of attack. General Erich von Falkenhayn (Chief of the German General Staff) concluded after the middle of June that there would be an attack in northern France from

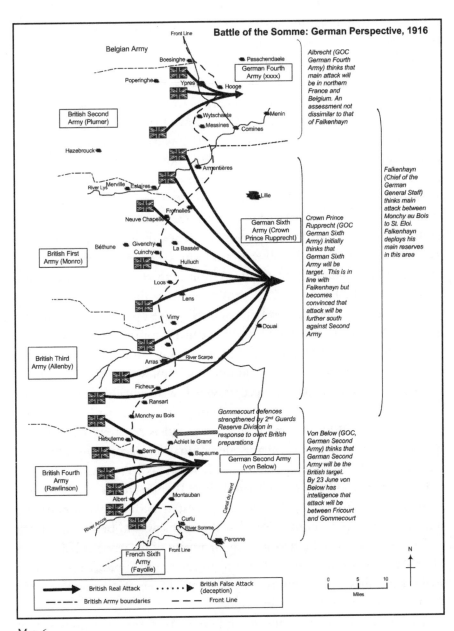

Battle of the Somme: German Perspective, 1916

Belgian Army

Boesinghe
Passchendaele
German Fourth Army (xxxx)
Poperinghe
Ypres
Hooge

Front Line

British Second Army (Plumer)
Wytschaete
Menin
Messines
Comines

Albrecht (GOC German Fourth Army) thinks that main attack will be in northern France and Belgium. An assessment not dissimilar to that of Falkenhayn

Hazebrouck
Armentières

River Lys
Merville Estaires
Lille

Fromelles
Neuve Chapelle

German Sixth Army (Crown Prince Rupprecht)

Falkenhayn (Chief of the German General Staff) thinks main attack between Monchy au Bois to St. Eloi. Falkenhayn deploys his main reserves in this area

Béthune
Givenchy
Cuinchy
La Bassée
British First Army (Monro)
Hulluch

Loos

Lens

Vimy

Crown Prince Rupprecht (GOC German Sixth Army) initially thinks that German Sixth Army will be target. This is in line with Falkenhayn but becomes convinced that attack will be further south against Second Army

Douai

British Third Army (Allenby)
Arras
River Scarpe

Ficheux

Ransart

Monchy au Bois

Gommecourt defences strengthened by 2nd Guards Reserve Division in response to overt British preparations

German Second Army (von Below)

Hébuterne
Achiet le Grand
Serre
Bapaume

British Fourth Army (Rawlinson)

Albert
Montauban

Canal du Nord

Von Below (GOC, German Second Army) thinks that German Second Army will be the British target. By 23 June von Below has intelligence that attack will be between Fricourt and Gommecourt

River Ancre
Curlu
River Somme
Peronne

French Sixth Army (Fayolle)
Front Line

N

British Real Attack → → → British False Attack (deception)
British Army boundaries — — — Front Line

0   5   10
Miles

Map 6

Monchy au Bois (just north of Gommecourt) to St. Eloi. This would have meant that the German Sixth Army (Crown Prince Rupprecht) would be facing the British First and large parts of the Second and Third Armies.

Both von Below and Prince Rupprecht were concerned by the build-up in front of their respective armies, in line with the British deception plan. They had both become increasingly alarmed by the growing numbers of trench raids, instigated since Haig had taken overall command. However, both eventually came to the same conclusion that von Below's Second Army was the most likely target and by 19 June Crown Prince Rupprecht was certain that the big attack was imminent. Von Below was also convinced of this, as his intelligence organisation reported additional artillery emplacements appearing in the British Fourth Army sector together with the registration of Second Army targets. On 19 June the transfer of four divisions from in front of the German Sixth Army to opposite the Second Army was reported along with the accompanying increase in trench digging and camp activity. This complemented the observation from the beginning of the month of an increase in gun emplacements in front of the German Second Army. The arrival of the French XXX Corps to reinforce the XX Corps south of the Somme was observed. Von Below's intelligence operation subsequently decided that the attack would be between Fricourt and Gommecourt with confirmation on 23 June from a German spy who had penetrated the deception plan, although this conclusion could simply be arrived at by reading the British and French newspapers, which were equally convinced. The comments of a British Minister to munitions workers regarding the postponement of the Whitsun bank holiday were widely reported! The German spy also suggested that only infantry demonstrations accompanied by artillery fire would take place in front of the German Sixth Army.

But neither von Below or Crown Prince Rupprecht were able to persuade the stubborn Falkenhayn, who persisted with his assessment and remained firm in his conviction that the attack would be further north and as a consequence he stationed the majority of his reserves behind the Sixth Army, with only three divisions in reserve to support the Second Army. Falkenhayn was supported by Albrecht, Duke of Württemberg, the GOC German Fourth Army in Flanders.

A wide-ranging geographically dispersed deception plan must target the Supreme Command as that was the only organisation that was in a position to see the whole of it. Initially, Crown Prince Rupprecht could only see the British Third and First Army activities and was convinced that he was the target, although he later changed his mind. Albrecht could see Second Army preparations and von Below observed the Fourth Army. Each man was convinced that his army was the target but Falkenhayn was able to assess intelligence gathered from all fronts and it was Falkenhayn and his intelligence officers that the deception plan was really targeting. The idea that Falkenhayn was the primary target and not the individual army commanders should be evident from Map 6.

Falkenhayn's conviction that the main attack would be against the German Sixth Army persisted in the face of mounting intelligence from the German Second Army front that it was the British target. In April, Falkenhayn suggested that the Sixth Army should mount a 'preventive attack', aimed at disrupting the British preparations, but insufficient men and materials precluded this. On 25 May when von Below suggested that the Second Army should mount a similar attack, although the Supreme Command agreed to the enterprise, it only committed an additional regiment of artillery, rendering the venture unfeasible. Falkenhayn simply did not believe the Second Army to be the target. At the same time as he responded to the overt British Third Army activities around Gommecourt by inserting the 2nd Guards Reserve Division into the line in mid-June, the German Second Army lost the 11th Bavarian Division, which was transferred to Galicia on the Eastern Front.

On 15 June, Falkenhayn informed the Kaiser who was visiting Crown Prince Rupprecht's headquarters that he could not understand why the Second Army would be attacked. There were no serious steps taken to reinforce either the Sixth or the Second Army until the afternoon of 1 July when the 3rd Guards, 11th Reserve and 12th Reserve Divisions were sent to bolster the Sixth Army! Even as late as 3 July, Falkenhayn still expected an imminent attack against the Sixth Army.

The British deception plan generated enough credible intelligence to hold Falkenhayn's attention in northern France, although the British cannot take total credit for this, as it was more or less an accidental application of Magruder's Principle. Falkenhayn's *idée fixe* left him oblivious to anything that might challenge the validity of his interpretation. On 29 August 1916, Falkenhayn was replaced as Chief of Staff by Field Marshal Paul von Hindenburg.

On 1 July on the left flank surprise was lost with the firing of the Hawthorne Ridge mine ten minutes early and in the centre an intercepted telephone message from the 34th Division opposite La Boiselle signalled the general offensive by the Fourth Army. Even so, the defenders at Fricourt were taken by surprise despite a Moritz listening station detecting activity. Apart from the listening stations the Germans were also able to intercept telephone conversations along badly insulated wires (before the Fullerphone) which meant that the conversations could be carried by any conducting materials, including the ground itself. The listening devices meant that the Germans did not need to conduct raids. There does not seem to have been a systematic attempt by the British to use these channels to their advantage although locally, one corps preserved a circuit, known as the 'Wolff Circuit' for feeding disinformation to the Germans. At the Battle of Bazentin Ridge (14–15 July), the British did make use of the situation (see below).

Room 40, Naval Intelligence Division in London, spread rumours of an amphibious landing on the Belgian coast which would create a flank and roll up the German line. This was the same idea that had come from Major-General G.M.W. Macdonough, Head of Intelligence at First Army headquarters, before the Battles of Neuve Chapelle (March 1915) and Loos (September 1915). This time however, the plan was more complex. Room 40 was headed by the brilliant Admiral Sir Reginald Hall. (For the full story of Room 40, see *'Blinker' Hall, Spymaster: The Man who Brought America into World War I* by David Ramsay.)

All troop leave was stopped early in June in Flanders and the rail centre at Amiens was put off limits to convey the impression that significant troop transfers northwards were planned by rail, from the Fourth Army sector to the Second Army sector. The plan also involved a bogus question being asked in the House of Commons in late June.[7] To maintain this northern focus a fake headquarters was set up at Cassel, less than twenty miles west of Ypres while the real advance GHQ was situated at Beauquesne, sixteen miles north-west of Albert. In response to all this intelligence, the Germans did transfer some troops northwards into Flanders but in insufficient numbers to have an impact on the 1 July battle.

The French XX and XXX Corps, on the right flank of the British Fourth Army, south of the Somme had a great deal of success on 1 July in achieving their objectives. The 85 French batteries outnumbered the eight German batteries in the area. They delayed their zero hour until 9:30, two hours after the British. This meant that the Germans were taken by surprise, the British effectively providing a deception plan for the French. German intelligence had also judged the French ill-prepared for an attack with a large number of divisions committed to the defence of Verdun, even though von Below had recently observed the movement of the French XXX Corps into the area.

For the first day of the battle, the deception plan included subsidiary attacks north of the Ancre as far as Serre (Fourth Army) and in the Gommecourt Salient (Third Army) with the aim of engaging the German reserves and distracting the artillery from enfilading the main attack. Haig in his Second Despatch reported that when it was felt that the troops had achieved these objectives, the battle should be broken off and the troops withdrawn.[8,9]

Battle of Bazentin Ridge, 14–15 July 1916

Within two weeks of the start of the battles of the Somme, the British Army altered its approach and adopted a short, intense bombardment with infantry forming up under the cover of darkness and the attack going in at dawn. Having issued a prior face-to-face verbal instruction, the British Fourth Army headquarters, using the knowledge that the Germans were able to overhear the telephone conversations of the British 62 Brigade, informed all companies of the brigade that the attack had been postponed. This ruse seemed to have succeeded as there was very little machine gun fire when the attack commenced as planned.

With the German first line taken, the British tried a new ruse. Royal Flying Corps aircraft flew over the battlefield at 13:00 and reported back via wireless that British cavalry were passing through the German second lines. This wireless message was intended to be intercepted by the Germans in the hope that they would not reinforce their as yet uncaptured second line. The ruse did not work and the Germans did not retreat to their third line.

On 5 July, GHQ had informed the various army commanders that the Fourth Army was advancing well but for continued progress it was essential that the other armies maintained pressure on the Germans to prevent the transference of German troops to the Fourth Army sector. As a result, the Third Army targeted the Hébuterne-Vimy Ridge sector, the First Army (initially commanded by Monro but after 13 September, by Lieutenant-General Sir R.C. Haking) targeted Vimy Ridge to Laventie and the Second Army, Laventie to Boesinghe. All three armies initiated demonstrations, minor actions and a large number of raids. To illustrate the scale of activity, during this period the three armies initiated 310 raids, of which 67 pre cent were considered to be successful, compared with 65 initiated by the Germans, of which a third were considered successful. The other actions to tie down the Germans included the attacks at Fromelles (First and Second Armies, 19–20 July), the Second Army's preparations for an attack at Messines and a large number of Chinese Attacks including those at Fromelles (17 July), Guillemont (7 August, 1 September), Switch Trench (16 August) and High Wood (4 September). There was also a Chinese Attack at Ovillers (2 July) which was a successful distraction from the British attack at La Boiselle, captured 24 hours after the scheduled date.

Fromelles, 19–20 July 1916

On 6 July, following on from Haig's call for action, General Sir Herbert Plumer (Second Army) notified Monro (First Army) that he was occupied with preparations for an attack at Messines, but would be prepared to partici-pate in a joint attack on his extreme right as part of the programme to distract the Germans. As a result, Monro ordered Lieutenant-General Sir Richard C. Haking (GOC, XI Corps) to develop a suitable co-ordinated plan based on XI Corps (First Army) and a division from the Second Army. The Haking plan identified the villages of Aubers and Fromelles as potential targets but Aubers Ridge was vetoed immediately by Monro who favoured an attack at Hill 70 to expand the Loos salient. However, Major-General R. H. K. Butler, Deputy Chief of the General Staff, advised them that as the Germans had already withdrawn nine battalions from the Lille area and moved them to the Somme, Haig wanted the attack to take place further north at the junction of the Second and First Armies, scheduled for 17 July following a bombard-ment beginning on 14 July. Despite the potentially disastrous narrow front, the attack had to be kept local with the express aim of teaching the Germans that they could not reinforce the main battle area with impunity.

By 13 July Monro notified Haking that the preliminary artillery bom-bardment should convey the impression that it was the prelude to a massive offensive but the infantry assault should have the limited objective of the German front line. The attack was to be conducted by the 61st Division (182, 183 and 184 Brigades) and the 5th Australian Division (15, 14 and 8 Australian Brigades).

Due to bad weather, the attack had to be postponed until 18:00 on 19 July. On 16 July the artillery began wire cutting. The heavy artillery commenced a steady bombardment of the German front line defences, which were not inconsiderable as they had been developed over time in relative peace. On 17 July from 04:00 until 07:00 there were four lifts to barrage lines and at each lift the infantry showed bayonets and dummy figures to induce the Germans to man their front line trenches.[10] At the end of each lift, which lasted about five minutes, the artillery shortened its range to the front line trenches. This deception tactic did not induce the Germans to man their trenches but Haig still thought that the artillery bombardment alone had already achieved the objective of holding German troops in that sector. Nevertheless, both Monro and Haking insisted that the infantry attack should go ahead, which resulted in serious casualties. The artillery had failed to destroy the wire, the defences were largely intact and the defenders were alert. The casualties were staggeringly high, 1,547 (50 per cent of the strength) from the 61st Division and 5,533 (over 90 per cent of the strength) from the 5th Australian Division. The failure to weaken the defences was unexplained at the time but Christopher Duffy has suggested that German primary sources indicate an Australian prisoner had given the Germans details of the plan and the troop deployments.[11] A critical factor in this failure is the lack of intelligence gathered to confirm that the deception plan had been accepted by the enemy. Although Fromelles has been portrayed as an unnecessary and bloody 'sideshow', it should be placed within the context of all the actions that were initiated post-1 July to maintain the illusion that British attacks were to be expected anywhere along the line so that German reinforcements could not be transferred south with impunity.

The Battle of the Ancre, 13–18 November 1916

One of the final acts of the Battles of the Somme, which had started almost five months earlier, was the Battle of the Ancre, an operation across the Redan Ridge designed to eliminate a German salient between the Albert-Bapaume Road and Serre. The main attack was delivered by V Corps (GOC, Lieutenant-General E.A. Fanshawe), north of the river, with the 63rd (Royal Naval) (Major-General C. D. Shute), the 51st (Highland) (Major-General G.M. Harper), 2nd (Major-General R.H.K. Butler) and

3rd (Major-General C.J. Devereux) Divisions. The II Corps were to attack south of the river. What had started with the Fourth Army was finished by the newly formed Fifth Army (COC, General Sir Hubert Gough).

The bombardment on the V Corps sector was designed to modify the expectations of the German defenders. Each morning, 30 minutes before dawn, after the night firing programme had finished, the heavy artillery fired a barrage on the German front line for 60 minutes, which concluded with intense firing, assisted by the field artillery to give the impression of an impending infantry attack. The artillery bombardment was attended by an infantry demonstration that lasted for 40 minutes, although artillery counter-battery work continued for the remainder of the day. On 13 November the same artillery programme was followed by the infantry attack after the troops had moved up into position under the cover of darkness. The outcome was a relative success with the capture of Beaumont-Hamel by the 51st (Highland) Division, Redan Ridge by the 2nd Division and Beaucourt by the 63rd (Royal Naval) Division, but Serre remained in German control.

The Battle of Le Transloy Ridges, 1–18 October 1916

Although the instruction from GHQ and the Army Commanders throughout 1916 had emphasised the need for surprise, within the lower units the message had not been fully assimilated. At Le Transloy on 12 October, the lack of success was attributed to the fact that the 6th Division (Major-General C. Ross) always followed a rigid pattern, with a two-day bombardment followed by an early afternoon infantry attack.[12] Further, the use of creeping barrages, far from assisting the infantry attack, had simply taught the Germans that machine guns sited in the front line were vulnerable and useless and as a result they placed them further back across the valley to catch the infantry as they came over the skyline. The battle failed to capture the Le Transloy Ridge and resulted in serious casualties.

The German Perspective

In October 1916, in line with Haig's instructions to distract the Germans, the amphibious invasion ruse was tried again. To counter this, the

Germans moved thousands of troops northwards. However, because of the need-to-know principle, the British Government, unaware of the deception, viewed the build-up of enemy troops on the Belgian coast as the prelude to an invasion of Britain. Haig, urged by the Government to release troops from the front for the defence of the mainland, was forced to admit that the British Government had been deceived. From a deception perspective, this was a perfect demonstration of the effectiveness of the need-to-know principle.[13] The rumours of the amphibious landing would have fitted well with the work that was being conducted by Plumer's Second Army, particularly the digging of the mines under Messines Ridge, of which the Germans were aware. It was probably these activities that persuaded the Germans that the British Army would switch the axis of their attack to Flanders as the Somme offensive was closed down.

On 12 October intelligence officers of the German General Staff concluded that the limited fresh divisions of the British infantry would be employed in small-scale attacks south of Arras. However, on 14 October the Bavarian representative at German Supreme Headquarters reported that despite evidence from the Flanders sector that the next attack would be on the British left wing, the actual attack would still continue by the Fourth Army along the same axis.[14] It was predicted that a big attack would come at the end of October or beginning of November, which would be accompanied by demonstrations of strength on other sectors.

Tanks

On 15 September at Flers-Courcellette the British launched their latest weapon, the tank, to crush wire defences and attack head on machine gun emplacements regardless of any intervening trench systems. Although not the outright success that was hoped for, the potential was there for all to see. Winston Churchill, the chief political advocate of the tank, recommended that all tank attacks should come as a surprise to the enemy and that their success was dependent on this. They should be assembled behind the front line in secrecy and be deployed under the cover of smoke. In 1916 the tank was of course a surprise because it was new. The surprise associated with the deployment of tanks in 1917 and beyond was by virtue of deception plans implemented by GHQ and the army commanders. The concealment of the tank represented a huge challenge, not simply in hiding the vehicle itself but also in obscuring their tracks from aerial reconnaissance and masking the engine noise, a tell-tale sign that required no specialist equipment to detect.

Lessons of the Somme

The analysis of the deception plans of the Battles of the Somme revealed that constraints in men and materials had had a significant effect on plausibility, consistency and predictability. The objective of concealing the time and place of the attack had arguably been achieved. All of the four principal German Army commanders, Falkenhayn, von Below, Crown Prince Rupprecht and Albrecht, were initially deceived, but the failure to maintain the strict plausibility, consistency and predictability compromised the plan at a local level.

The commanders of the British Third, First and Second Armies had embraced the idea that each had a significant role to play in the Fourth Army's attack, though the officers, NCOs and soldiers from the lower units, not being privy to the plan, might question the activities and regard them as foolish, especially as significant casualties resulted.

The British Army in general and Sir Douglas Haig in particular considered that the use of deception, despite the large investment in men and materials, did bring significant benefits to British offensive operations. Throughout the whole campaign, from June until November, Haig insisted that the Third, First and Second Armies should engage the Germans, primarily although not exclusively, through deception activities, to prevent the Germans transferring reinforcements south to oppose the British Fourth Army.

In his Second Despatch to the Secretary of State for War, printed in the *London Gazette* supplement of 29 December 1916, General Haig acknowledged that the subsidiary attacks had achieved their objective of holding Germans to their sectors. In reference to the Gommecourt operation he pointed out that as soon as the attack had fulfilled its objective of holding the German reserves and artillery, the troops were withdrawn. Haig explained that pressure had to be applied to the rest of the front so that the Germans could not devote themselves to the Fourth Army advance and he acknowledged the role played by the other Armies in 'keeping the enemy on their front constantly on the alert'. In his retrospect written in 1938 Captain Wilfred Miles, the author of the second volume of the 1916 Official History, summarised the British deception plan.

To carry out such a policy on an extensive scale required a preponderance of strength greater than the Allies possessed in 1916 ... but the activities of the British Third, First and Second Armies during the preparations for the Somme offensive certainly left Falkenhayn and Prince Rupprecht in doubt as to where the main blow would fall.[15]

The deception plans had been carefully thought through but as Miles had rightly assessed, the British Army did not possess sufficient resources to make the plan truly plausible and consistent. The fake preparations generally lacked sufficient strength and the transfer of resources southwards to bring the Fourth Army up to the desired strength was eventually detected by von Below and Crown Prince Rupprecht. The plans however were saved, somewhat fortuitously, by the application of Magruder's Principle. By chance, rather than strict design, the British deception plan aligned with Falkenhayn's beliefs and although there was evidence to the contrary, he remained firm in his conviction even after the British Fourth Army attack had begun.

Post-war appraisals and re-appraisals of the battles of the Somme have concentrated on the horrendous casualty figures, the lack of ground gained, the offensive approach adopted and the apparent failings of the senior commanders. The assessments have focused on the British Army's failure to nullify the main German defences with worn out, inaccurate guns and dud shells, based on poor intelligence. Gommecourt and Fromelles have been seen as actions resulting in high casualties for very little apparent gain. But they should really be placed within the context of the overall deception plan as implemented by the Third, First and Second Armies. These subsidiary attacks were just a small part of Haig's plan to divert the attention of the Germans from the British Fourth Army sector. Overall, this plan, aimed at the German Commander-in-Chief and the Supreme Command structure, achieved its objective. As late as 3 July, Falkenhayn remained convinced that the German Sixth Army was the real target and the offensive by Rawlinson's Fourth Army was merely a feint.

From 1916 the implications of the two golden rules of deception established in 1915 were better understood. The use of a multi-sector, multi-unit deception plan was still the key to a successful outcome but the target of the plan had become another major factor. A plan that was initiated across geographically dispersed sectors could only be appreciated by the enemy commander who could 'see' all those sectors. If a deception plan could only be implemented at local level as at The Bluff, then this plan must target the local commander and not the Commander-in-Chief. The first additional rule to emerge from 1916 was that the aim of deception was to elicit a response, and not necessarily simply to cause confusion, and must target the appropriate enemy commander who had the authority to order that response. The second additional rule was that prolonged deception could not be achieved by simple simulated activity alone and it was for this reason that throughout the second half of the year Haig encouraged his Third, First and Second Army commanders to continually engage the Germans either through minor attacks or deception activities.

6

The Western Front 1917: Reaping the Rewards

You can be sure of succeeding in your attacks if you only attack places which are undefended.
Sun Tzu

There were significant engagements throughout 1917 which utilised deception, but the major offensive, the Third Battle of Ypres (Passchendaele, 31 July–10 November 1917) was poorly supported by deception activities through constraints in men and materials. The intention had been there from the early planning phases but the preparations for Third Ypres had soaked up the men, materials and artillery, so that the deception plans could not obey the rules about plausibility and consistency. However, Third Ypres aside, there were other engagements where deception played a significant role, particularly at Vimy Ridge and Cambrai.

Whereas 1916 had focused on the British Fourth Army's actions across the Somme, in 1917 the spotlight would fall on the Third, First and particularly Second Armies at the northern end of the Western Front. In November 1916, an Anglo-French conference was held at the French General Headquarters (Le Grand Quartier Général, GQG) which agreed that the strategy for 1917 would consist of a number of integrated and timed Allied offensives, each designed to maintain pressure on the German front and prevent the transference of reserves. This whole approach was in essence a type of deception plan, except that the British and the French both agreed that all actions would be invested with men and materials and that all would have real strategic or tactical objectives.

General Joseph Joffre was replaced on 13 December 1916 by General Robert Nivelle; in 1917 Joffre became head of the French Military Mission to the United States. Nivelle proposed a new plan as he confidently claimed that his major offensive for 1917, to be known to posterity as the Nivelle Offensive, would rout the German Army with minimal French casualties and end the war within a matter of months. Nivelle planned his major offensive to fall initially on the Chemin des Dames, a twenty-mile ridge that ran south-east of St. Quentin between the Laon-Soissons road and Corbeny and covered the valleys of the Aisne and the Ailette. This would revisit the 1914 battlefields across which the Germans had fallen back after the Battle of the Marne. But Nivelle changed the emphasis of the original 1917 plan, with the agreement of David Lloyd George, at a meeting in London in January 1917. Nivelle proposed that the French offensive along the Chemin des Dames would be the axis of the Allies' major effort in 1917, with the British operations acting as diversionary attacks. At a conference in Calais on 26 February, the Calais Agreement was drawn up to give Nivelle operational command over the British Army. There were immediate objections from the British Army establishment and the powers were subsequently diluted as it was agreed that Haig would remain in command of the British Army, but which would now act in support of French requirements. Nivelle's offensive was planned to commence on 9 April and in order to divert German attention, the British First Army would launch a simultaneous offensive in front of Arras. For the British, this would become known as the Second Battle of Arras (9 April–24 May 1917) and would comprise the Battle of Vimy Ridge (9–14 April 1917) and First Battle of the Scarpe (9–14 April 1917), although the British would advance along this axis until 4 May (Second Battle of the Scarpe, 23–24 April; Third Battle of the Scarpe, 3–4 May).

Battle of Vimy Ridge (Second Arras), 9–14 April 1917

The British First Army (GOC, General Sir Henry Horne) engagement at Vimy Ridge involved all four divisions of the Canadian Corps commanded by Lieutenant-General Sir Julian Byng against units of the German Sixth Army (GOC, General Ludwig von Falkenhausen). The Vimy Ridge heights had been the object of previous offensives. The French Army had made two earlier unsuccessful attempts to capture the positions (Second Battle of Artois, May 1915, Third Battle of Artois, September 1915). Vimy Ridge was a strategically important objective as it would provide the Allies with a panoramic view over the Plain of Douai towards the important communications centre of the town of Douai. As the centre of a rail network that ran north-south behind the German lines, Douai had been the focus of Allied attention since the beginning of 1915. If Douai fell under Allied control, there would be serious repercussions for the stability of the whole of the German front line. The capture of Vimy Ridge would be the first step towards this goal. However, with the change of French commander, the Allied focus had shifted and whereas Joffre had recognised the important of Vimy Ridge as a strategic target, Nivelle downgraded the attack to capture it as merely diversionary.

The timing of the attack had to fit with the French preparations for their offensive against the Chemin de Dames and was to commence on 9 April, a week before the main offensive. The British attack was to be conducted by all four divisions of the Canadian Corps together with a brigade from the British 5th Division in support of the 2nd Canadian Division. The attacking units formed up under the cover of darkness. At 05:30 precisely the artillery barrage opened up and seconds later mines laid under No-Man's-Land and various German strong points were detonated. The barrage lifted 100 yards every three minutes as the infantry attacked behind it. Tunnels had been dug which enabled the troops to get close to their jumping off positions in relative safety. On 9 April 1917 – Easter Monday – the attack was a complete success as the British advanced almost five miles and achieved their primary objective, with the entire length of Vimy Ridge under British control by 12 April. The Canadian Corps suffered over 10,600 casualties compared with at least 20,000 German casualties.

Success was due to the fighting abilities of the Canadian Corps, but the plan of attack embraced elements of intelligence, new offensive measures and secrecy and built on the lessons learnt on the Somme.[1] So success was also due to the methodology of Byng, who organised a comprehensive intelligence organisation that collated information from every possible source, from aerial reconnaissance and counter-battery artillery to snipers, observers and prisoner interrogators, to build up a picture of the German defences. He placed emphasis on infantry tactics, especially the effectiveness of small units and the all-arms approach and ensured that his personal philisophy pervaded throughout by getting to know all his company and battalion commanders individually. He invited groups to his headquarters throughout the preceding months, not only the commanders but also the NCOs, to study and analyse the tactical problems. His overall plan and its implementation was studied and understood in detail by all ranks. Byng made extensive use of technology including novel methods to locate German batteries and the relatively new 106 fuse, which meant that shrapnel shells reliably burst above ground, rather than in it, to destroy wire; its success led to a shortage of supply. This attack would act as a blueprint for the approach adopted by Byng at the Battle of Cambrai later in the year when, promoted, he commanded the British Third Army.

Byng also made use of a few deceptive measures. He employed a novel ruse in that the initial artillery fire plan, which began on 20 March, only employing half the batteries to conceal true strength.[2] The Germans would in view of the low volume of fire assume that it was a poor and transparent attempt to distract them from the French activities further south. This tactic changed within a week of the attack as the full weight of the artillery became apparent. As the front line defences were destroyed the guns switched targets to destroy the German batteries, while machine guns targeted the devastated defences to ensure that they could not be re-built. This was similar to the approach adopted by Plumer at The Bluff in March 1916.

Byng also utilised the *Behaviour Modification* tactic of the back barrage. Up to 9 April, artillery barrages rolled forward to each of the barrage lines in turn, but, as a back barrage, it returned to its original line as the Germans emerged from shelter and were manning their defences in anticipation of an infantry attack. Through this simple ruse the Germans became reluctant to man their defences as soon as a barrage had been lifted for fear of being exposed to a second sweep of the deadly shrapnel. On the morning of the actual attack the situation was further confused for the Germans. As the final high explosive (HE) bombardment lifted, the shrapnel barrage arrived so that, in the comparative safety of their dugouts, they were unaware of the change. The switch from an HE bombardment to a shrapnel barrage gave the British soldiers the opportunity to advance across No-Man's-Land in relative safety.[3] As the shrapnel barrage lifted, the Germans, who were 'conditioned', remained in their dugouts with the result that the British infantry, who had 'leant' on the barrage, were immediately on top of their objectives.[4] Although front line soldiers were able to distinguish between the different types of artillery fire, the subtleties would have been lost on the Germans due to the preceding exercise and the non-stop shell fire of the bombardment and the barrage. The situation was further improved for the attackers by the explosion of a number of mines that destroyed numerous German strong points.

Byng had managed to conceal the time of the attack only by a matter of minutes, but these were vital as they allowed the Canadian Corps to cross in comparative safety. However, unlike Plumer at St. Eloi in March 1916, Byng also addressed the problem of concealing the point of attack. Byng enlisted the assistance of 24th Division from I Corps (Lieutenant-General A.E.A. Holland) (First Army) to advance north of the Souchez River and the XIII Corps (Lieutenant-General Sir W.N. Congreve) (First Army) to advance in the south. This coincided with the VI (Lieutenant-General I.A.L. Haldane), VII (Lieutenant-General Sir T. D'Oyly Snow) and XVII (Lieutenant-General Sir. C. Fergusson) Corps from General Sir Edmund Allenby's Third Army advancing in what was known as the First Battle of the Scarpe (9–14 April 1917). The Third Army units advanced north of the Arras-Cambrai road, along similar ground to the 1918 advances, which resulted in the 12th (Eastern) Division pushing along Observation Ridge to Feuchy while the 3rd Division pressed on to Tilloy-dès-Mofflaines. The latter pushed on towards Monchy-le-Preux before meeting resistance owing to the intact nature of the wire entanglements. The geographical locations of the Third Army advances, which can be seen on Map 10, produced territorial gains equal to those of the First Army. While the latter gained strategically important ground with commanding views over the Plain of Douai and the 1915 goal of the all-important communications centre, the Third Army advances threatened Douai from the south-west. Further south on 10–11 April, Gough's Fifth Army, spearheaded by the 62nd (2nd/West Riding) Division from V Corps and the 4th Australian Division from I ANZAC Corps, engaged in a flanking action at Bullecourt. At 04:30 on 15 April, the Germans launched a counter-attack at Lagnicourt which penetrated the British line, although by 13:00 the British had responded and the original line had been restored.

These offensives were diversionary attacks designed to distract German attention away from what Nivelle, in his estimation, considered to be the main attack, the advance by nineteen divisions of the French Fifth and Sixth Armies against the Chemin des Dames between Soissons and

Rheims. In the event Nivelle's offensive was a costly failure, with 187,000 casualties, while the 'diversionary' attacks made significant advances, especially at Vimy Ridge and further south, which posed a potential threat to Douai.

Von Falkenhausen, the German Sixth Army commander, even as late as 7 April was convinced that no offensive would take place before the French Army attacked in Champagne, which German intelligence had determined was set for 16 April (Third Battle of Champagne – Second Battle of the Aisne, 16–20 April). Von Falkenhausen was surprised because his intelligence reports and prisoner information had indicated that the assault on Vimy Ridge was merely a diversionary attack in support of Nivelle's Champagne Offensive and that preparations were consistent with this. However, the front line troops had a different perspective. General Ernst von Bachmeister (GOC, German 79th Reserve Division) observed the preparations of the Canadian Corps, despite Byng's security measures, but his reports to his commander that something bigger than a mere diversion was in preparation were ignored.

As the British actions around Arras settled down, Haig turned his attention further north to the British Second and Fifth Army sectors in Flanders, specifically around the Ypres Salient. On 7 May Haig explained to an audience of British and French generals that the major offensive within the Ypres Salient would aim to capture the Passchendaele-Staden-Clercken ridge. In order to deceive the Germans, there would be a major attack at Lens by the British First Army and an attack at Frelinghen, three miles south of Warneton by the Second Army to create the impression that Lille would be the next objective. Lille, of similar importance to Douai, would distract German attention as its capture would disrupt the north-south railway supply line and threaten the stability of the German defences.

Battle of Messines, 7-14 June, and Third Battle of Ypres (Passchendaele), 31 July–10 November 1917

General Sir Henry Rawlinson had originally been requested by Haig to develop a plan for this offensive, which consisted of six stages. As there was a week between the first and third stages to provide sufficient time for the artillery to move up, it was proposed that the second stage should involve

A road screen made of natural material representing the crops growing in the fields. In the foreground is the road along which troops and materials would have travelled. (Royal Engineers Museum 5.7.163.A5)

Quaker guns at Confederate winter quarters, Centreville, Virginia, 1861–62. (Library of Congress LC-B811-334)

Photographed at Zillebeke in the Ypres Salient, one of the Quaker guns, a term derived from the American Civil War. (Royal Engineers Museum 23.522)

LIEUT.-GEN. SIR CHARLES FERGUSSON

An observation post made to resemble a devastated tree, complete with bark. The photograph shows the entrance at the bottom through which the observer had to crawl. The photograph is taken from the British side on La Bassée road; the entrance was of course invisible to the enemy. (Royal Engineers Museum 23.86)

Lt.-Gen Sir Charles Fergusson, GOC of XVII Corps that fought at the First Battle of the Scarpe (9–14 April 1917) and made a subsidiary attack during the Battle of Cambrai (20 November–7 December 1917) to the north of the main effort.

German machine-gun posts under camouflage screens. These are light in colour to blend in with the chalky soil. These appear to be 08-15 Maxim machine-guns.

In a field on the Somme, British Engineers are building a dummy Mark II Tank from wood. It appears to be a Female tank with representations of four machine guns. Visible beneath the structure are the large wooden wheels that made it possible for the troops to pull it some distance across No-Man's-Land over the rough terrain. (Tank Museum 410/B/2)

A wooden mock-up tank is manhandled by troops and hitched up to a team of horses ready for towing to the forward areas. (Tank Museum 410/B/4)

The horse team pulls the tanks towards the front supported by a number of troops. The large wheels beneath the tank are again visible. (Tank Museum 4962/C/5)

The tank is pulled through intact villages on the way to the front with the support troops on bicycles leaving all the effort to the horses. Local French farm workers are interested bystanders. The name 'HMLS (His Majesty's Land Ship) John Collins' is visible on the back of the tank. (Tank Museum 410/B/6)

The support troops are required in the narrow village streets and tight corners to 'shuffle' the dummy tank sideways to get around. The lightness of the tank is evident as only two soldiers are required to lift it around the corner. The sight attracts the attentions of the local inhabitants. (Tank Museum 1525/A5)

The impressive depth of barbed wire in front of the Hindenburg line; either tanks or artillery had to force a way through it.

Abandoned dummy tanks, a Medium A Whippet together with two either Mark IV or V tanks. Clearly, these tanks were just large, empty wooden boxes. (Royal Engineers Museum 23.604)

A German dummy tank factory, pointing to the lack of an effective German tank force and the reliance on captured British tanks. This factory is mass producing the Medium A Whippet, which first saw service in March 1918. (Tank Museum M10.22)

It is all too easy to bring a misleading modern sensibility to command, control and communications to bear when looking back and considering some of the deception plans followed – and conclude that they could not possibly be effective. This is the VI Corps pigeon loft, August 1917. (Imperial War Museum Q 27093)

Men of I Corps, RE Signals burying telephone cable in a wooden case. Such lines were sometimes tapped.

African American infantry unit on the road in 1918, probably somewhere north-west of Verdun. Note the camouflage netting in the trees. (Library of Congress LC-USZ62-116442)

an attack at Neuve Chapelle. This would maintain the pressure on Douai begun during the Arras offensives. The plan was subsequently altered by Plumer who retained the element of the subsidiary attacks, but as artillery was required to move from the First and Third Armies areas to the Second and Fifth Army sectors to support the fire programme proposed for Third Ypres, it became apparent that the proposed subsidiary attacks would not be viable. As a prelude to the main Flanders offensive, an attack along the Messines Ridge (7–14 June) was planned, but the timing of this had to fit with the disengagement of the Arras operations to provide men, materials and particularly artillery pieces. This constraint would have serious repercussions for the main offensive.

The lack of sufficient ordnance to support the subsidiary attacks did not prevent Haig from issuing orders to units of the First and Third Armies and other units not involved in the attack to maintain pressure on the Germans in front of them. Even the lowest level of activity, provided that it was sufficient not to be classed as 'normal' for that sector, would tie down German troops, especially near the sensitive area of Douai, which had been a strategic target all year.

As a prelude to the main attack within the Salient, the Messines Ridge, south of Ypres, would have to be captured to deny the Germans the observation point. The Messines attack by the IX, X and II ANZAC Corps from the Second Army lasted a week from 7 to 14 June and Haig issued instructions that within the Arras area the units of the First and Third Armies had to continue to actively engage the Germans, although he recognised that this was not easy, qualifying his orders as mentioned in his Fourth Despatch by stating that these engagements were to be conducted with 'such force as were left to them.'[5] Haig thought that by a careful selection of targets and by a combination of real and feint attacks, the Germans could still be deceived and prevented from transferring troops northwards into the Salient. In his despatch, Haig claimed that these actions were extremely successful, as the Germans consistently reported that they had repulsed major British attacks, which Haig gleefully claimed never took place but which he could not publicly deny!

Horne finalised the plans for the subsidiary, diversionary actions in the First Army sector to commence on 26 June on a broad front between Arras and Lens. The XIII Corps (Lieutenant-General W.F.N. McCracken) was to 'improve its position' over a 2,300-yard front between Gravrelle and Oppy while the Canadian Corps (Lieutenant-General Sir A.W.

Currie) and the British I Corps (Lieutenant-General Sir A.E.A. Holland) were to advance on a 4,800-yard front astride the Souchez River against specific objectives. The geographical location of these positions can be seen on Map 7.

On 26 June the Canadians launched an attack near the Souchez River with the objective of capturing the fortified post between Souchez and Avion, close to Lens. At the river, the Canadian Corps linked up with the British 46th (North Midland Division (Major-General W. Thwaites) from I Corps, which had been attacking Hill 65 (Reservoir Hill) south-west of Lens. Two days later the 3rd and 4th Canadian Divisions and the 46th (North Midland) Division attacked across the Souchez River and although successful, there was little exploitation beyond the initial objectives as heavy rain caused the river to flood and on the opposite bank the British troops were counterattacked fiercely.

Haig invested a great deal in men and materials to create the illusion that the next major thrust, after Messines, was further south than the Ypres Salient. On 28 June, the First Army launched a feint attack over fourteen miles from Gavrelle to Hulluch, which encompassed the town of Lens. The attack consisted of infantry demonstrations, discharges of gas, HE shells and Thermit (incendiary) together with mock raids. For instance, on 28 June at 19:20 5/Leicestershire Regiment moved forward as the barrage started, supported by real and dummy gas attacks north of the Lievin-Lens road. This confused the German defences and the 5/Leicestershire Regiment met no defensive barrage and very little machine gun fire.[6]

All of the feint attacks were mixed in with real attacks by the 31st Division (Major-General R. Wanless O'Conor) and 5th Division (Major-General R.B. Stephens), opposite Oppy on 24–25 June and by the Canadian 3rd and 4th Divisions and the British 46th (North Midland) Division on a two-and-half mile front astride the Souchez River on 28 June. The feint attacks used over 300 animated dummy soldiers and demonstrations by infantry – bayonets above the parapets, cheering and rapid rifle fire.

Slightly further north, pressure was also maintained. On 21 and 26 June, the 3rd Australian Division (Major-General Sir John Monash) attacked outposts north of Douve. This attack towards Warneton was originally envisaged by Haig but was probably too weak in terms of the overall deception plan to influence the Germans. The capture of the Messines Ridge had indicated an offensive in the Salient and a strong attack was

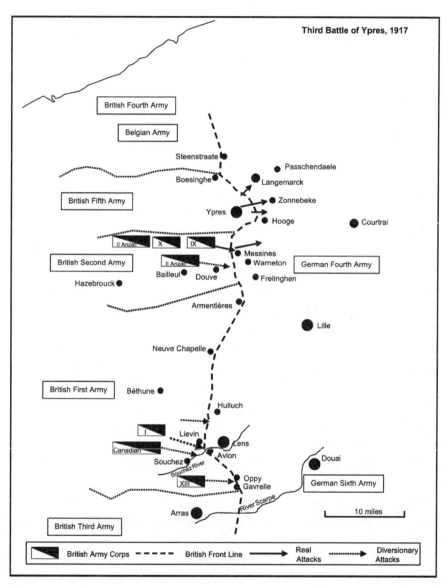

Map 7

required from the southern end of the ridge towards Lille to change German intelligence assessments.

These 'attacks' by themselves would have been soon revealed as fakes except for the fact that they were interspersed with real attacks. This created the impression of real attacks along the complete twelve-mile front and the Germans assumed that their efforts to repulse the attackers had been spectacularly successful in some instances. It would be the German claims of these successes that Haig was unable to deny in June 1917. His Fourth Despatch published in December 1917 explained the reality.

The combination of real and feint attacks appeared to show an advance towards Lille and Douai but in reality the attacks were too weak and sporadic to pose a credible threat. The cancellation of the attack at Neuve Chapelle created a 'gap' in the advance, which further contributed to the lack of credibility. In view of the Flanders offensive, these actions did not transfer significant numbers of German troops from the Salient, in fact ten divisions from the German Sixth Army, defending the Lens-Lille sector, were transferred in June to the German Fourth Army defending the Salient. These moves came despite the fact that German Sixth Army headquarters were expecting an imminent attack against Lille. Crown Prince Rupprecht overruled their concerns on the basis that the British did not have sufficient men and materials to mount simultaneous offensives in Flanders and against Lille. This indicates that the British deception plan had failed to target Rupprecht and that the preparations within the Salient were insufficiently concealed. On 16 November, Rupprecht would find himself in a similar situation but this time he would interpret the real threat against Cambrai as a minor action. In June, the Germans did move a number of troops from the French sector in the south to counteract the perceived threat against Lille as a precautionary measure. This was fortuitous as on 7 June, General Pétain, who had replaced Nivelle as the French Commander-in-Chief, had informed Haig that a number of French divisions had refused to go to the front line, thereby potentially destabilising the Allied front.

The attack within the Salient gained some ground for the British but at a high cost. Alongside the massive artillery bombardments and infantry advances, the British still employed some of the more subtle approaches to neutralising defences. On 28 July 1917, three days before General Sir Hubert Gough's Fifth Army's attack at Gheluvelt Plateau at the start of the Third Battle of Ypres, 300 dummy soldiers were used in a Chinese

Attack to disclose German machine gun emplacements and to target them with shrapnel. After the barrage had ceased, the dummy figures were left standing to show the Germans that they had been fooled, in the hope that when the real attack came, the Germans would take extra time before ordering their troops from their dugouts to man the front line and engaging their artillery.

On 26 September, the Germans reported that between Langemarck and Hollebeke, they were attacked by British troops who came in behind a screen of dust and smoke. The Royal Engineers in their post-war manual confirmed that these were Chinese Attacks using 280 dummy soldiers worked for twenty minutes to support an infantry brigade by attracting fire that would have enfiladed the advance. Over most of this sector only the dummies were used, though the Germans reported that the English infantry attacked many times but were 'continuously beaten back by our fire'.[7]

Battle of Cambrai, 20 November–7 December 1917

The Battle of Cambrai was the fourth British offensive of 1917. Over a six-mile front the Third Army advanced a distance of between three and four miles. In just over four hours, the much vaunted Hindenburg Line had been breached with over 500 tanks advancing en masse on day one. The British suffered about 4,000 casualties (killed, wounded or missing) on the first day and the total over the eighteen days of the battle was 44,207 casualties; the total German casualties have been estimated at 53,000. The attack, between Hermies in the north and Gonnelieu in the south, was assigned to the 12th (Eastern), 20th (Light) and 6th Divisions of the III Corps (GOC, Lieutenant-General W. Pulteney) and the 51st (Highland) and 62nd (2nd/West Riding) Divisions of the IV Corps (GOC, Lieutenant-General Sir C. L. Woollcombe). The attack targeted the German Second Army (GOC, General Georg von der Marwitz).

The initial attack, intended as a joint Franco-British offensive with the French attacking at St. Quentin and the British at Havrincourt, had been planned as an attempt to shift German attention and troops from the Ypres Salient further south to Cambrai. The task was assigned to the Third Army. However, ten days before the scheduled start of the Battle of Cambrai, the Third Battle of Ypres (31 July–10 November) was closed down. Although the original aim of Cambrai had disappeared there was nevertheless pressure to continue in order to unleash the tanks. The Third Army was now commanded by General Sir Julian Byng who had taken over from General Sir Edmund Allenby in June 1917; Byng employed all of the methods which had been so successful at Vimy Ridge with the Canadian Corps earlier in the year.

The initial instructions for Operation 'GY', issued by Byng on 13 November 1917 contained the deception details. To avoid the build-up being detected a large order for camouflage material was placed with the Special Works Parks at Wimereux and Aire. All the tanks were moved into camouflaged positions during the night with all daylight movements banned and for the first time large concentrations of the assaulting infantry were also hidden under horizontal camouflaged covers that concealed their bivouacs. Byng had placed an order for at least 100,000 square yards of camouflage netting for the III Corps to conceal the 476 tanks, 1,003 guns and an additional 150 gun emplacements plus ammunition dumps. The whole area was scoured for woods and shelled-out houses, anywhere capable of hiding the build-up of the artillery and tanks. Byng's instructions indicated that special attention should be paid to the concealment of the tell-tale tank tracks visible from the air. The RFC flew daily missions to detect and report back on any camouflage scheme shortcomings so that from the air there was no trace of the force, which gradually moved into position from 7 November onwards.[8] On the night of the attack, the tanks crept forward to the start line with the engines on tick over, with their tank commanders walking in front. As the artillery concentration built up, using the cover of darkness to move the guns into their camouflaged emplacements, their registration on their allotted targets was surreptitiously achieved by following a strict schedule so that there was no increase in artillery activity other than that expected from the sector during 'quiet' periods. An even stricter rule was applied that any gun that occupied a newly formed position or was of a calibre heavier than that previously present, was not allowed to open fire at all and these batteries would have to rely on bearing pickets to register the guns. Major-General Louis Vaughan, General Staff Third Army issued Artillery Instruction No.20 on 14 November, which stressed that right up to zero hour the normal firing programme should be maintained and there should be no discernible increased rate of fire. With a real appreciation of deception, he emphasised the point that not only should there be no increase in firing but equally importantly the period should not be abnormally quiet. In a similar vein he instructed the RFC that all flights over the sector should follow the pattern set over the previous four months with no attempt to screen troop movements and all Corps attacks, whether real or subsidiary, should be equally supported up until zero plus two hours; through these deception activities the British were hoping to tie down the German reinforcements for at least those two hours.

Although the ground was ideal for tanks, being firm and based on a chalk layer with little surface water, this dryness caused a logistical problem. The Royal Engineers had to create horse watering and cart-filling points, 500–700 yards from the front line which would have to blend into the background despite the large volumes of traffic turning up there. No unusual activity was allowed on the ground or in the air, artillery registration was stealthy and all home mail was stopped for the incoming troops. The thin screen of troops which held the sector was kept in position in the trenches until the last possible moment when they were replaced by the assault troops.

The area was divided into Front, Central and Back Zones. The Front Zone, an area directly visible in daylight from the German front line trenches, covered the ground between the front line and a notional line, the 'Daylight Line', two miles back. In this area, daytime working parties could not consist of more than two men and individual working parties had to be at least 100 yards apart to create the impression that they were engaged in low level area maintenance and not the overture to a major battle, creating assembly trenches and opening lanes through the barbed wire defences. Behind, in the Central Zone, an area visible from German balloons, the restrictions were slightly relaxed while in the Back Zone, visible only from German aircraft, the activity was more frantic although this did depend on the RFC being in the ascendancy.

From a German perspective, the front opposite Cambrai-Havrincourt displayed no abnormal activity. As a further, but inadvertent, ruse, some units of the Third Army had been ordered to the Italian Front and Army orders were issued to all officers who spoke Italian to identify themselves. In the event, the order to move Third Army units to Italy was rescinded as the potential of the battle became realised, but the issuing of the real orders had added to the Germans' sense of complacency when they discovered them. Plumer and his Second Army were sent to the Italian Front on 13 November to bolster the Italian Army against the Austro-Hungarians.

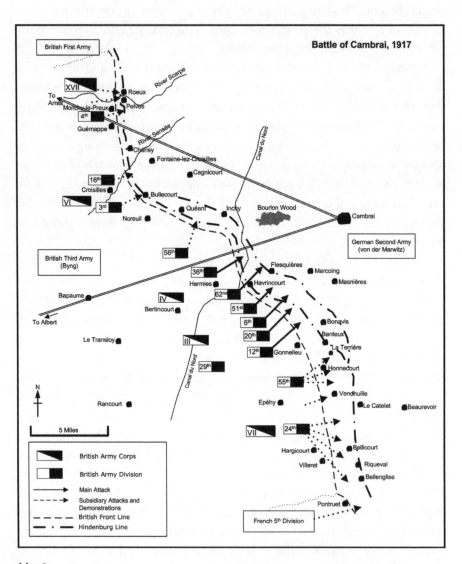

Map 8

To disguise the point of attack, disinformation measures and fake preparations were instigated. The Tank Corps Headquarters at Albert, which would control the Cambrai attack, was labelled as the 'Tank Corps Training Office' part of a permanent tank and infantry school. Officers in the back areas were informed of this 'in confidence', which conveniently explained the presence of tanks. To shift the focus away from Cambrai, the 1 Tank Brigade Headquarters at Arras, 30 miles north-west of Cambrai, created a specially locked room with a 'No Admittance' sign on the door.[9] The room contained maps of the Arras sector and a number of 'secret' plans. It was hoped that a curious person would look in and spread rumours of an impending attack. To ensure consistency, each evening six tanks were detrained from a railway siding in the Arras XVII Corps sector. The tanks moved across country and 'hid' in a nearby wood. During the night, the tanks moved slowly and quietly out to another siding and were returned to their tankodrome. For a few weeks, the process was repeated with the same six tanks until rumours began to circulate of a mass tank build-up around Arras. As a result the wood received frequent German artillery attacks. So the Germans were expecting a mass tank attack – but 30 miles from the real thing!

For the main attack, the troops of the 12th, 20th, 6th, 51st and 62nd Divisions were assembled behind the lines and brought up just before 20 November under the cover of darkness and hidden in villages or woods or lying out under camouflaged canvas erections, which looked like ammunition or supply dumps.[10] The extensive railway network laid down by the British meant that the troops could remain stationed a relatively long distance behind the front and could be brought up in large numbers during the night before the attack. The troops would not have to endure for too long the cramped, uncomfortable conditions of their hidden bivouacs. These troops had been specifically trained to work in conjunction with their tanks and the two groups were reunited during the night before the attack. The camouflaged congestion within the forward areas meant that the three divisions of V Corps, the strategic reserve, had to be stationed twenty miles away at Bapaume before zero hour, but the rail network would again speed their arrival. With the troops stationed a distance from the front, they had been able to undergo specialised training with tanks on a ground model, although the troops were not made aware of what terrain it represented.

On 20 November the main attack was supported by subsidiary artillery attacks to lengthen the frontage of the attack. Artillery bombardments were the primary weapon used to pin down the Germans to their sectors. In his initial instructions, Byng had suggested that subsidiary actions should take place in the sectors either side of the main attack with a view to 'distracting the enemy's attention and weakening his power of resistance'.[11] The units involved with subsidiary attacks and demonstrations also began discreet camouflaged preparations on their fronts, shielded by the same strict level of security that characterised the main attack.

As the main attack commenced at 06:00, so did the subsidiary operations. South of the III Corps sector at zero hour on a ten-mile front the VII Corps (GOC, Lieutenant-General Sir Thomas D'Oyly Snow), began a bombardment with a mixture of high explosive and smoke. On the extreme right, near Pontruet, the artillery of the French 5th Division joined in to extend the apparent frontage of the attack even further. On the immediate right flank of the main attack, artillery targeted the German batteries around La Terrière that had revealed themselves following a Chinese Attack with dummy figures on the front of the 55th Division (GOC, Major-General H. S. Jeudwine). Within the same division, the 164 Brigade (Brigadier-General C.I. Stockwell) mounted an assault against two prominences, the Knoll and Gillmont Farm, but were repulsed with serious casualties. Meanwhile, across the divisional front, G Special Company, Royal Engineers discharged 1,320 gas drums against Honnecourt Wood and other local targets. On the 24th Division (Major-General A.C. Daly) front, Q Special Company RE set fire to 200 oil drums in Quennet Wood, the 73 and 72 Brigades launched a series of raids east of Hargicourt, a Chinese Attack was mounted south-east of Villeret, six fougasses were exploded south of Villeret and Bangalore Torpedoes and bombs were exploded opposite Bellenglise.[12] The VII Corps were extremely busy and were proud of the fact that not a single German battalion opposite them was transferred to the main battle area until after 23 November.

Within the main attacks, Chinese Attacks with dummy soldiers and tanks were also mounted by 6th Division (GOC, Major-General T.O. Marden) to distract the German machine gunners in particular, providing them with targets amidst all the smoke, gas and dust.

North of the main attack, subsidiary operations were carried out by the IV, VI and XVII Corps. The 56th (1st London) Division (GOC, Major-General F.A. Dudgeon), the IV Corps division not involved in the main attack, kept up a Chinese Attack all day with artillery, dummy soldiers, canvas tanks and copious amounts of smoke.[13] The 56th Division had apparently brought motorcycles up into the front line so that during the attack their engines could be revved to simulate the noise of tank engines. This might be a myth as the noise would have had to compete with the artillery and machine guns! However, if the same ruse was used during the night of 19/20 November, especially in quieter moments, maybe the imitation of the sound of tanks moving up would have given the threat posed by the dummy tanks, visible amidst the smoke in the early morning, more credibility.

In the VI Corps (Lieutenant-General J.A.L. Haldane) sector, the No. 3 Special company RE fired a special smoke bombardment along the divisional front, while Q Special Company RE discharged 300 drums in Reincourt and 75 drums into trenches south-west of Fontaine-lez-Croisilles. J Special Company RE put down 500 drums south of Chérisy and the 16th (Irish) (GOC, Major-General W. B. Hickie) and 3rd (Major-General C.J. Devereux) Divisions mounted attacks with dummy infantry and tanks behind a smoke screen. These Chinese Attacks had the express aim of supporting the important attack by 9 Brigade against the Bovis and Tunnel Trenches on the front between Bullecourt and the Sensée, in order to remove a salient. The effort was designed to look like a pincer attack and had the objective of making the Germans abandon their positions. Although the British entered the trench system, the attack was eventually repulsed. Further north, the XVII Corps (Lieutenant-General Sir Charles Fergusson) with the 4th Division (GOC, Major-General L.J. Lipsett) targeted the area east of Monchy with gas shells in support of a raid while the gas projectors shelled Pelves and the chemical works at Roeux.

Through these subsidiary and feint attacks the original attack front of six miles was extended to over eighteen miles, from Vendhuile (three miles south of Baneux) to Fontaine-lez-Croisilles (Sensée); and the fake headquarters and tanks operations around Arras attempted to shift focus from Cambrai-Havrincourt back to the areas fought over earlier in the year during the Arras Offensive. The deception plan was aimed specifically at von der Marwitz, in command of the German Second Army. However, throughout the year, from the attack on Vimy Ridge to the actions around the Souchez River, the demonstrations and operations to support the Flanders offensive as well as the current operations north of Cambrai would have been of great concern to Ludendorff. These various actions, real, subsidiary and fake, from April through to November, created the impression that Douai could be the real Allied target. In reality the British were focused on Flanders and the front south of the Scarpe. Douai and the surrounding plain were sandwiched between Flanders and Cambrai and the German line here was ideally placed to reinforce and support defenders both north and south. In the Final Hundred Days in 1918, the British threatened Douai once more as Horne, the Commander of the First Army at the Fourth Battle of the Scarpe (26–30 August 1918) initiated a deception plan indicating he would attack north of the Scarpe, which could be interpreted as an advance against Douai. Four weeks, later at the Canal du Nord, Horne tried the same ruse, threatening to turn his main force northwards, rather than across the canal, to support his forces still deployed north of the Scarpe to pose a threat from the south to Douai. In 1918 this would tie down the German defenders and prevent their transfer to the threatened sectors north and south. The left flank of the First Army finally directly attacked and captured Douai on 17 October 1918, an action threatened more or less continually since March 1915 through deception plans.

On 16 November, four days before the attack, von der Marwitz reported to Crown Prince Rupprecht that no attack was expected in the near future.[14] Two days later, there was a sense that an attack near Havrincourt was in preparation but Rupprecht interpreted this as a minor attack to draw down German troops from Flanders; this of course was indeed the original objective of the Cambrai offensive. But by 19 November signs of unusual activity were being reported along the whole of the Cambrai-Havrincourt sector. Lieutenant-General von Moser from the Arras Group on the right flank of the Second Army warned that the attack might involve tanks, although this observation could have been a response to the games that the British were playing with tanks around Arras as part of the overall deception plan. Such tanks would be on the line of advance towards Douai.

After the day one successes of the surprise tank and infantry attack, the following days became a disappointment, as the German reinforcements attacked the British who had now overreached their artillery support and had their deception activities exposed. The advantage that deception and secrecy had afforded them on day one could not be maintained as the nature of the threat of the various demonstrations and feints evaporated. This inherent problem with deception plans was never really solved. Just as Haig had recognised this inherent weakness and attempted to counteract it on the Somme in 1916 by instructing the Third, First and Second Armies from 5 July until the closedown of the campaign to keep pressure on the Germans in their sectors through real and implied threats, so Byng similarly insisted that the subsidiary actions and feints should threaten the Germans right through to 21 November. XVII Corps even continued with a variety of activities astride the Scarpe until 27 November and the Germans did bolster their defences in this sector in response.

No army has managed to resolve this problem. The best that could be hoped for was that the implied threat remained as real as possible for as long as possible. From 1914 until mid-1918, there was often an overly optimistic assessment made of the potential of offensive operations. Coloured by that optimism, to the thinking of the commanders there was no reason even to try and maintain the threat posed by deception beyond 24 hours.

Haig in his Fifth Despatch (Cambrai Operations) on 20 February 1918 mentioned the use of surprise against the sector, which had already been weakened because of the transfer of troops to Flanders. Haig stressed the fact that the tanks had greatly assisted in the surprise nature of the attack as they made it possible to dispense with wire cutting and destruction of strong points. Haig's general message, which reiterated the approach that he had adopted on the Somme a year earlier, was that the Germans had to be taught that they could not transfer troops to other sectors at will. This theme ran throughout 1917 and was reiterated in Haig's Fourth and Fifth Despatches to the Secretary of State for War.

In the Fourth Despatch, dated 25 December 1917, Haig mentioned the role that deception and the feint attacks had played through the year prior to Cambrai. He said the operations had been worth the investment to extend the apparent frontage of attacks. The success of these activities was measured by the Germans' response to them. Clearly impressed, Haig paid tribute to the 'forethought and ingenuity' of the commanders and their staffs and the troops who planned and implemented these activities. As many of the deception activities had crossed army bureaucratic boundaries, this level of cooperation has to be attributed to Haig himself.

7

The Western Front 1918:
The Learning Curves Coincide

When we are near, we must make the enemy believe we are far away. When far away, we must make him believe we are near.
Sun Tzu

The endgame of 1918 saw the Allies' all-arms offensive approach, with tanks, artillery and infantry in co-ordinated, symbiotic relationships, come of age. Not only had the fighting units been trained in the use of new weapons systems and fighting techniques, but they were also given a higher degree of control with brigade commanders endowed with an autonomy of command over their brigades and at a lower level, the 'fighting platoons' made decisions on the battlefield. As we have argued, the deception learning curve had always been more advanced than that of the offensive. (At the same time the German assault detachments that had been born under Hauptmann Rohr back in September 1915 had matured into the highly effective Stoßtruppen, small, autonomous units that achieved success in Operation Michael, from March 21, 1918.) Throughout 1915 to 1918, the Allies had the ability to distract enemy defences and to weaken them through deceit, but they were not strong enough offensively to take full advantage. In 1918, the deception and offensive learning curves finally came together. The effectiveness of the Allies' offensive abilities only became apparent towards the latter half of the year however, as for the first six months they had to endure successive onslaughts that threatened to break open the Western Front.

German Spring Offensives: March–July 1918

As the Germans realised the limitations of their diminishing resources and the ever growing menace of the United States Army, they switched tactics from the defensive to an out-all, major offensive gamble. For most of the previous years, the Germans had learnt lessons in defensive strategy but their offensive approach arguably lagged behind that of the Allies. This changed with the introduction by General Ludendorff of the new concept of Stormtroopers (Stoßtruppen) to the Western Front. These elite troops would push forward and bypass resisting strong points to be dealt with by the follow-up troops, in order to maintain momentum. This basic concept was not strictly novel as some British attacking units on the Somme in 1916 had operated under similar instructions and the approach was codified in manual SS135 in February 1917, which made provision for the capture of bypassed strong points. Ludendorff also now decided that reinforcements would be sent to support progress and not to alleviate situations where the advance was held up. In a continuous defensive line, like a chain, the weak points can effectively nullify any strength than the line possesses. By supporting progress, Ludendorff effectively annulled the strong points simply by bypassing them.

Ludendorff planned a number of grand offensives on the Western Front with the aim of separating the French Army from their British Allies. The split would create a flank which could roll up the French and British lines and threaten the Channel Ports, the lifeline of British communications and supplies and the route for the incoming Americans. Over the next four months, the Germans launched a series of pre-planned offensives beginning with Operations Michael (Kaiserschlacht) (21 March–5 April 1918), Georgette (9–29 April) and Gneisenau (9–12 June) against the British, and Operations Blücher-Yorck (27 May–6 June) and Marne-Rhiems (15–17 July) against the French Army.

The Germans' initial target was predominantly General Sir Hubert Gough's British Fifth Army, which had recently taken over the sector from the French at the conjunction with the French Sixth Army to their right. To compound Gough's problems, his army, who had taken over an additional 28 miles of front on his right flank from the French in January, found that the defences were not as well developed as they should have been. In some places, the term 'red line defences' was coined since although they were marked with red lines on the French maps, there were very little actual defensive works on the ground. The Germans also targeted the right flank of the British Third Army, on Gough's left flank.

The attack, Operation Michael, planned for 21 March across a 50-mile front, was to be launched by the Eighteenth Army (von Hutier) from the Oise at La Fère to just north of St. Quentin ('Michael 3') and from there to the Scarpe by the Second (von der Marwitz) and Seventeenth (von Below) Armies ('Michael 2' and 'Michael 1'). To maintain the momentum, Operation Georgette, the Germans' second offensive, was scheduled to be launched around Armentières on 9 April while later advances would target the French Army fronts. For the main front of the first attack the Germans targeted the twelve divisions of Gough's Fifth Army which held a 42-mile front from the boundary with the French Sixth Army northwards to the Péronne-Cambrai road. The Germans intended to use the new tactics and the elite Stormtroopers.

The Germans struck at 04:40 on 21 March amidst thick fog with high explosive and gas shells falling on the British Third and Fifth Army fronts. Simultaneously, they bombarded the First Army front in the Lens-Mericourt sector together with an unusually strong raid against Hill 70, north of Loos. The British were taken by surprise and by the end of the day the Germans had advanced in some places between the Oise and the Sensée up to three miles. During this offensive, the British Army faced novel infantry tactics against defences weakened through a lack of physical preparation, and with inadequate reinforcements available. This situation had arisen in part because of well-planned German deception activities. Ludendorff had issued instructions that the attack (Operation Michael) should come as a complete surprise and be based on intensive training undertaken during the winter. There was no artillery pre-registration, the infantry were held well back and only brought up into concealed positions during the final 24–36 hours. The German troops moved up only at night using wagons with muffled wheels and any troops spotted by German aircraft marching towards the front during the day were immediately ordered to march in the opposite direction.[1] There were no distinctive unit markings on the vehicles and no obvious concentration of troops or material in the back areas, especially around railway stations.

Throughout January and February the Germans made secret preparations for Operation Michael. But Ludendorff had adopted a complete Western Front strategy and implemented a plan which would, through a series of real and feint attacks, seem to threaten both the British and the

French Armies. Ludendorff's deception plan was designed to move the perceived danger along the line in a manner that would prevent the Allies from moving reinforcements from sector to sector to nullify the real threats. With historical hindsight, this is exactly what the British, and their French allies, had been incorporating into their deception plans since the first structured plan at Neuve Chapelle in March 1915. Besides the 'Michael' preparations, there were more overt preparations for 'Georgette' and 'Roland' that the British and French airmen were allowed to detect. Operation Georgette was split into 'George I' and 'George II'. The latter targeted the sector around the Ypres Salient, the former focused on Armentières. 'Roland' created the impression that the sector around Rheims was similarly threatened. The overt preparations were actually part of the preparations for later real offensives, which showed that the Germans were sufficiently confident in their offensive operations to split their forces, rather than concentrate them against the Allied defences around the Arras-St. Quentin sector. This would prove to be a mistake and goes against the basic deception principle of 'strength where there is weakness and weakness where there is strength'. By committing real forces to distract the British and French, Ludendorff ran the risk that, in the event of failure, his line would be weakened as all his forces would be committed. From their first battle the British had simulated 'strong' threats through 'weak' demonstrations and feint attacks. However, despite the over-commitment of troops, the Germans still showed good practice in employing other aspects of deception.

They concealed over 800,000 troops and 6,500 guns in front of the British Fifth and Third Armies and created dummy sites, amidst the real preparations for the later offensives, to create the illusion of a larger attacking force and that the offensives would be launched further north against the Second Army and south against the French. The false preparations were accompanied by feints and demonstrations in the appropriate sectors, which were most numerous in mid-March and were designed to indicate that the British and French defences were being tested as a prelude to a major attack. As a quirky deception contribution, Ludendorff had no cinematography units covering the start of Operation Michael; the units were deployed to other parts of the front to confuse the Allies with regard to the point and timing of the attack.

By 10 March, British air observers had spotted large-scale troop movements by road and rail into the sector opposite the Fifth and Third Armies and deserters' statements told of the construction of large ammunition dumps, which confirmed the Arras-St. Quentin area as a prime candidate for an attack. On 19 March, Gough had even predicted in a letter home that the attack would likely commence on 21 March.[2] However, although Ludendorff's attempts at concealment of 'Michael' were a failure, the diversionary activities were of sufficient quality to distract the Allies' attention. This lesson had already been learnt by the Allies by the end of 1915: that multi-unit, multi-sector deception plans were the most effective because even if the real preparations were detected, provided that the criteria of consistency, plausibility and predictability were maintained, then the deception was still viable. The Germans ensured that their activities complied with these criteria even though the diversionary nature of the preparations lacked any serious infantry activity. When the initial assault came against the British Fifth Army, the French in particular were convinced that this was a feint and that they were still the main target. The French refused to release their strategic reserve to support the British even though they were not attacked until 27 May (Third Battle of Aisne, Operation Blücher-Yorck). Bean, the Australian Official Historian, considered this offensive to have been the most effective diverting offensive ever achieved on the Western Front, as both Haig and Pétain were deceived.[3] They had interpreted the intelligence correctly that major attacks would be launched against the British in Flanders and south of the Oise against the French, but they were deceived with regard to the timing. Edmonds considered that the most successful trick, which convinced Pétain in particular, was the 'escape' of a normally tethered balloon containing details of the forthcoming attack against the French, confirmed through the interrogation of prisoners who were primed with false intelligence. This was a variant of the Haversack ruse used at Gaza in 1917. The information confirmed Pétain's existing belief and hence followed Magruder's Principle. Haig was also taken by surprise owing to the narrow front of the attack, as he expected actions along most of the British Army front line.

Bean summed up Ludendorff's Spring Offensives: 'By deceiving his opponents with preparations in three sectors – and more – and then flinging his whole strength against one of these, [he] had actually placed it beyond the power even of a Napoleon to stop the rapidity of his advance in the first stages.' This statement is not quite accurate as Ludendorff had indeed loaded the 'Michael' offensive with a disproportionate number of troops but he still built up large numbers of troops in the other sectors ready for the other pre-planned, timed offensives.

The other basic issue with Bean's assessment is that military historians have tended to think that for the Allies, Gallipoli (1915), Gaza/Beersheba (1917) and Amiens (1918) aside, there was a lack of any deception planning throughout the war and that the Germans led the way during their Spring Offensives. As we have seen, on the contrary the British implemented serious deception plans beginning with Neuve Chapelle (March 1915) and continued to use them for every other major offensive. The deception plan at Amiens, implemented in August 1918, has been held up as a shining example of what would have been possible on the Western Front if only the British had employed it earlier – but if the British had attacked at Amiens using waves of infantry, uncoordinated with the tanks or artillery, the result would have been failure and the deception activities would have been granted little space in the literature. In terms of deception the Germans in support of Operation Michael did not employ any tactic that the British had not been using since 1915.

The British and the French were effectively deceived by the orchestrated deception plans of the Germans. In the spring of 1918, in the absence of intelligence to the contrary, the Allies had to react to these deceptions and recover from them before their turn would come to practise the art.

However, in the midst of retreat and whilst on the defensive, the British still applied their hard learnt lessons. At Monchy le Preux, south of Arras, in March for instance, as the eleven divisions of the German Seventeenth Army swept down on three Canadian divisions, they were repulsed. The Canadians had withdrawn the majority of their forces away from the battle zone but had positioned their machine gun teams in camouflaged emplacements created by the theatrical designer L. D. Symington.[4] The emplacements were well concealed both from the air and the ground as the firing apertures were only visible when the guns were in operation and the gun was set so far back that the flash was not visible at ground level.

'Michael' ended on 5 April with the Battle of Dernancourt (4–5 April) although this was not appreciated at the time by the British. The Germans' last desperate attack in this sector, three miles south-west of Albert, was repulsed by the Australians.

As 'Michael' slowed unproductively, Ludendorff switched his attentions northwards for an attack ('George I') between Armentières and La Bassée

Canal in an attempt not only to breakthrough in that sector but also to draw off troops from the Flanders region, where the German Fourth Army planned to strike ('George II'). The overall offensive known as Operation Georgette, or the Battle of the Lys, was launched on 9 April. The success of the advance of George I resulted in George II being launched the following day. Haig appealed to Foch for reserves to bolster the British First and Second Armies but he refused to send reinforcements northwards, still under the spell of the deception plan. On 17 April, the Germans launched an attack towards Mount Kemmel and when they attacked over 100 miles further south at Villers-Bretonneux on 24 April, it was assumed it was a continuation of the 'Michael' offensive and was not seen for what it really was, an attack to divert British attention from Flanders. This action resulted in 1,455 Australian casualties and served to confirm French fears that they were still the main focus of the offensives.

By 20 April Operation Georgette had slowed and Ludendorff therefore switched the focus further south to the French sector. Foch's fears were confirmed on 27 May when the Germans attacked the right flank of the British Fourth Army and the French Sixth Army at the Battle of the Aisne (Chemin des Dames) (Operation Blücher-Yorck).[5] The movement of German troops and artillery into the region, primarily from Flanders, was covered by darkness and the noise of low flying aircraft. To deceive the Allies, the Germans left 30 divisions in Flanders, but lit extra bivouac fires, marched around large numbers of troops and generated large volumes of telephone, wireless and visual signalling traffic. The German Air Force also stepped up attacks against the British rear areas. The Germans maintained a threat in Flanders that through deception was perceived by the Allies to be bigger than it really was. With hindsight and better intelligence, the British would have recognised all of these activities. They had heard about them at Staff College being practiced by Magruder (1862) and Baden-Powell (1900), they had practised them themselves at Gallipoli (1915), Gaza (1917) and Cambrai (1917) and would use them again at Amiens (August 1918) and Megiddo (September 1918). However, just because you knew about it and could do it, didn't mean you could necessarily spot it being done to you!

The series of German offensives up and down the Western Front all exhibited a similar pattern in that initial success was characterised by significant territorial gains but no breakthroughs. As the Germans drove deeper into the Allies' back areas so their lines of communication and supply were stretched. The failure to capture a major communications centre, such as Amiens, left them dangerously exposed. As the advance gradually slowed down due to a lack of men and materials and a basic inadequacy in logistics, the Allies began to push back. As the British and French staggered and then gradually recovered, their defensive stance increasingly changed to one of offence. There were some small engagements that began the fightback but the British planned a secret offensive operation which would begin the sequence of battles that would ultimately lead to the Armistice. The final four months of the war, now known as The Final Hundred Days, were typically characterised by a 'static' first day of an offensive followed by days of 'mobile' warfare. This period was typified by army-level deception plans on the first day and more local deceptions during the mobile phases which, slowly at first, moved the front back to where it had been in March.

The Action of Le Hamel, 4 July 1918

The Germans had been stopped ten miles short of all-important Amiens, but as the key to future Allied operations around the River Somme and the defence of Amiens, the capture of Le Hamel represented a strategic target that straightened the Allies' line. The objective was a ridge stretching northwards from Villers-Bretonneux to the Somme with the principal features of Vaire Wood and the well-fortified village and wood of Le Hamel. The 4th Australian Division (GOC, Major-General E.G. Sinclair-MacLagan) of the Australian Corps (GOC, Lieutenant-General John Monash) from Rawlinson's Fourth Army was given the task, a combined infantry, artillery and tank operation. It would be supported by some American units despite the insistence of General John Pershing (Commander-in-Chief, American Expeditionary Force) that they should not participate owing to a lack of combat readiness.[6] The planning for the operation followed a familiar pattern with secrecy paramount. Very few instructions or plans were committed to paper, verbal conferences were the norm and the final conference to inform the brigade and company commanders took place only three days before. Troop movements were restricted to the hours of darkness and machine gun and artillery harassing fire was maintained as the troops and tanks moved into position in order to ensure that enemy observation was restricted. To maintain secrecy in the event of capture, the troops moving in were simply told that they were reinforcing the existing units to repel an expected German attack. Those troops already holding the line were withdrawn at the last possible moment and had no orders issued to them until behind the lines so that any prisoners were ignorant of the build-up of the Australians and the imminent British attack. Although Lieutenant-General Sir John Monash (GOC, Australian Corps) asked for aerial support to bomb installations in Le Hamel, he also asked for older planes the engines of which created sufficient noise to cover the advance of the tanks. Over 200 guns moved into the sector over a five-day period into pre-prepared camouflaged positions but the majority remained silent until the morning of the attack. As Private Lynch of the Australian Corps reported: 'Dozens of guns hidden everywhere ... and not one has fired a shot yet, so Fritz can't have any idea of their positions.'[7] Limited 'normal' shooting was used to register the existing guns on their targets but this was mixed with 'promiscuous' shooting, which scattered the fall of the shells and disguised their true intent. From 1 July, in order to get the artillery and ammunition across the river Somme near Vaire, the 12th Company of Australian Engineers erected a pontoon bridge, camouflaged against aerial observation, which was partially demolished each morning. To divert attention, eight dummy bridges made of hessian and canvas strips were erected elsewhere, which the Germans systematically bombed. These bridges also came under attack from a local British battery commander who thought they drew fire on his guns.[8] When the attack began at 03:10 on 4 July, the German artillery, pre-registered on the dummy bridges, targeted them as the Australians crossed relatively unmolested over the real bridges. This ruse with the dummy bridges had previously been practised by the Japanese at the Battle of Yalu (1904) and by British engineers and the Egyptian Labour Corps at Fig Tree Camp, Tel el Fara in the summer of 1917 as part of the railway built by Allenby to Wadi Ghazze.

To broaden the apparent attack frontage, the 2nd Australian Division on the right extended the artillery barrage. This was supplemented by French units, on their right, who targeted artillery groups at Marcelcave and Wiencourt which could have enfiladed the main attack. On the left flank, north of the main attack, the 5th Australian Division (GOC, Major-General Sir J.J.T. Hobbs) carried out a minor action on a 1200 yard front, while on their left, III Corps (GOC, Lieutenant-General Sir R.H.K.

Butler) fired a creeping barrage intermixed with smoke shells to hide the lack of any infantry attack. To maintain the characteristics of a good deception plan during the build-up to the main attack, the supporting units on either flank had constructed dummy installations of camouflaged fake ammunition dumps and CCS, together with spurious troop movements, so that the real attack sector was lost amongst all the offensive preparations.

The main barrage contained a percentage of smoke to create the impression of gas to force the defenders to don their gas masks. To conceal the time of the attack, similar barrages containing smoke and gas, mixed in with explosive shells, were fired for three successive days prior to zero-day. The smoke concealed the attacking troops from the defenders but caused major navigational problems for the tanks. However, it did serve to conceal the true nature of the attacking force. Dummy tanks, built by the engineers, simulated a much larger attacking force. The attack at Le Hamel resulted in a British victory with approximately 1,000 casualties.

Within days of the attack at Le Hamel, the Germans mounted another major offensive operation (Operation Marne-Rheims, 15–17 July) which was interpreted by the French as an attempt by Ludendorff to achieve a decisive breakthrough. Haig, on the other hand, interpreted this correctly as another attempt to draw British troops south from the Flanders sector in order for the Germans to launch another major offensive against the Channel ports before the build-up of American power became decisive. Hence despite these diversionary pressures, Haig remained steadfast and at the northern end of the line, the British began to fight back against the now over-extended Germans through a series of actions as a prelude to the Fourth Battle of Ypres.

Action of Meteren, 19 July 1918

During the capture of Meteren, the 9th Divisional artillery during their bombardments to flatten the village to prevent falling masonry injuring the infantry, performed the usual trick – including a mixture of gas and smoke shells amongst the high explosive – to force the Germans to put on their gas masks. On the day of the attack, only smoke was mixed in. In order to conceal the presence of the attacking troops, the 9th (Scottish) Division (GOC, Major-General H.H. Tudor) adopted a novel ruse and completely covered their assembly trenches with 2,000 yards of coconut matting, the same colour as the exposed soil, stretched on poles with only small openings for sentries. A twelve inch wide line of black tar was painted down the centre so that from the air the trench appeared empty. Beneath the matting the attacking troops were completely concealed from the ground and the air, although the sentries occasionally poked their heads out through special holes to ensure that they did not become the victims of a surprise attack. The Germans has used a similar ruse at Aubers Ridge in 1915 when they covered their trenches with hurdles to make them indistinguishable from the surrounding ground and difficult to target by the artillery. At 07:30 on the morning of the attack a German plane flew low over the trenches and reported accordingly that there was no direct threat. At 08:00, only 30 minutes later, the infantry emerged from their concealed positions, attacked and were successful as the Germans were taken completely by surprise. Elated with their simple ruse, the 9th (Scottish) Division repeated it again successfully during the Action of Outtersteene Ridge (18 August 1918) when the British trenches were similarly covered with coconut matting and the black 'shadow'. Having experimented with camouflage at St. Omer in the summer of 1917, it became apparent that even the simplest device could prove effective against aerial reconnaissance.

It has been generally accepted that the Battle of Amiens was the beginning of the end of the First World War. As all the British Armies were involved, it became increasingly difficult to plan overt multi-army deceptions as this need was obviated by the very real orchestrated actions of all the armies along the entire length of the Western Front. As a result, the Germans became unsure where the next attack would come from, so the British came to rely on local deceptions. However it must be stressed that dogged German defences ensured that in terms of casualties, this would still be the most costly period of the war. Hence to strike the first major blow against the over-stretched and worn out German military, the British planned a battle whose success was dependent on the marriage of an efficient all-arms offensive and a cunning deception plan.

Battle of Amiens, 8–12 August 1918

The concept behind the British deception plan for the Battle of Amiens had been elucidated by Sun Tzu, 2,500 years before – 'When we are near, we must make the enemy believe we are far away. When far away, we must make him believe we are near.' The battle has been portrayed in some post-war literature as a 'headline' example, along with Gallipoli (1915) and Gaza (1917), of what could have been achieved if the British Army had employed deception. There is no doubt that deception was a key factor in success at Amiens. But the deception employed was simply an extension of the work of Haig and his commanders, begun at Neuve Chapelle three-and-a-half years previously. There was no doubt that the deception plan significantly contributed to the victory at Amiens, but there is evidence to show that the plan was flawed and had been penetrated by the lower units of the German Army who gathered the intelligence directly from their own sectors. As on the Somme in 1916, the German Supreme Command (OHL) was faced with intelligence of offensive preparations emanating from multiple sectors but Ludendorff, not unlike his predecessor Falkenhayn, judged that the next major offensive by the British would be further north in the British Second Army sector around the Ypres Salient rather than south of the Somme, at Amiens. Once again, this demonstrated that for wide-ranging deception plans, the primary target was the commander who assessed the intelligence from across all affected sectors. The local commanders were only secondary targets, but still had to be deceived.

Amiens was chosen as the sector to launch the fightback against the Germans whose offensive had ground to a halt having just failed to capture this important communications centre. It became apparent through intelligence gathered from raids by the Australian Corps that the Germans facing the Fourth Army around Amiens were not the formidable troops of the generation faced the previous March. The elite stormtroopers had been decimated in the Spring Offensives. Raids also discovered that the defences were poorly maintained and that the low grade troops were easily driven from their trenches during these raids. Further, the ground chosen was well suited to tanks which it was hoped could be used to redress the relative imbalance of attackers over defenders. Although the tanks up to the Mark IV were less potent than had been hoped for, the Mark V, was launched in July as a faster, better armoured, better armed, more manoeuvrable and more reliable model. The introduction of this new tank would come as a real surprise to the Germans who still expected only to face the less reliable, more vulnerable Mark IVs. After specialised training and the success at Le Hamel, the tanks and infantry came together to develop a mutually beneficial relationship. The troops trained with their 'own' tanks and tank crews and an *esprit de corps* was built up so that the tank crews and the infantry platoons became single fighting units. The army units chosen for the attack at Amiens were from the British III Corps, the Australian Corps and the Canadian Corps. The Australian Corps and the British III Corps were already under Rawlinson's Fourth Army command, but the Canadians were part of the British First Army (General Sir Henry Horne) and were stationed in the sector east of Arras, 35 miles to the north of Amiens. It would be the Canadian Corps who would be the subect of Sun Tzu's *legerdemain*.

The Amiens deception plan had the specific objective of concealing the presence of the Canadian Corps in the sector opposite the German Second Army (GOC, General Georg von der Marwitz). The British made the Canadian Corps disappear from one sector, only to apparently re-appear somewhere else. By this stage of the war, the deception template was being routinely and innovatively applied. However, at Amiens, under GHQ and Fourth Army HQ direction, the multi-sector, multi-army plan demonstrated their real potential in support of effective offensive operations.

Once again GHQ issued instructions which stressed that secrecy was key to success.[9] Since the end of 1917, Bean, the Official Historian of the Australian Imperial Force, considered Haig was convinced that complete surprise was the key to *any* offensive operation.[10] To add emphasis, the Fourth Army HQ also issued a general instruction on 4 August that the operation had to come as a surprise and that the scope and date of the attack was to be concealed. The plan was implemented through the energetic and enthusiastic work of Major-General A.A. Montgomery (Chief of General Staff, Fourth Army) and Major-General H.C. Holman (Administrative Chief). The planning stages were held, on a need-to-know basis, at different places at different times to avoid the congregation of red-tabbed officers becoming a regular sight.

The plan revolved around the relatively fresh Canadian Corps who had taken little part in the spring fighting against the successive German offensives.[11] The plan was designed to make the Canadian Corps 'disappear' from the First Army sector, 're-appear' in the Second Army sector whilst secretly transferring it to the Fourth Army. Obviously, this plan was high risk if exposed by the Germans and therefore all the soldiers were simply told 'Keep Your Mouth Shut' in a message pasted into their small book, carried by every officer and man, and not to gossip, to stop others gossiping and how to act if taken prisoner.[12]

Montgomery issued a series of instructions beginning on 31 July that all movement into the sector by troops, guns and materials had to be conducted at night and he instructed the Royal Air Force to fly sorties over the Fourth Army sector and immediately report any abnormal activity to the appropriate Corps HQ for immediate rectification. The plan was initially worked out only amongst the corps commanders; the divisional commanders were excluded until 30 July. The brigade commanders were let into the secret even later and the troops only 36 hours before the off.

The plan was initiated on 26 July as the Canadian Corps withdrew from the First Army and its sector, east of Arras, was taken over by divisions from the XVII and VI Corps. The intelligence associated with this move was deliberately not overly secure and was relatively easily gathered by the German intelligence units. Raids and captured prisoners testified to the fact that the Canadian Corps had indeed been withdrawn. Edmonds reported that the German Second Army (von der Marwitz) had been notified by OHL that the Canadians had been relieved from their front line positions and their whereabouts should be determined as a matter of priority and, worryingly, that they should pay particular attention to the British Third and Fourth Army fronts.[13] In a situation analogous to the Somme, the British instigated a multi-army deception plan that primarily targeted Ludendorff and OHL and not the individual army commanders. It is interesting to note that it was OHL which informed von der Marwitz of the withdrawal of the Canadian Corps divisions but as the German Second Army's intelligence organisation had not reported any unusual activity, Ludendorff was satisfied with Marwitz's defences. Although they were not as advanced as those of the Eighteenth Army (von Hutier) on Marwitz' s left flank, facing the French, there was little concern as Marwitz expected only strong local diversionary attacks.

In Ludendorff's estimation, the main British threat was expected over 100 miles further north around the Ypres Salient, based on the intelligence generated by the British for the consumption of the Germans indicating that the Canadian Corps had moved north to the Second Army sector in Flanders. In reality Rawlinson had ordered the northwards movement to Mount Kemmel of only two Canadian battalions, the 4th Mounted Rifles and the 27th Battalion, two Casualty Clearing Stations (CCS) and

a wireless section. The task assigned to these troops was to generate sufficient activity and intelligence to represent the whole of the Canadian
Corps. The two infantry battalions were ordered to make enough preparations to simulate a corps attack against Mount Kemmel, lost to the
Germans on 25 April. The close proximity of the CCS was a clear sign of
an impending attack. These troops also conducted a number of raids to
make the Canadian presence in the area obvious to the defenders opposite them. The wireless section generated frequently transmitted dummy
traffic using the Canadian call-sign. This created the impression that the
Canadian Corps was in Flanders and would attempt to re-capture the
position as part of a Second Army offensive, while in reality it was 110
miles further south.[14, 15, 16] Some British troops within the sector wore the
Maple Leaf badge on their uniforms to 'bolster' the force, whilst others,
simply to cause confusion, wore Australian slouch hats.[17] The British
accent amongst Canadian or Australian units would not have seemed
strange to the Germans as pre-war emigration, the expediency of joining
Canadian units at Liverpool Docks and simply local recruitment, saw
Britons assigned to Canadian and Australian units. The apparent movement of the Canadian Corps into the Flanders sector resulted in the
Belgian Army on the left flank wanting to know why they were not
involved in the forthcoming offensive. There were also complaints to the
War Office emanating from the Canadian HQ in London regarding the
fact that the Canadians had been sent to this area of the front without
their consent.[18] Both of these actions illustrated that the need-to-know
principle was in operation and both lent credence to the deception plan.
The Canadian units in the Second Army sector rejoined their comrades
at Amiens two days before the attack. Before the transference of the
Canadian Corps to the Fourth Army, it was to have mounted an attack
against Orange Hill, east of Arras. Although the operation was cancelled,
General Sir Arthur Currie (GOC, Canadian Corps), in real appreciation
of the deception plan, ordered that the incoming troops should continue
with the preparations, to enhance the illusion that the northern end of
the line was where the next offensive would be launched.[19]

The main bulk of the Canadian Corps moved south, mostly by rail and
bus with the rest on foot. The troops did not know their final destination.
Moving only at night, according to sealed orders, a few senior officers led
the majority of the soldiers south by following a nightly itinerary of villages. Before each dawn the troops were moved into concealed billets and

the previous night's orders were burnt. During the journey and period
before the attack, the Army Post Office did not accept any letters from
the Canadians. Officially the troops were informed that they were going
to assist the Second Army which expected an imminent German attack.
However it rapidly became apparent, even to those with a poor sense of
direction, that they were moving south rather than north, but to allay suspicions the troops were subsequently informed that they were to join the
GHQ reserve, which would provide support to the British First or Fourth
Armies or even the French forces on the Rheims-Soissons front.

Besides the apparent presence of the fresh Canadian Corps troops
within the Second Army, the RAF was ordered on 27 July to occupy
additional aerodromes between Ypres and Hazebrouck and gradually
to increase landings, take-offs, patrols and aerial reconnaissance until 6
August. Further south the RAF between 6 and 8 August also busied itself
on both the Third and First Army fronts. Dummy tanks were moved into
the Second Army area and the wireless section, besides sending Canadian
call-sign messages, transmitted a volume of messages in the First and
Second Army areas on the Tank Corps wavelength, which was known
to the Germans. During the day false troop movements were carried out
and a great deal of dust was created at St. Pol, eighteen miles from Arras
with a few real machines visible on the road on the heights above Notre
Dame de Lorette. Dummy tanks were constructed from a wooden framework on an old chassis, covered with tarpaulin and left where they could
be spotted from the air despite an abundance of woods in the area where
they could have easily been hidden. By leaving the dummy tanks, albeit
camouflaged, in the open, this would seem to be breaking the cardinal
rule of deception, of not to 'present' the enemy with intelligence. Any
information that was easily acquired would normally be treated with
suspicion. In this case the Germans must have misinterpreted the intelligence and concluded that the woods were already full of tanks and that
the dummies were unable to be concealed properly due to the size of the
tank build-up. The tank call-sign wireless traffic would have strengthened
this interpretation. Tank officers were also brought forward to observation platforms, visible from the German positions, where the lie of the
land was studied through binoculars.

In the Amiens sector, the 'opposite' activities were taking place. Real
tanks were 'walked' into the Amiens sector by their commanders to
occupy pre-prepared camouflaged positions.[20] The tanks were fitted with

horn covers to disrupt their distinctive shadow when under the camouflage sheets so that they could not be spotted from the air. All Tank Corps
personnel were ordered to remove their insignia in case of capture.[21]
Officers were taken to open observation posts in sectors distant from
Amiens and at Amiens reconnaissance was restricted; Canadian Corps
officers were attached to the Australians to perform their reconnaissance.[22]
The Canadian and British III Corps were ordered not to open any wireless traffic and were strictly forbidden from entering their battle zone
before day zero. The Canadian Corps moved into the Fourth Army area
on successive nights between 31 July and 4 August into their camouflaged
positions between the junction of the Somme and the Ancre and Boves,
south of Amiens. All of the roads in the area were covered with cut straw
and the wagon wheels wrapped in rope to deaden the noise of any movement. The last units of the Canadian Corps moved into Picquigny, eight
miles west of Amiens, on the night of 7 August. The RAF flew over the
area to detect and report back any breaches in the camouflage which were
immediately rectified.

To convince the Germans that this sector was truly dormant and that
the British would not attack between Albert and Moreuil, III Corps took
over an additional mile-and-a-half front from the Australians, between 31
July and 1 August. The latter for their part took over an additional four
miles (7,000 yards) of front, as far as the Amiens–Roye road, from the
French, releasing them for the impending Marne Battle. The Australians
immediately made their presence felt by target shooting and with ill-
advised raids which ran the risk of capture and disclosure of the Allies plan.
Although these Australian moves were made seven days before the offensive, the troops were only informed 36 hours before zero hour of their
actual tasks. These moves of the III Corps and Australian Corps resulted
in troop concentrations which were now too low for any offensive operation. As the Canadian Corps secretly moved into the Amiens sector, they
were followed by the 1st Australian Division from the Hazebrouck sector.
The apparent lateness of these moves not only portrayed a relaxed front
within days of a major attack but was also a measure of the ability of
the British Army to mount an all-arms offensive at relatively short notice.
As the additional troops moved in, the III Corps and Australian Corps
regrouped to present troops concentrations suitable for an attack.

As the artillery concentration increased within the Amiens sector, one
thousand guns were camouflaged in the open rather than in pre-dug

gun pits which would have more easily detected from the air. However, at this point the quantities of camouflage became scarce so out of necessity the troops covered them in netting and intertwined them with grass and wheat. These guns were registered within the normal activity for that front and were consistent with a front that was 'dormant'. The same applied to the Royal Artillery's counter-battery work.[23] At Loos in 1915 the Germans had fooled the British artillery into thinking that if a shell landed close to them that it had scored a direct hit and ceased activity. These 'destroyed' batteries came back to life when it came time for the British infantry to cross No-Man's-Land. As the ability to register against targets was now feasible without firing a shot, it was time for the British artillery to gain their revenge. During the build-up to Amiens, as part of their normal fire programme, the British targeted the German batteries. To avoid destruction, the Germans frequently moved their batteries to 'secret' locations, which were silently registered using maps and aerial reconnaissance. However, the British continued to fire at the old gun pits until just prior to the attack when the new locations were targeted and the German inroads into the attacking infantry and tanks was severely diminished.[24, 25]

The German Supreme Command had estimated that the British had 80 divisions available on the Western Front but they lacked detailed knowledge of their dispositions. OHL assumed that the British would hold their strategic reserves behind the Flanders front and near Arras for the next offensive. The apparent low concentration of the troops in the Fourth Army sector precluded this as an area of concern and they expected only minor attacks around Villers-Bretonneaux. This fitted well with OHL's estimation on 20 June that the British would maintain weaker forces on their southern wing, so the British deception plan adhered to Magruder's Principle. The Canadian Corps did not move into the front line trenches until two hours before zero hour with the Australians moving north into their own sector to establish the necessary troop concentrations for the attack and to link up with their 'personal' tanks. The move coincided with the generation of dust, noise, tanks and dummy wireless traffic, twenty miles north-east of Arras near St. Pol, indicative of a troop build-up for an attack in that sector.[26]

To maintain the illusion of the defensive stance throughout, the British labour companies in the Fourth Army sector continued work on strengthening the defences, only ceasing their efforts on the morning of the attack.

Throughout the build-up, the British had conducted raids to gather intelligence to determine whether the deception activities were affecting the German's OODA Loops with respect to troop depositions and defence readiness. Analysis of the prisoner information indicated that the German were expecting an attack astride the Scarpe, in the Arras sector. They intended to counter this by an attack towards Vimy as soon as the withdrawal to consolidated positions on the Vesle, after the failure of the Marne-Rheims offensive, was completed.

The British build-up was not without its anxious moments, however. On 3 August, five days before the attack, an Australian sergeant and four men were captured near Hourges, but they revealed that they knew nothing of an attack and were expecting a long quiet spell in the trenches. The need-to-know principle was yielding unexpected dividends once again. In response to all the intelligence from all sources the Germans re-aligned their troops. On 3 August the German withdrew their forward troops between Montdidier and Moreuil, opposite the French First Army, and from between Dernancourt and Aveluy Wood opposite III Corps. On 5 August they withdrew from the line between La Bassée and Kemmel, giving up ground gained in the April Lys Offensive. These troop withdrawals and their subsequent transfer northwards showed that the British deception plan was effective.

Locally the German Second Army expected strong but minor attacks near Villers-Bretonneux despite the efforts of the RAF, which kept German aircraft away from the British back areas. A continuous barrage from 26 June onwards prevented direct observation of these rear areas and as by now the troops were infused with the culture of secrecy, this area, the favoured haunt of German spies, was effectively closed down. Even British airmen, captured on 7 August, maintained that a great attack was in preparation between Dickebusch and Meteren, in the direction of Armentières towards Mount Kemmel.

Despite all this, in the front line, opposite Amiens, suspicions were growing. German troops reported the noise of tanks as the attack preparations advanced, but the senior officers attributed this to 'phantoms of the imagination or nervousness'.[27] There was an element of truth in this as the first report of tanks was on 3 August near Villers-Bretonneux, which was actually before any of tanks had moved into the area! As this report was dismissed, no additional tank defences were implemented. On 6 August, Crown Prince Rupprecht's Group of Armies, to which the Second Army belonged, issued an intelligence summary that reported, apparently falsely, the presence of hundred tanks on the Ailly-Morisel road (Moreuil) but again this did nothing to alert the defences. Edmonds quoted a German staff officer in the Official History: 'We were anxious because anyone who brings up a hundred tanks is not planning a joy-ride.'[28] Edmonds thought that tanks had as great a psychological effect as they did offensively, that they impinged on the front line soldiers' morale to the extent that 'The German infantry saw and heard them when they were not present, and always exaggerated their numbers.'[29]

On 4 August, Ludendorff released an Order of the Day indicating that the troops should not be apprehensive about an attack provided they remained vigilant. Ludendorff justified this by stating that they had only been tactically surprised once, on 18 July by the French between the Marne and the Vesle. He pointed out that subsequently they had inflicted significant casualties on the French. He dismissed the innate value of tanks putting any success down to the element of surprise; although it must be assumed he was referring to the older models and not the latest Marks Vs.

Although the Germans had detected the presence of the Canadian Corps within the Second Army, they did not draw the right conclusion. The Germans spotted that the Canadian Corps had been relieved by the XVII and III Corps in the First Army sector, but the High Command concluded that it had moved south and thought that an attack in the Fourth Army sector by the Canadian Corps was expected but not imminent.[30, 31] The Germans thought the same situation held true within the Flanders region and believed that the next northern attack would be astride the Scarpe in front of Arras.

The attack at Amiens on 8 August at 04:20 with 414 Mark IV and V tanks came as a complete surprise and the Allies advanced seven miles in seven hours. Although the advance pushed the Germans back and gained ground, above all its effect was on the morale of the German Army. It justified Ludendorff's description of 8 August as the 'Black Day of the German Army'. One of the many surprises for the Germans to emerge from the Battle of Amiens was the effectiveness of the Mark V tanks and their co-operation with the infantry. The front line troops began to realise that the tank was a weapon of dread which could only be stopped by a direct hit with an artillery shell or with their newly developed 13mm bolt action rifle. Although with an effective range of 250 yards, it still took at least four or five direct hits to stop a tank.[32] The mechanical unreliability of the tank or driver error were still factors but these had been significantly diminished with the introduction of the Mark V and the protection that the tanks received from the British infantry, who now appreciated their real worth.

Not only did the tanks fire shells and have machine guns but they had also developed the nasty habit of simply crushing machine gun emplacements. The appearance of a tank caused panic in all but the most resolute of defenders and as a consequence the German High Command issued a series of documents for coping with them. These documents were captured, translated and published by the American Army on 9 November 1918.[33] It was clear from these documents that tanks were a major physical and psychological force and defences were weakened and liable to collapse when they were involved. The Germans recommended that their front line troops improvised anti-tank obstacles. Deep trenches in front of defences were undoubtedly effective provided that they were the correct shape and deep enough and there was sufficient time available to dig them, but barricades of furniture, farm implements and assorted metalwork bordered on desperation! It was this effect that deception sought to exploit in the following months and although multi-unit deceptions were still planned, at a local level whenever there was a hold-up or a strong position was encountered, and real tanks were not available, the engineers were immediately called in and dummy tanks were built and deployed. 'The British did not hesitate whenever they did not have enough tanks to deploy fakes [although they were] mere tractors camouflaged with painted canvas attached to a wooden frame.'[34]

Despite the momentum generated by the British Army, the Germans still played a few tricks of their own. On 15 August, the 52nd Battalion entered the village of Demery, which had been the strong centre of resistance in front of 9 Brigade, with comparative ease. The easy passage of the final advance rightly created suspicion, justified in the afternoon as the German artillery accurately shelled the village against pre-registered targets housing the British troops and causing significant casualties. As the bombardment lifted the German troops of the 60th Regiment attacked but, as a sign of the current fortunes of this war, still found the British troops too strong.

Battle of Albert, 21–23 August

As the operations at Amiens gradually slowed after a fourteen-mile advance, the Allies switched their point of attack to the line in front of Albert, fifteen miles further north. The operation, scheduled for 21 August, was on the British Third Army (Byng) front. Haig instructed that their wireless traffic should be maintained at the 'normal' level. The transfer of the Cavalry Corps from the Fourth to the Third Army was concealed through wireless deception. The wireless sets and operators of the Cavalry Corps were retained in the Fourth Army sector as the cavalry moved north. Haig's obsession throughout the war with exploiting any breakthrough by sending through the cavalry was used to good effect to mislead the Germans. The detection of the Cavalry Corps within the Third Army sector would have been an unequivocal signal of an impending attack. The assault was undertaken by 200 tanks in the direction of Bapaume. The only negative aspect of the operation was that the now usual method of masking the presence of tanks by covering their approach with aero engine noise failed as thick fog prevented the RAF flying their usual patterns above the front. As a result, the advance initially stalled before momentum was regained as the left flank of Rawlinson's Fourth Army joined in the attack.

As the dust settled around Albert, the British Army switched its point of attack 23 miles further north to the Arras front where the British First Army under the command of General Sir Henry Horne lay in readiness to inflict another defeat. This ability of the British to switch the point of attack was real and was not something that needed to be simulated through the use of deception plans, which had been the case from March 1915 to the beginning of August 1918. The Battle of Arras (26 August–3 September) resulted in a number of battles at the Scarpe, Cagnicourt and the Drocourt-Quéant Switch where the First Army was supported by the Third Army.

Battle of the Scarpe, 26–30 August

General Sir Henry Horne planned an attack for 26 August, south-east along the axis of the Arras-Cambrai road. He intended to attack south of the River Scarpe, which ran to the north of the road, but to weaken the German defences a deception plan was initiated designed to convince the enemy that the attack would be north of the river. As at Amiens, the presence of the Canadian Corps south of the river had to be concealed. Deception plans were by now *de rigueur*. North of the river, Horne initiated an artillery fire programme, combined tank and infantry training exercises, established dummy ammunition dumps and casualty clearing stations. To simulate the build-up of troop concentrations, an orchestrated programme of high volume false wireless traffic was maintained.

While the majority of the preparations north of the river were relatively easily detected, the real preparations south of the river were surrounded by strict security and an energetic camouflage programme. As a result, the Germans north of the river supported their troops through the deployment of reserves to counterattack. When the attack was launched south of the Scarpe at 03:00 on 26 August, without a preliminary bombardment, the Germans were taken completely by surprise. The 2nd Canadian Division attacked south of the Arras-Cambrai road on the left flank of the British Third Army, while the 3rd Canadian Division advanced north of the Arras-Cambrai road, between it and the Scarpe. To complete the deception, the 51st (Highland) Division simultaneously attacked north of the Scarpe with no specific objectives other than to tie the Germans to their front and prevent them from transferring units to repel the main thrust. The Canadian Corps attack was successful and Chapel Hill was taken by 06:00 and Monchy-le-Preux by 07:40, despite the late arrival of the tanks. Success was significantly aided by accurate artillery and machine gun barrages. For the lines of the advances and the deception perpetrated, see Map 9.

As the advance continued from Albert to Arras, the prospect of an offensive against the formidable and much vaunted Hindenburg Line (Siegfried Line) became a real possibility. The offensives launched by the British generated a momentum in their First, Third and Fourth Armies as the true nature of the German defences became apparent. With the Hindenburg Line in front of them the British Armies mounted coordinated attacks from St. Quentin to Douai, over a 50-mile front, where the defenders could expect little support as the British Second Army was engaged in its major offensive around the Ypres Salient and potential German reserves were tied down as they tried to staunch this advance.

By this stage of the war, as it became more mobile in nature, the infantry-tank relationship had the firepower capability to defeat German defences. The combination had also developed a relationship with the RAF to mask their approach. Typically, as the First Army progressed, the Mark V tanks on the 4th Division sector on 1 September were taken to within 320 yards of the German front line by using RAF aeroplanes to drown out the noise.[35] The high operational tempo was threatening the Germans with final defeat.

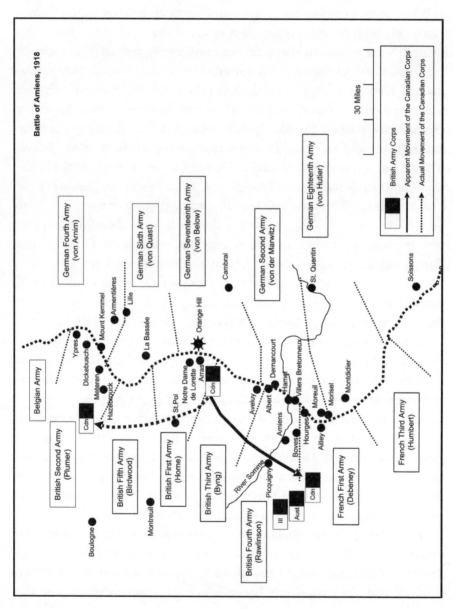

Map 9

Battle of Drocourt-Quéant Line, 2–3 September 1918

The Drocourt-Quéant Line, in front of the main Hindenburg Line, ran northwards from Quéant to Drocourt. This attack was still considered part of the Second Battle of Arras and continued with the momentum generated from the Battle of the Scarpe. The 1st and 4th Divisions of the Canadian Corps from the British First Army attacked the Drocourt-Quéant Line between Dury and Etaing at 05:00 on 2 September. The British utilised a range of methods similar to those used at Amiens with diversionary activity by the British Third and Fourth Armies around Bapaume further south. As a result and also because the Battle of Mont St. Quentin had also gone badly, Ludendorff was forced to withdraw his Seventeenth and Third Armies initially behind the Sensée and then the Canal du Nord.

Battles of the Hindenburg Line, 12 September–9 October 1918

The Hindenburg Line, the last great defensive barrier, covered the central section of the Western Front from Lens to Verdun. It aligned with the trenches network through Flanders to connect through to the Belgian coast. Construction on the central section had begun in September 1916 and although incomplete as the Allies approached in 1918, it still posed a formidable obstacle. Built to a depth of ten miles, it was a system of linked fortified areas or positions (*stellung*), each of which was a complex network of concrete strong points, trenches and barbed wire entanglements designed to maximise the effect of supporting firepower. There were five major *stellung*: Flanders, Wotan, Seigfried, Alberich and Hunding. The Wotan *Stellung* ran from Lille to north of St. Quentin and at its northern end linked with the existing trench system in Flanders (Flanders *Stellung*) to complete the defensive barrier at the northern end to the North Sea. The Seigfried *Stellung*, the strongest position, covered the 45 miles from Arras to St. Quentin, while the next section, the Alberich *Stellung* continued for 30 miles on to Laon. The Hunding *Stellung* consisted of a northern portion, the Brünhilde *Stellung*, which ran through Craonne to Rheims for about 32 miles and a southern section, the Kreimhilde *Stellung*, which continued for 70 miles to Verdun. A further extension, the Michel *Stellung,* extended the Hunding *Stellung* 50 miles to Metz.

The British approach to the defences north of St. Quentin continued along the lines already established, with Horne's First Army in the north, Rawlinson's Fourth Army in the south, and Byng's Third Army between the two. The attacks of all three armies were co-ordinated, which dispensed with the need for multi-army deception plans. Each army, or combination of armies, attacked in a manner co-ordinated by GHQ which prevented the Germans from optimising their defences or redeploying their reserves as the attacks switched focus from sector to sector. However the attacks still relied on local deceptions which could, in some instances, cover considerable distances.

As the First Army regrouped after the capture of the Drocourt-Quéant Line, the Third and Fourth Armies further south maintained pressure on the Germans, giving them very little respite to marshal their forces and denied them the capacity to transfer troops northwards to defend against the advancing First Army.

Battle of Épehy, 18 September 1918

Although the left flank of the Third Army had supported the First Army at the Drocourt-Quéant Line, Byng now found himself involved with another major assault against sections of the Hindenburg Outpost Line. At Épehy, the combined British Third and Fourth Armies attempted to capture the village that sat on top of a ridge and presented an observational and artillery advantage over the surrounding countryside and down to the Hindenburg Line proper. The Germans fought hard to keep the British Army away from their much vaunted defensive system and through determined defence had repulsed a previous attack on 10 September. As a result, the British offensive approach changed as they employed a re-run of the tactical deception plan that had proved so successful at Amiens six weeks previously.

There was a reliance on counter-battery work, tanks, smoke and gas, surprise achieved through a lack of a preliminary bombardment and well concealed troop concentrations and, of course, the almost omnipresent dummy tanks. The dummy tanks were dragged forward a short distance by the pioneers using ropes before dawn, so that as the sun came up and while the visibility was still poor they were at their most impressive. The infantry from units of the IV, V and VI Corps (Third Army) and the

III, Australian and IX Corps (Fourth Army) attacked at 05:20, on a seventeen-mile front from Holnon to Gouzeaucourt against the German Second and Eighteenth Armies. The British Third Army attacked north of Épehy while the Fourth Army attacked the southern sector. Although the tank force was limited, there was sizeable support from 1,488 artillery pieces and 300 machine guns, including teams that Monash from the Australian Corps had 'borrowed' from other non-attacking divisions to augment the initial barrage. There were only twenty tanks available for the Fourth Army attack and eight were assigned to III Corps attacking Vendhuille to the north, eight to the Australian Corps in the Bellicourt-Bellenglise sector and only four for the IX Corps north of St. Quentin.

With such limited tanks numbers, the inclusion of the dummy tanks was vital. Orders were relayed that the tanks would advance behind the infantry and would be used to attack any strong points that the fighting platoons were unable to deal with and which they bypassed. Although the tank advance behind the infantry placed them at a disadvantage, it significantly aided the deception, making the detection of the dummy tanks less likely. The eight tanks which supported the 4th Australian Division attack were supplemented with ten dummy tanks made by the 4th Field Company Australian Engineers. The lightweight dummies were supported on two eight-foot-diameter wheels which held the tank six inches off the ground ensuring that only six troops were required to pull them fairly easily over the rough ground. For added realism, the engineers had added names and regimental colours to the tanks, which were painted with camouflage to ensure that detection was difficult and that there would be a 'shock' value as the shapes were gradually discerned.

This massive force of eighteen tanks was so impressive that only one tank was disabled by machine gun fire, which resulted in slight injuries to two crew members. However, the value of the dummy tanks elsewhere at the Battle of Épehy was questionable, not because they were detected but because the real tanks found the ground slippery and heavy German fire made progress slow. The infantry attack on the right by the 6th Division, IX Corps and on the left by the 18th (Eastern) and 58th (2/1st London) Divisions from III Corps, in the absence of effective tank support, made slow progress under the heavy German fire from well-concealed positions, even though they were supported by a creeping barrage. As a consequence the fight through the village of Épehy was slow and costly.

Despite these tactical setbacks, the British and Australians still advanced to a depth of three miles and success at Épehy and previously at Havrincourt (12 September) together with the American success further south at St. Mihiel (12–16 September) persuaded the Allies that German resolve was weakening and that they should push on to the main defences of the Hindenburg Line.

Battle of Canal du Nord, 27 September–1 October 1918

As the Hindenburg Outpost Line was being attacked by the Third and Fourth Armies, the Canal du Nord, incorporated into the Hindenburg Line, was the next daunting and final major defensive obstacle in the way of the British First Army's easterly advance. Work on the Canal du Nord had begun in 1913, and although interrupted by the war, it still represented a fearsome barrier, 113 feet wide and filled with water of varying depth to an average of eight feet. The Germans had fortified the far bank with wire entanglements and machine gun emplacements with interlocking fields of fire. Once across, however, Bourlon Wood would be vulnerable to attack by the First Army, which would threaten Cambrai, the Germans' all-important communications centre, with the Third and Fourth Armies closing in from the west and south. The Canadian Corps would spearhead the attack, to begin at 05:20 under the cover of darkness.

They would cross the canal between Sainslez–Marquion and Moeuvres where reconnaissance had shown that the banks were firm and the canal was dry. Once the attack commenced, the remainder of the troops would cross using lightweight wooden bridges constructed by engineers from the 11th (Northern) Division. Further south over a weaker section of the canal, the crossing would be attempted by units from Byng's Third Army. As this was a daring and high risk plan, especially from the Canadian's perspective, Horne initiated a deception plan which had echoes of that used earlier at the end of August during the Battle of the Scarpe, when the Germans had been deceived into expecting that north of the Scarpe was where the First Army's major offensive would be launched. However, the First Army continued its south-easterly approach, through the Drocourt-Quéant Line until faced with the Canal du Nord. Now

Horne played the same game to convince the Germans that the point of the attack would now switch north of the Scarpe and his forces at the Canal du Nord would swing northwards to support the other First Army units still there. This movement would apparently threaten Douai and would leave Cambrai to be captured by the Third and Fourth Armies. As previously mentioned, the threat against Douai was credible as the town was the centre of a north-south rail network that was a vital element in sustaining the German front line throughout the war. Douai had held Allied focus, particularly in 1915, when the battles of Neuve Chapelle and Aubers Ridge were fought in conjunction with French offensives with the ultimate objective of advancing across the Douai Plain and capturing the rail centre to initiate the collapse of the German trench system.

In the two weeks before the attack on the Canal du Nord, Horne ordered the corps, cavalry and tank commanders of VIII Corps north of the Scarpe to engage in false preparations for a large-scale attack. Cavalry and tank officers began to reconnoitre the ground in front of them while the artillery initiated a low level but systematic programme of wire cutting and registration against fictitious targets. The infantry patrolled the area and engaged in raids to probe the German defences, while in the British back areas, visible only to German aircraft, tank and infantry co-operation training took place. At the same time, Horne launched a number of aggressive activities north of the Scarpe, which included on 11 September the capture of the Quarries west of the Cité Ste Elie by 15th (Scottish) Division (Major-General H.L. Reed) and the line of the railway west of Auchy lez la Bassée by the 16th (Irish) Division (Major-General A.B. Ritchie). On 13 September this latter division went on to capture Fosse 8 ('the dump') which had been in German hands since the Battle of Loos in September 1915.[36] Further north the 55th Division (Major-General Sir H. Jeudwine) took Rue des Marais and Violaines, before transferring to the British Fifth Army on 19 September. Despite these actions, the seasoned British troops realised the difference between real preparations and the activities they were engaged in, but from the German side of No-Man's-Land, the intelligence gathered indicated only one possible scenario and as a consequence they moved in three additional divisions north of the Scarpe whilst virtually ignoring the southern front where all Allied preparations were conducted in strict secrecy and camouflaged to conceal the build-up.

As these First Army fake preparations distracted the Germans, so too did the preparations of the Third and Fourth Armies for their assault on the Seigfried *Stellung* across the St. Quentin Canal. As the threat from the First Army across the Canal du Nord was seemingly weak, the Germans moved reserves away from this sector southwards to counter the threat against the Hindenburg Line posed by the Third and Fourth Armies.[37] Throughout the Final Hundred Days, the Germans maintained numerical superiority in divisions opposite the British Third and Fourth Armies through the movement of reserves and by thinning fronts where they perceived the threat to be minimal.[38] This level of co-ordination required direction from Haig and GHQ.

The main attack was scheduled for 27 September. The 20th (Light) Division (Major-General G.G.S. Carey), VIII Corps (Lieutenant-General Sir A. Hunter-Weston) on the left wing of the First Army, north of the Scarpe, launched a successful diversionary attack against the Fresnoy sector, but as it was still west of the Drocourt-Quéant Line, it did not press the attack home. On the left of the main attack, from XXII Corps (Lieutenant-General Sir Alexander Godley), the 51st (Highland) Division (Major-General G. Carter-Campbell, north of the Sensée launched a Chinese Attack with the 4th Division on their right engaged in similar activities, as did the 167 Brigade of the 56th Division (Major-General L.J. Lipsett) in the direction of Palluel. These attacks lasted from 05:35 until 06:30, with an artillery barrage which supported the operation of animated dummy soldiers attached to wooden frames. The German defenders failed to react to the dummies, which was attributed at the time to the early morning poor visibility. Further left, north of the Scarpe, another brigade Chinese Attack was launched by the 8th Division (Major-General W.C.G. Heneker) of VIII Corps (Lieutenant-General Sir A. Hunter-Weston).[39] All of these demonstrations shifted the apparent focus of the attack front further north in the direction of Douai as well as concealing the time of the attack (see Map 10).

The actions around the Givenchy area, begun by the First Army, were continued by the re-formed Fifth Army now commanded by General Sir William Birdwood. At Aubers Ridge, between 1–4 October, the 59th (2nd North Midland) Division conducted two minor operations supported by M Special Company Royal Engineers firing a mixture of smoke and innocuous gas. The division met very little resistance and encouraged by this, the Fifth Army pushed across through the La

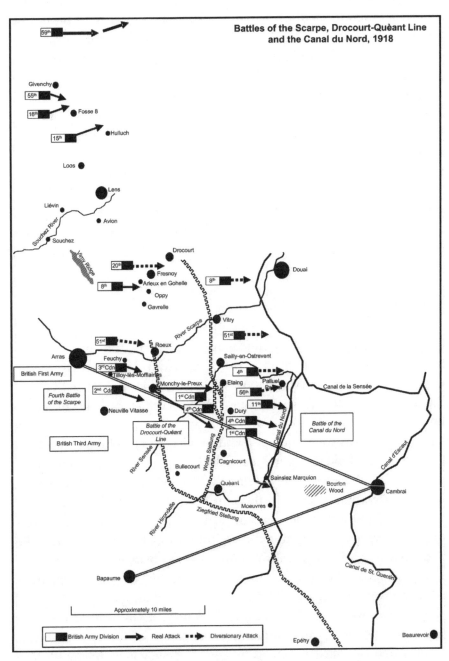

Map 10

Bassée-Neuve Chapelle-Aubers area with the I Corps going across La Bassée Canal and XI Corps through the Fournes-Lorgies-Fleurbaix area, in advances reminiscent of the attempted attacks of 1915 to break out onto the Douai Plain. With the First, Third and Fourth Armies advancing against the Hindenburg Line south of the Scarpe and the Second Army pushing forward around the Ypres Salient, there was a gap in the British advance between Arras and Armentières, filled by the left flank of the First Army and the Fifth Army. Although there were no major battles in this area, as recognised by the Battles Nomenclature Committee, a series of actions through this region maintained pressure on the Germans. As a result, the Germans were unable to transfer troops either north or south. Prior to August 1918, this threat would have been maintained by deception but now the threat could be real as the Germans were no longer in a position to repulse it through the transfer of reinforcements to create strong counterattacks.

Battle of St. Quentin Canal, 29 September–2 October 1918

At the southern end of the Hindenburg Line, the British advanced four miles on a thirteen-mile front as the St. Quentin Canal was crossed by troops of the Third and Fourth Armies as the Allies penetrated behind the formidable defences. The crossing had been achieved using collapsible boats that took four men to carry and twenty seconds to open up and launch. The boats were equipped with mud-mats and scaling ladders to combat the mud and the steep canal walls. Over 3,000 life belts were requisitioned from the leave boats crossing the channel, which enabled soldiers, even non-swimmers, to carry their kit across the water.[40] However, the initial assumption that the Germans had destroyed all the bridges across the canal, which had prompted these measures, proved inaccurate. The 46th (North Midland) Division found that the bridge at Riqueval was intact and broke through the Hindenburg Line; the ensuing celebrations resulted in one the First World War's most iconic photographs.

With the Hindenburg Line broken in several sections by the First, Third and Fourth Armies, the communications centre of Cambrai was now vulnerable to a multi-front attack on 8–9 October, which duly resulted in its capture. While the 3rd and 4th Divisions of the First Army's Canadian Corps advanced on Cambrai from the north, the 1st Canadian Division,

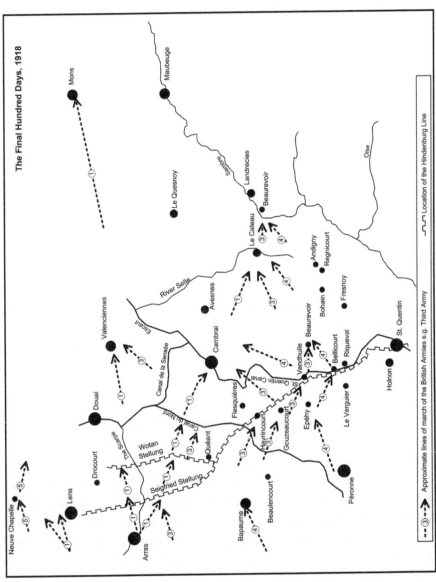

Map 11

moving towards Sailly-en-Ostrevent, attempted on several occasions to cross the River Trinquis and the Sensée. The Canadians used the well-rehearsed deception technique of a series of Chinese Attacks with dummy soldiers, smoke and a creeping barrage to probe the German defences and to distract the defenders from the activities of the 3rd and 4th Canadian Divisions. Through these activities Horne ensured that additional German troops on the Trinquis and Sensée could not be diverted to the Cambrai front.

After the capture of Cambrai by the First, Third and Fourth Armies, all three armies advanced ten miles between 9 and 12 October until the River Selle was reached, an advance that became known as the Pursuit to the Selle.

Battle of the Selle, 17–25 October; Battle of Le Cateau 17–18 October 1918

As the river was reached, a battle ensued to cross it, just one of a series of co-ordinated attacks across the Western Front. Besides the Battle of the Selle, on 17 October the left flank of the First Army attacked and captured Douai. This advance was in support of the British Courtrai (Kortrijk) Offensive (14–19 October) as it prevented the Germans reinforcing northwards to stem the advance of the British Second Army.

On 17 October the British Fourth Army attacked across a ten-mile front south of Le Cateau with the objective of gaining the Valenciennes-Sambre line. The 137 Brigade (GOC, Brigadier-General J.V. Campbell) of 46th Division maintained its position in front of Riqerval Wood but conducted a feint attack with dummy tanks and soldiers in order to draw fire away from the 138 and 139 Brigades attacking at Andigny-les-Fermes and Regnicourt. The Chinese Attack, supported by a barrage from the XVI Army Brigade of the Royal Horse Artillery and machine gun fire, was completely successful. The dummy tanks and troops were placed in such a position as to appear that they were attacking the Bois de Riqerval from the west.[41] A rolling barrage was brought down on the wood in the expectation that part of the enemy's defensive barrage would be wasted against this sector. The 'attack' was perforce at right angles to the main attack and advanced in a north-easterly direction with the specific aim of engaging the German defenders and pulling down some reinforcements from the other sectors. The real attack, further north towards Le Cateau, involved the South African Brigade (GOC, Brigadier-General W.E.C. Tanner) of the 66th (2nd/East Lancashire) Division, XIII Corps of the Fourth Army. The Third Army on its left was not involved in the attack, but its rightmost division, the 38th (Welsh), cooperated with their own Chinese Attack with a machine gun and artillery barrage, although the infantry remained well concealed.[42] The early morning fog greatly assisted in the concealment of the true nature of the feints on both flanks of the real attack, although it did cause some confusion amongst the attacking troops as some of the units became mixed up. Priestley, in his account of the 46th (North Midland) Division written in 1919, acknowledged that the capture of Andigny-les-Fermes was in part the result of the deployment of dummy tanks to distract the enemy defenders.[43]

On 19 October, the focus of this attack switched as Horne's First Army attacked to the north of Le Cateau and were joined on 20 October by the units of Byng's Third Army. Beginning on the 23 October at 01:30, a co-ordinated attack by all three armies resulted in an advance of six miles in two days, as the Germans withdrew to the Valenciennes-Sambre line, now twenty miles behind the 'impregnable' Hindenburg Line.

On the night of 20 October the advance was held up on the banks of a river which Lieutenant Frank Mitchell, a tank commander in the 1st Battalion, the Tank Corps, identified in his 1933 account as the Selle, although there were several other streams and channels in the area that had to be crossed. The far bank was defended by German machine gun emplacements that were not well developed because of the defenders' confidence in the formidable tank barrier that was the river.[44] Under the cover of darkness the Royal Engineers constructed a submerged bridge from railway sleepers. In the morning the tanks simply 'walked' on water and captured the German defences. During the same period, between the Selle and Landrecies, as tanks became scarce and aware of the effect that they were having on German defenders, the Engineers built a number of dummy tanks of canvas and wooden lathes strapped to the backs of mules. Each mule was led by its handler, also under the canvas, who viewed the terrain through a slit. The Engineers had constructed a number of lightweight bridges over the series of trenches so that from a distance it appeared that the 'tanks' were easily traversing these obstacles. The tanks had to be behind the infantry, often the case with the dummies. Their presence often panicked defenders who did not remain in position to test the tanks' armoured skin and firepower. Mitchell reported that close-up there was a comic element to the four hooves and two regulation army boots that stuck out underneath. He also described how, depending on the mule-driving skills of the driver, these tanks suffered a high number of 'breakdowns' as the frightened animals refused to advance. Nevertheless, and this was the main objective, the Germans reported that they had been attacked by a large formation of tanks. The ruse of using mules to create tank movement was used on a number of subsequent occasions.

The Germans failed to develop the tank during the First World War although they came to appreciate its potential, especially after 8 August at Amiens. Given the opportunity they would capture, repair and use British tanks, four of which would be encountered in the battle at Valenciennes on 1 November. This practice even extended as far as creating dummy wooden models of the British tanks in an effort to forestall the advancing soldiers. Mitchell wrote 'The mere sight of advancing tanks created panic in their ranks.' The deployment of dummy tanks often meant that 'large numbers of Germans surrendered at once, and the remainder fled in haste.'[45] Mitchell's assessment was supported by German documentation acknowledging the impact the tanks had on their front line troops and although they suggested several measures to combat this, these were ineffective.[46]

As the First, Third and Fourth Armies marched across the region, approximately south of Arras in an easterly direction, the British Second Army were achieving their own advances through the area around Ypres. These advances mutually supported each other and effectively prevented the transfer of German troops from one sector to the other.

The Second Army had suffered the onslaught of Operation Georgette in June but following the same pattern as Operation Michael, as the advance slowed the British began to regain the initiative and go on the offensive. There were minor actions around Meteren and Outtersteene Ridge before the main thrust at Ypres.

Fourth Battle of Ypres, 26 September–2 October 1918

At the northern end of the Western Front, Army Group Flanders under the command of King Albert I of Belgium prepared to take the offensive. The force consisted of twelve divisions from the Belgian Army, six divisions from the French Sixth Army and ten divisions from the British

Second Army. The preparations for the main advance of the British Army within the Ypres Salient followed a familiar pattern. General Sir Herbert Plumer issued instructions to the Second Army prior to the battle for the movement of all troops and guns to be at night and that there was to be no preliminary bombardment with only a discreet registration of the guns. Further, there was to be no disclosure of an increase in artillery strength prior to the battle to the extent that all new batteries sent to reinforce the XIX and II Corps had to remain completely silent until zero hour; these batteries had to engage in silent registration. The supporting infantry barrage also had to rely on silent registration. Finally, Plumer ordered that certain field batteries of six-inch howitzers and 60-pounders were to select forward positions which were developed and camouflaged in readiness for the artillery to rapidly move forward to maintain effective artillery support for the infantry. These were all 'standard' deception measures within the British Army, but this approach was not followed by the other partners. The Belgian Army had originally planned a four-hour bombardment at night, prior to the dawn attack. There were British objections that not only would surprise be lost but in their sector the German lines were ill-defined and did not follow the logical contours and as observation would not be possible, the whole exercise would be counter-productive. Regardless, the Belgians instigated a three-hour bombardment. In truth, at this stage of the war maintaining pressure on the Germans was the primary concern and as a consequence on the first day they advanced over six miles. By 2 October the Allies supply lines were stretched after an eighteen-mile advance and the battle was closed down. The British suffered 4,695 casualties. After a twelve-day respite, while the pressure on the Germans was maintained by the other armies further south, the Second Army advanced and captured Courtrai on 19 October.

With the front rapidly collapsing the British regained Mons on 11 November, just before the Armistice came into effect – they were back where that had started 1,540 days before. During the Final Hundred Days, the nature of the deception plans had changed. The last multi-army plan, which had been the norm since March 1915, was implemented at the Battle of Amiens on 8 August. After that the deceptions had been confined to single armies as each army commander had initiated his own plan. The need for the multi-army deception plans had passed as Haig and GHQ implemented a multi-army strategy characterised by real attacks by all armies along the Western Front.

8

1915–1918: Other Theatres, Similar Stories

All men can see the tactics whereby I conquer, but what none can see is the strategy out of which victory is evolved … And if we are able thus to attack an inferior force with a superior one, our opponents will be in dire straits.
Sun Tzu

Throughout the whole of the period of the Great War, the eyes of the six major protagonists (Great Britain, France, United States of America, Germany, Austro-Hungary and Turkey) were firmly focused on the Western Front, with a few distracted glances towards Gallipoli and Palestine. The conflict did spread however, regardless of any strategic value, to wherever the protagonists found themselves in close proximity to each other and where post-war aspirations might be strengthened. As a consequence, there were twelve recognised land theatres, some obvious, some less obvious and some downright difficult to find on a map: the Western Front, Eastern Front, Italian Front, Mesopotamia, Persia, Sinai and Palestine, the Balkans, Gallipoli, East, West and South-West Africa and the Caucasus. From the British perspective the Army maintained different commands in the majority of these theatres, all operating under the authority of the British Government and the Secretary of State for War. At a strategic and tactical operational level the commands were autonomous but there were personality connections amongst most of them: for instance, General Sir Herbert Plumer, Western Front and Italy, General Sir

Edmund Allenby, Western Front and Palestine, General Sir Charles Monro, Western Front and Gallipoli and General Sir John Monash, Gallipoli and Western Front.

Hence although commands were distinct, the commanders were still members of the British Army trained at the Staff Colleges, which meant that their approach was fundamentally the same regardless of the theatre. The commanders who had experience of more than one theatre often transferred the lessons learnt on one battlefield to more distant ones. Deception was no exception in this and it was apparent that the template that emerged from the conflict on the Western Front in 1915 was applied elsewhere. Some theatres, notably Gallipoli and Palestine added their own contributions. Some techniques within the template were universal and would have appeared spontaneously in the other theatres regardless – the feint attack to distract enemy defences for one. However, despite the pre-eminence of the Western Front, it was from the non-European theatres that the more celebrated examples of the deceptions of the First World War emerged, particularly at Gallipoli, Gaza, and Megiddo. There were also examples of deception being practised in a minor role to support offensive operations throughout all the theatres. The following are a few examples to illustrate the point, before the major contributions are described.

Italian Front (23 May 1915–4 November 1918)

A series of battles was fought in the frontier region of northern Italy between the Italian and Austro-Hungarian Armies with the involvement of some British, French, American and German units. Following a familiar pattern, these soon became trench warfare. Between 13 November 1917 and 17 March 1918, General Sir Herbert Plumer's Second Army was temporarily transferred to the Italian Front to bolster the Italian Army, although some units remained in theatre for most of the war. Prior to the Second Army's move, units of Byng's Third Army had been ordered to Italy during the preparations for the Battle of Cambrai. Inadvertently, the request for Italian-speaking officers from the Third Army had served only to reinforce Byng's deception activities.

The British troops had been sent to the Italian Front following the Battle of Caporetto (24 October–9 November 1917, also known as the Twelfth Battle of the Isonzo or the Battle of Karfreit). The Austro-Hungarians, reinforced with German units, broke through the Italian Front and routed the Italians using the soon-to-be familiar stormtrooper and infiltration tactics (*stosstrupptaktik*). The Germans instigated a number of ruses which seemingly targeted another sector almost at the far end of the front, 150 miles away. Wireless stations were set up in the Trentino, spurious orders were generated referring to non-existent troop formations, while as a tried and trusted method, troops were marched around to simulate the build-up of a significant attacking force. A programme of raids was instigated to test and understand the defences in the Trentino. Meanwhile at Caporetto, troop concentrations were built up in the valleys of the Drave and the Save, behind the Julian Alps, which were off limits to the Italian Air Force. 300 artillery batteries were manually moved up at night into camouflaged positions and more or less left unguarded so as not to arouse suspicion. All of these activities would have been standard on the Western Front.

In February 1918 the Italians planned an attack from the Sile bridgehead with the objective of driving the Austrians back over the Piave. To distract their attentions the British were asked to cross the river within their sector below Nervesa. Two brigades from the British 5th Division were tasked with the crossing and while one brigade would cross on improvised bridges, the other would simulate on attack further south using dummy soldiers. In the event the incessant rain raised the water level in the Piave by four feet and the Italians were forced to abandon the whole venture. This nevertheless showed that the British were willing to bring Western Front experience to other theatres. This was amply demonstrated in July 1918 when Lord Cavan, Commander-in-Chief, British Force in Italy – Plumer had returned to the Western Front on 17 March – ordered all British artillery to remain silent from 6 to 10 July, except in emergency. The objective was to detect new hidden enemy batteries. As Cavan rightly assumed, silence, famously used at Gallipoli, had an unnerving effect, especially amongst the Austrian wireless operators who thought that the British behaviour was 'extraordinary'. The Austrians fired bursts of shells all along the British front – not with any specific aim but in the frantic hope that it would disrupt any British troop movements. As all British guns remained silent, the sound-ranging and flash-spotting tasks of the artillery were simplified and eight new batteries were detected and subsequently targeted. Cavan also pointed out the period of silence meant a deserved rest for the RFC and a saving in precious ammunition.

Mesopotamia (6 November 1914–30 October 1918)

In Mesopotamia, British units engaged in standard deception activities. Edward Roe in his diary reported that on 8 January 1917 near Kut, to divert Turkish attention from a real attack at Abdul Hassan, they staged a demonstration amidst smoke by marching up and down their trench with fixed bayonets showing above the parapet. The sight of fixed bayonets was indicative of an imminent attack and as a deceptive measure was first used at Loos in September 1915. The demonstration drew Turkish fire.[1]

Later on, as Roe and the 1/East Lancashire Regiment advanced towards the Tigris, the Turks retreated leaving behind empty trenches. But the regiment had previously been at Gallipoli and were unnerved and tentative about approaching the silent trenches. Throughout the First World War, the weapon of silence had proved to have benefits. In the East Lancashires' case the silence indicated that they had done a good job and the Turks had retreated, nothing more sinister.

East Africa (15 August 1914–23 November 1918)

The East Africa Campaign should have been familiar to the British in its echoes of the Boer War, the Germans under their commander Colonel Paul Erich von Lettow-Vorbeck waging a guerrilla style war, never engaging the British head on in a battle that he knew he could not win. In the early phases, the British force of three battalions – 1,800 men under the command of Brigadier-General Michael Joseph Tighe – reached the River Umba after landing on the coast on 20 December 1914, meeting only minor opposition from Abt von Boemken. The weakness of the German response can be attributed at least in part to the feint attacks of the Royal Navy, which bombarded several towns along the coast to disguise the actual location of the landing and forced the Germans to split their forces to protect the various targeted sectors. This classic tactic was actually more characteristic of Lettow-Vorbeck than the British for the remainder of the war.

After months of chasing the enemy and as a much needed boost to morale, Tighe took the initiative and decided on an amphibious attack against Bukoba on the western shore of Lake Victoria. Bukoba was a strategic target with a wireless station that was the hub of the colony's communications network. It was defended by a garrison that doubled as reinforcements in support of the Kagera Line (along the Kagera River). Bukoba's weakness was that it occupied an isolated position on the western shore of Lake Victoria, which made the rapid reinforcement of it very difficult. Beginning on 16 June 1915, a series of feint attacks were carried out along the Kagera Line to attract the attention of the Bukoba defenders, obliging them to transfer troops to support the threatened sectors. At dawn on 22 June 1,600 British troops, two mountain guns and twelve machine guns landed on the shore under the command of Brigadier-General James M. Stewart. Although opposition was encountered, the weakened defences gave way as the Germans retreated and the town was captured. The wireless station was destroyed. The force re-embarked on 23 June and returned to Kisumu, buoyed by this demonstration that through the employment of deception and proper offensive preparations, successful operations could be achieved.[2]

Gallipoli (The Dardanelles Campaign) (25 April 1915–9 January 1916): The Disappearing Army

It was in Gallipoli and Palestine that the most elaborate, most effective ruses of the First World War were perpetrated. These ruses were to have long reaching consequences. The landings at Gallipoli acted as a blueprint for the D-Day landings 30 years later and the Haversack Ruse at Gaza was the inspiration for 'Operation Mincemeat' in support of the Sicily landings in 1943.

As the awful reality of the Western Front became apparent to the military and politicians alike, the British Government sought to focus the attention of the Germans away from France and Belgium. Winston Churchill (First Lord of the Admiralty) proposed the opening of another front, which found favour with the British cabinet, particularly David Lloyd George (Chancellor of the Exchequer) and Andrew Bonar Law (Colonial Secretary). This led to the formation of a group within the government known as the 'Easterners' who believed that the war could be won without necessarily beating the Germans on the Western Front. As a consequence, the ultimately disastrous Dardanelles Campaign was launched with the strategic aim of opening a route through to the Black Sea that would neutralise Turkey, keep the remainder of the Balkans out of the war and ensure a free passage through to Russia. The achievement of these objectives would cause Germany to divert resources to the existing Eastern Front and thus weaken the Western Front.

The amphibious landings on the Gallipoli Peninsula that started with such high expectations in the spring of 1915 ended in disaster for the Allies as the Mediterranean Expeditionary Force (MEF) became bogged down in Western Front-style trench warfare. By the autumn of 1915, it was apparent that the MEF would have to evacuate the peninsula, which resulted in the most famous of all the ruses perpetrated during the First World War. The approaches and trickery adopted by the British to achieve the evacuation had a precursor in the American Civil War when Major-General Pierre G. T. Beauregard evacuated Confederate troops from the town of Corinth under the noses of a superior Union force in May 1862.

Prior to the evacuation, the Allies undertook opposed landings on the peninsula twice, in April and August 1915. These high risk ventures were supported by complex multiple-front deception plans, which reinforced the beliefs of the Turkish commander as per Magruder's Principle.

On 25 April 1915, the MEF waded ashore at multiple landing sites at Cape Helles, codenamed the S, V, W, X and Y beaches, while farther north the Australian and New Zealand Army Corps (ANZAC) landed at a beach (Z beach) destined to be known forever as Anzac Cove. The French Army landed on mainland Turkey, on the eastern shore of the Dardanelles near Kum Kale, and acted as a diversion for the main British landings. The invasion was a more sophisticated and complex affair than the usual multiple offensive operations as it also included fake operations against positions the Turks believed were vulnerable. General Sir Ian Hamilton, commander of the MEF at the start of the Dardanelles Campaign, wrote in his post-war diary that the invasion plans were designed to 'upset the equilibrium' of Field Marshal Otto Liman von Sanders, the German Army commander of the Turkish Fifth Army defending the Dardanelles.[3] Von Sanders was unable to concentrate either his men or his mind to meet the threat.

As the Allied forces began to assemble in Egypt and the Greek islands, von Sanders stationed two of his six available divisions in the peninsula at Bulair to protect what he considered to be the prime invasion spot. He stationed another two divisions at Besika Bay on the Asian side, close to the Allied fleet, to meet the probable target. Hamilton and his staff devised a deception plan that targeted von Sanders pre-determined beliefs and divisional dispositions so that these redundant divisions would be tied up and could not be immediately transferred to those sectors where the Allies were coming ashore.

The forthcoming landings were common knowledge following a period of build-up in Egypt and the Greek islands, where security was particularly lax. Newspaper reports in the western press also published 'details' of the proposed landings while the British and French, who underestimated the fighting potential of the Turkish Army, decided to rely on firepower to force a landing. As the amphibious landings were a new venture, the decision was taken to cloak them in deception. The British planned a feint attack at Bulair, 40 miles north of Anzac Cove, to engage the 5th and 7th (Turkish) Divisions, while the French Army were to mount a diversionary landing at Kum Kale supported by a demonstration ten miles further south at Besika Bay to attract the attention of the 3rd and 11th (Turkish) Divisions. All three elements of the deception plan obeyed Magruder's Principle of reinforcing an enemy's belief rather than creating a new one. The simulated landing at Bulair, which was at the narrowest part of the peninsula, would threaten the Turkish supply and communications lines throughout the peninsula, while both Kum Kale and Besika Bay with its suitable terrain would threaten the Turkish guns protecting the Dardanelles and allow the Royal Navy through to attack Constantinople (see Map 12). Von Sanders, had recognised the military potential of the threats against these targets and deployed his divisions according. In the main area of the peninsula where the actual landings and attacks would occur, he primarily deployed only the 9th Division with the 19th Division in reserve.

The diversionary attack at Kum Kale led by General Albert d'Amade, commander of the French forces, was initially successful. However, it was always vulnerable to being surrounded; as soon as the Besika Bay threat dissolved, the Turkish troops could be easily transferred north-west to threaten the French at Kum Kale. The feint at Besika Bay was instigated by French naval vessels that appeared off the shore on the morning of 25 April, but the Turks soon realised the impotent nature of the threat and redeployed the 11th Division to reinforce Yeni Shahr, a village south of the French diversionary landings, which immediately compromised their line of retreat. This feint was conducted by the French Army alone, as Lord Kitchener had expressly forbidden the landing of any British troops on the Asian coast.

The European coast, however, was not off limits. Eleven transports of the Royal Naval Division together with three warships, two destroyers and a number of trawlers arrived just after daybreak on 25 April off Bulair

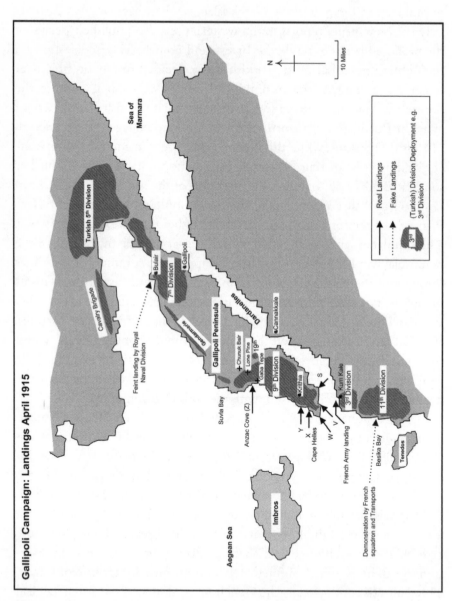

Map 12

and began a slow bombardment of the Turkish positions. Later in the day, the ships' boats were ostentatiously swung over the sides and the trawlers towed eight cutters ready for the landing. The feint landing in the Gulf of Xeros, south of Bulair, in darkness, was originally planned to consist of a platoon from the Hood Battalion, Royal Naval Division, but the plan was changed by Lieutenant Commander Bernard Freyberg, who decided that it was too risky a venture. Instead, Freyberg, acting alone, was dropped into the water at 00:40 on 26 April, two miles offshore carrying a waterproof bag filled with oil flares, calcium lights, a signalling lamp, a knife and a revolver. After a 90-minute swim he reached the westernmost of the three northern beaches. There he lit one of the flares before continuing his swim to a second beach where further flares were lit. In the dark, the presence of the flares should have alerted the Turks that a possible landing was taking place. At the second beach, Freyberg entered what appeared to be deserted Turkish trenches but found that they were simply two-foot-high piles of earth over 100 yards long. From the sea these dummy trenches appeared to be real and were intended to deter the British from selecting the area for a landing. His job done, Freyberg, after a further two-mile swim, was picked up by the cutter that had originally dropped him off. For his extraordinary escapade Freyberg was awarded the Distinguished Service Order (DSO). In 1916 in France he went on to win the Victoria Cross. Lieutenant Commander Bernard Freyberg, together with Lieutenant-Colonel Richard Meinertzhagen at Gaza (1917) were the names that became synonymous with deception during the First World War as they captured the imagination of post-war readers. It took the Turks two days to understand the nature of the threat posed at Bulair, before they sent the redundant troops from the 7th (Turkish) Division (GOC Colonel von Sodenstern) and the 5th Turkish Divisions (GOC Colonel Remsi Bey) south to reinforce the Anzac Cove defences.

The main landings on the peninsula, begun just after 03:30, were supported by the Royal Navy with an artillery bombardment. Amongst the flotilla were old liners that were painted, funnelled and bedecked with dummy guns to resemble HMS *Tiger*, *Inflexible* and *Indomitable* as diversionary targets for the German submarines known to be operating in the area. When Liman von Sanders was woken at 05:00 on 26 April with news of the activity at Besika Bay, Kum Kale, Bulair, Helles and Anzac Cove, he immediately assumed that the main attack was at Bulair where he was most vulnerable.[4] In response he ordered units of the 7th (Turkish)

Division, which were stationed lower down the peninsula, to march further north to reinforce the Bulair defences. Potentially significant numbers of troops were removed from the Allies' real target. As a piece of deception this must be seen as a 100 per cent success. However, with hindsight and in view of the significant casualty figures to come, it is interesting to speculate whether the Allies were too rigid in their adherence to Magruder's Principle. Liman von Sanders considered Bulair the Achilles Heel of the peninsula as it occupied a position able to cut off supply and communication lines. Should the Allies' plan have been reversed? Should they have initiated feint attacks at Helles and Anzac Cove to draw down the 5th and 7th (Turkish) Divisions and engage the already present 9th and 19th (Turkish) Divisions while making Bulair their real target to cut off the peninsula, trap four Turkish divisions and threaten the Dardanelles?

As for the real landings, which took place between 03:30 and 08:30, the casualty rates varied depending on the landing beach. The major weakness with all deception plans, not only in the First Word War, was illustrated at Gallipoli. Initially the four Turkish divisions were contained as a result of the deception activities at Bulair and Besika Bay; but feints could rarely be sustained beyond the initial phase of the battle and as a result the true nature of the threat became apparent and the 'spare' troops could be redeployed to support units under real attack. This weakness was seen in all theatres and was an especially serious defect where attrition followed the initial phase. This problem was partially addressed in the later stages of the war on the Western Front in 1918 and in those theatres where No-Man's-Land was not so precisely defined. At Gallipoli the situation was exacerbated by a failure of the local commanders at Helles and Anzac Cove to seize the initiative and break out of the bridgeheads that were defended by relatively low numbers of Turks.

In the months following the April landings, the Allies suffered a high rate of attrition as trench warfare ensued. Having spurned chances early on to make progress, they were pinned down to not much more than the landing beaches and dominated by the Turkish-held high ground. The British now resorted to the familiar tactics of the Western Front and used Chinese Attacks to force the Turks to reveal their machine gun locations and to act as diversions for real attacks. On 28 June, the 29th Division attack was supported along the line with demonstrations while on 12 July at Helles the 52nd (Lowland) Division attack was assisted by a demonstration at Anzac. There was machine gun fire and simulated preparations for an attack and although small parties of soldiers actually left the trenches, the demonstration was not of sufficient strength to prevent the Turks sending their reserves to repel the attack of the 52nd Division.

The Turks were neither strong enough nor sufficiently militarily adept to force the MEF off the landing beaches back into the sea. While they resorted to futile offensive operations, the Allies decided to resolve the deadlock through another landing further north at Suvla Bay. This would attempt to outflank the Turkish positions and threaten the Turkish supply and communication lines, although as the peninsula was as its widest at this point, cutting it off and trapping the Turkish Army was not feasible. As Hamilton recognised that any preparations for another landing could not be hidden from the vast network of spies in Greece and the Aegean Sea, he decided that their landing preparations should, once more, be cloaked within a deception plan, which had the same aims as their real operation, to cut off Turkish lines of communication and supply.

At 22:30 on 6 August 1915 the British, under the cover of darkness and in an attempt to open an additional front on the peninsula, landed two divisions of approximately 20,000 troops at Suvla Bay, about five miles north of Anzac Cove. As before, there were feint attacks planned for Bulair and the Asian coast, south of Besika Bay, together with a series of offensive operations on the peninsula in an attempt to confuse the Turks.

In August 1915, von Sanders commanded sixteen divisions and of these, three divisions, commanded by Feizi Bey, protected the Bulair region while a further three were deployed along the Asiatic coast, in total 37 per cent of von Saunders' strength. The British deception plan targeted these divisions. Interestingly, von Sanders had deployed only three battalions, a force of less than 1,500 men, to protect the Suvla Bay area. These deployments are shown on Map 13.

At Bulair, the feint was no different and probably no more effective than that used for the 25 April landings. As soon as the hollowness of the threat was realised, on 8 August von Sanders transferred two of the defending divisions, the 7th and 12th (GOC Ahmed Feizi Bey), 30 miles south as the true nature of the Suvla Bay landings became apparent.

Prior to the invasion and without asking for permission from the Greek Government, six battalions of the 10th (Irish) Division were landed at Mitylene (now Lesbos). The island was used as a convenient concentration area together with the islands of Mudros and Imbros, for troops destined for Suvla Bay. The appearance of large troop concentrations together with

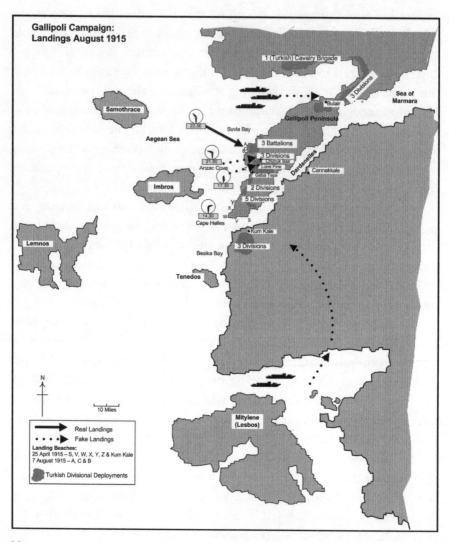

Map 13

their exercises convinced the Turks that the British would attempt a landing on the Asiatic coast. The landing on the Asiatic coast was a viable aim as the occupation of the coast between Eren Keui and Yeni Shehr would protect the British trenches at Helles from enfilade fire. Hamilton embellished this deception by ordering his officers to ask the local inhabitants about the availability of water supplies and suitable encampment areas on the mainland. Maps of the Asiatic coast were distributed. On 3 August Hamilton visited and inspected the troops, which further convinced the Turks. On 6 August spare French transports appeared in the area.

To coincide with the landings at Suvla Bay and prevent a redistribution of the Turkish troops throughout the peninsula, attacks were launched at Helles by VIII Corps, against Lone Pine by the Australians and against Chunuk Bair by the New Zealanders.

The attack at Helles by the VIII Corps (Lieutenant-General Sir F.J. Davies) was on a mile-wide front astride Kirte Dere with the aim of straightening the line. The previous more ambitious plans were abandoned due to an estimated high casualty rate for an operation designed to divert Turkish attention from Suvla Bay. The less ambitious operation effectively achieved the same aim.

The attacks at Lone Pine and Chunuk Bair both had strategic objectives over and above their deceptiveness but the timing of these operations would distract the Turks from Suvla Bay. In preparation for the attack against Lone Pine, Lieutenant-General Sir W.R. Birdwood, GOC ANZAC, ordered that new caves be dug throughout his sector capable of holding an additional 25,000 British troops and their equipment drawn from the 13th (Western) Division (Major-General F.C. Shaw), the 29 Brigade from the 10th (Irish) Division (Lieutenant-General Sir B.T. Mahon) and the Indian Infantry Brigade. These troops together with the equipment were brought ashore under the cover of darkness over four successive nights. Most of the transport ships had disappeared over the horizon by daybreak to maintain secrecy. The only exception was the ship disembarking the Indian Brigade on the morning of 6 August, which had arrived late and was still in view at daybreak. The Turks shelled the ship. The horses were brought ashore each with a full nose-bag, so that they concentrated on eating and not neighing. The new men were forced to remain hidden in the caves but had spells outside when an equivalent number of the original troops changed places with them. The former were under strict instructions not to look up when a Turkish plane flew over and not to engage in small arms fire, as their pale faces would have betrayed the presence of fresh troops. The concealment of these troops for three days under the direct observation of the nearby Turkish positions has been considered one of the major military feats of the First World War. The plan was that at zero hour the additional troops would emerge from the tunnels and caves and overwhelm the Turkish defences. As the Turks were aware of the build-up of men in the area of the Dardanelles, when the Lone Pine attack started they would assume that these were in fact those men that they had already observed and hence would not expect that there would be sufficient men left for the Suvla Bay landings.

The plan for the attack on Chunuk Bay had it own deception plan, which was imaginative and effective. Every night for a couple of weeks at 21:00, the destroyer that was regularly stationed off Anzac Cove shone a searchlight onto the Turkish line at Post 3 and for 30 minutes bombarded the positions. The Turks became accustomed to this activity and every night would retire from their positions only to return once the bombardment had ceased. On the night of the Chunuk Bair assault, the ANZAC troops crept forward in darkness either side of the beam and entered the trenches immediately as the bombardment ceased – classic *Behaviour Modification*.

The preparations for the actual landing at Suvla Bay had at Hamilton's insistence been shrouded in such strict secrecy that Lieutenant-General Sir F. W. Stopford, chosen to lead it, was unaware of the operation until 22 July.

The various operations were originally planned for different dates but circumstances forced them all to be initiated on 6 August. At 14:30 explosions were set off at Helles, at 17:30 the Lone Pine operation commenced, at 21:30 Chunuk Bair was assaulted and at 22:30, as the moon began to rise, the landings took place at Suvla Bay. Off Bulair, Royal Navy vessels together with a number of trawlers arrived in the evening when their presence would be detected, in what was a re-run of the ruse perpetrated on 25 April.

The deception plans meant that the landings at Suvla Bay were successfully achieved against minimal defences that remained weak as von Saunders maintained the concentration of his troops in those areas which he considered to be the most vulnerable. Despite this success, delays in action ultimately meant the rapid onset of the stalemate that was characteristic of Anzac and Helles. The deception plan had achieved its objective of 'neutralising' the Turkish reserves but the offensive operation was still low down on the learning curve, in a situation that mirrored the Western Front.

The stalemate, the casualties and the state of the Western Front ultimately led to the decision being taken on 22 November to evacuate the peninsula.

The possibility of evacuation had been first put forward in the middle of October by Sir Ian Hamilton, a suggestion which saw him dismissed and replaced on 26 October as Commander-in-Chief of the MEF by General Sir Charles Monro. Monro, having assessed the situation in the peninsula also recommended evacuation, which immediately saw him sent to Salonika to command the British Army there. At this point Lieutenant-General Sir William Birdwood (GOC, Australian and New Zealand Army Corps) was put in charge. Following a visit by Kitchener it became apparent that evacuation was the only practical course of action. Kitchener, now with a better appreciation of Monro, appointed him Commander-in Chief of all British forces within the Mediterranean, with subordinates Birdwood in charge of the Gallipoli Peninsula and Lieutenant-General Sir B.T. Mahon in charge in Salonika. Instructions were issued for the evacuation of the Gallipoli Peninsula with the explicit caveat that it had to be achieved with minimal casualties. Initially Birdwood planned an aggressive withdrawal as the only method of achieving this, but gradually the advantages to be gained from a well thought out and well executed deception plan aimed at maintaining the status quo at Suvla and Anzac became apparent.

As on the Western Front, the British were overlooked by the Turks, the only difference being that in the Gallipoli Peninsula the height was greater and gave commanding views over all the landing beaches. As the British had found out at S beach, Cape Helles, the high ground, not only granted an observational advantage but a line-of-sight field of fire along the beach. Prior to the landings and after a further nine months of occupation, the Turkish artillery would have registered on all of the occupied and potential landing beaches. How could an army of 134,000 men, 14,000 animals and 400 guns disappear without the enemy knowing? In some quarters, particularly in London, it was argued that because of the enemy's observational advantages and the close proximity of the Turkish trenches, which in some instances were only ten yards away, high numbers of casualties were unavoidable and to be expected. To exacerbate the problem it was known that German submarines operated within the area with the express aim of observing beach activity from the seaward side. Hence the British positions were under observation from every direction.

General Monro charged Birdwood with developing an appropriate scheme to disguise the evacuation and minimise the casualties. Birdwood and his staff devised a plan consisting of a number of relatively simple activities that would require a high degree of discipline, phenomenal organisation and meticulous timetabling. The complex plan must be regarded as one of the best ever deceptions in all military history.

The evacuation plan was devised in several stages for the gradual reduction of troop numbers, stores, guns and materiel. The last troops would leave by 04:00 on 20 December 1915. Throughout, the impression had to be created that troop numbers were remaining constant or even increasing.

Throughout November and December various individual measures within the beachheads were initiated. On 23rd November, Major-General A.J. Godley, GOC New Zealand & Australian Division and later GOC I ANZAC Corps, ordered that from 7 December there would be occasional periods of ceasefire. Any Turkish patrols sent out to investigate were to be shot. Through this ruse, the Turks were taught that complete silence in the British trenches did not mean that the garrison had been withdrawn.

The artillery gradually ceased firing, along with machine gun and rifle fire, after dark prior to the evacuation, so that the Turks became accustomed to a period of silence during the night. The artillery also gradually scaled back their day-time activities prior to the withdrawal. The reduced level of firing gave sufficient headroom so that there would be no discernible decrease in artillery activity as the artillery pieces were withdrawn.

The gradual decrease in artillery fire followed one of the principles of good deception plans identified by the United States Army in 1988, 'Susceptibility to Conditioning'. This referred to the inability of the enemy to detect small, gradual changes even if the cumulative change over a period of time was large. Had there been a step change in the level of activity, the Turks would have been alerted and would almost surely have taken some form of offensive action. As the guns were removed, there came a point where the remaining guns had to fire an increased number of shells daily to maintain a credible level. The empty abandoned gun pits were manned with dummy soldiers, dummy guns and old worn out guns – no useful ordnance was left.

To conceal diminishing troop numbers, dummy soldiers were used while the remaining troops lit numerous camp fires, all tents remained standing and sniper fire was apparently kept steady by the snipers constantly moving around from one location to another. The troops were also ordered to show themselves to the Turks and to march around the dirt tracks to create levels of dust associated with large concentrations of troops. One can imagine the reaction to such an order. As mentioned earlier, Private Edward Roe (6/East Lancashire), in his Gallipoli diary entry for for 16–17 December described parading along 'C' beach at Lala Baba in full view of the Turks as a 'sacrifice duty'.[5] The 6th Battalion war diary for the same period by the adjutant, A.C. Bailey simply stated that 'the whole four companies were then engaged in digging and rebuilding trenches'.[6] This was a less hazardous task than deliberately exposing oneself to the Turks, something everyone had been trying to avoid during the previous ten months. The trench building activities were also part of the British Army's deception plans to create the impression that the situation was normal. At Amiens in August 1918, the Fourth Army Labour Corps had continued to build defences until the day prior to the attack. These were simple activities that conveyed a lot.

To prevent the dwindling garrison being surprised, contact mines were placed in front of the trenches with the British troops under strict orders not to venture out into No-Man's-Land to avoid the new danger. Troops returning to their units did so during the day to add to the illusion of increasing troop numbers. This illusion of a growing force was reinforced by special squads with mules who walked up to the front line each morning carrying 'disembarked' stores; the boxes carried were empty. On their return trip, the mules carried 'empty' boxes full of spare ammunition and stores. Each evening empty 'jingling' ration carts went up to the front line, as usual, only to return silently later, laden with stores. On 19 December, Birdwood instructed the VIII Corps under Lieutenant-General Sir F.C. Davies to mount a small offensive action at Helles. Two attacks took place accompanied by the detonation of mines, to distract Turkish attention away from Suvla and Anzac.

As the last troops left on 20 December, the abandoned trenches were booby-trapped and automatic firing rifles were set up using a variety of devices, including weights, candles and fuses, to ensure that they fired randomly after the troops had left. The most common and famous contraption involved two kerosene cans, one placed above the other. The top can was filled with water while the lower can, attached by string to the trigger of a rifle, was empty. Holes were then punched into the upper can and the water dripped into the lower can. The weight gradually increased and the tension on the string built up until the rifle fired. By varying the size and number of holes punched into the upper can it was possible to have rifles firing for all of the desired thirty minutes after the troops had abandoned the trenches. Bean attributed the invention of this device to Lance Corporal Scurry of the 7th Battalion, 2 Australian Brigade, 1st Australian Division. Even after the final rifle fired, the Turks kept their distance from the British trenches thanks to 'Godley's silence'.

As the final Australian troops on the right hand of the line crossed
Brighton Beach south of Anzac Cove, they were in full view and vulnerable to the Turkish lookouts on Gaba Tepe. To counteract this, the British
destroyer, at anchor off Anzac, had for 30 minutes on several successive
nights shone its searchlight on the beach, south of the embarkation point.
The Turks had become accustomed to this and, on the final night, were
unable to see through the intense light as the last troops scrambled over
the beach to the lighters.

During the last phases of the evacuation, between the 8 and 20
December, 83,048 officers and men, 186 guns, 2,000 vehicles and 4,695
mules and horses were withdrawn. The success of the deception scheme
was such that at Suvla there were no casualties, while at Anzac two men
were wounded.

The evacuation of the Suvla and Anzac areas immediately created the
thorny and dangerous problem of the occupation of Helles, held by the
13th (Western) (Major-General F.C. Shaw), 29th (Major-General H. de
B. de Lisle), 42nd (East Lancashire) (Major-General W. Douglas), 52nd
(Lowland) (Major-General G.G.A. Egerton) and Royal Naval (Major-
General A. Paris) Divisions. The French Army had withdrawn almost
immediately and by 24 December only a French Colonial (Senegalese)
Brigade remained, on the extreme right, and even these were soon
replaced by troops from the 29th Division. The British had initially considered holding Helles but all estimates predicted that this would be too
costly. The only practical solution was the evacuation of the cape. This
would have to take place before the end of January when the weather
and sea conditions would render an evacuation impracticable.

Birdwood again decided that hoodwinking the Turks was the only
practical, although incredibly difficult, solution. His adversary, General
Liman von Sanders, thought that a withdrawal would be attempted and
was adamant that the Turks would not be fooled twice. Testimonies from
Turkish prisoners showed that patrols were regularly sent out to test
British defences to determine their readiness and to make sure that the
trenches were still adequately manned.

Birdwood's plan and the method of implementation were very similar
to that executed at Suvla and Anzac and all the same ruses were tried again.
The evacuation was to be carried out in three stages with the final withdrawal planned for a single night. This had to be modified when General
Davies (GOC, VIII Corps) estimated that 22,000 troops were needed in

the front line to resist any attack and the Royal Navy determined that the most troops that they could evacuate in a single night was 15,000. As a consequence the final stage was extended to two nights, the last night a calculated gamble. On 25 December all animals and material not needed for winter were removed and on 28 December the official order to evacuate Cape Helles was received.

As the British area at Helles was laid out like a map for the Turkish observers on Achi Baba, and with their increased vigilance, it was important that normal activities were maintained. The levels of bombing, sniping and raiding were kept up to the end. From 30 December onwards all firing ceased at midnight and the trenches fell silent but any approach by the Turks was vigorously repulsed, although as the Official Historian noted, the jumpiness of the sentries who fired at anything throughout the night probably reduced the effectiveness of this ruse.

The Turks themselves helped in the attempted deception. Liman von Sanders ordered an attack for 7 January by the 12th (Turkish) Division to test the strength of the British defensive lines. The Turks massed for attack and the trenches could be clearly seen by the British to be bristling with bayonets. Despite the low morale of the defenders after the withdrawal of their comrades from Suvla and Anzac, the British 13th (Western) Division, aided by the Royal Navy with counter-battery fire, laid down such a volume of rifle fire that the majority of the Turkish soldiers refused to leave their trenches and high levels of casualties were inflicted upon them. The vigour of the repulse was interpreted by the Turks as showing that the British were at full strength and were possibly intent on remaining in the peninsula. This attack probably ensured a smoother evacuation than could have been expected, as the Turks never seriously threatened the British positions again.

As the last troops left, all the automatic rifle firing devices were in place and on 9 January 1916 the remaining 16,918 troops were withdrawn. As at Suvla and Anzac there had not been a single loss of life throughout the evacuation as 35,268 officers and men, 3,689 horses and mules, 127 guns, 328 vehicles and 1,600 tons of materials were withdrawn. Again, the Turks had been hoodwinked.

There is no doubt that without deception the Turkish Army, with the high ground and supported by the patrolling German submarines, would have caused many casualties amongst the evacuating troops. It should be remembered that not only during the evacuation but also during the landings deception played a significant part, particularly at Suvla Bay where the entire invading force attained landfall opposed by only three Turkish battalions. The subsequent delays and confusion that resulted in another stalemate should not be attributed to the deception plan but to the fact that offensively in 1915 the British Army was not able to finish the job.

The Sinai and Palestine Campaign (3 February 1915–27 October 1918)

After General Sir Edmund Allenby took command of the Egyptian Expeditionary Force (EEF) in June 1917, deception was central to all his endeavours. There is some debate as to the actual deception plans employed in Palestine and in particular that implemented at Gaza (1917). The British had advanced through Sinai and into Palestine but were held up and had suffered greatly in front of Gaza, which resulted in a change of leadership and with it a change in tactics. Some contemporary military personnel and latterday historians have not been convinced of the merits and effectiveness of the deception plans instigated by the new commander, despite the fact that the line was broken and the Turks were in full retreat within a week of the start of the Third Battle of Gaza.

The fight for Palestine had begun on 3 February 1915, two months before the Dardanelles Expedition, when Turkish Forces attempted to threaten Britain's lifeline to India, the Suez Canal. The Turkish attack on the canal was aborted as they learned a lesson that was to have a bearing on all actions in Palestine, that prior to any action, water supplies had to be secured. The Turks learnt the lesson; and Allenby would in effect risk his whole campaign on securing water.

Third Battle of Gaza (Beersheba), 31 October– 7 November 1917

Even before Captain Cyril Falls, the Official Historian of the battle, had completed his account, controversy surrounded the deception plan. Lieutenant-Colonel Clive Garsia contacted Falls to ensure that his view was well represented in the document. He did not question the success of the deception but simply questioned whether the deception was necessary at all, a view that became known as the 'Gaza School'. Garsia argued that the Gaza defences in October 1917 were susceptible to a frontal attack and would have been overwhelmed without any elaborate deception plan. Such an approach would have avoided the problems with water supply subsequently suffered by the EEF. This in turn would have enabled the British to pursue the fleeing Turks and capture Jerusalem earlier than 9 December 1917, when it was taken. Garsia estimated that this would have considerably shortened the war in Palestine, which ended on 30 October 1918. There is no doubt that on 31 October, the Gaza defences were weakened, but whether this was their natural state or was a result of the deception plan is open to question.

The EEF under General Sir Archibald Murray had previously failed to capture Gaza in March and April 1917. On 26 March 1917 the EEF had launched an attack against the defences surrounding Gaza (First Battle of Gaza) with a numerical superiority of two-to-one. With victory in their grasp, General Sir Charles Dobell, Murray's subordinate, misread the intelligence and assumed that the infantry attack had failed, at which point the British cavalry were withdrawn. On the Turkish side, the German commander, General Kress von Kressenstein, initially and correctly believed that the situation was lost but seeing the British withdrawal, immediately reinforced his defenders. When the British resumed their attack on 27 March they failed against the bolstered defences and suffered 4,000 casualties, compared with 2,400 Turkish defenders.

On 17 April Murray initiated a second offensive against Gaza (Second Battle of Gaza) with three British divisions of the EEF supported by eight Mark I tanks and 4,000 gas shells. Murray, having signalled his intentions during the first battle, was now up against defences that had been significantly strengthened by von Kressenstein in the intervening period. The British suffered 6,500 casualties compared with approximately 2,000 Turkish casualties. After the battle, the British were left demoralised by the failure.[7] The Turks then strengthened their defences along the Gaza-Beersheba line in the expectation of a third offensive although, due to shortages, these defences lacked extensive barbed wire entanglements.

Despite these failures, the British still maintained pressure on the Turkish defences using raids and the tactic favoured on the Western Front, the Chinese Attack. Morrison in his account of the Highland Light Infantry described one such attack.[8] On 11 June 1917, in support of a raid by the 5th Battalion, King's Own Scottish Borderers against Belah Post, the 5th Battalion, Highland Light Infantry set up dummy soldiers about 300 yards from the Turkish lines, half way across No-Man's-Land. The dummies were raised and lowered from the shelter of a nullah (a dry river bed) and the 'attack' was supported by rifle fire. For the first hour the Turks remained inert but then opened up with continuous fire for the next 50 minutes and advanced to capture the dummies. These types of tactics, together with the raids, created the impression that the British were 'feeling out' the defences in preparation for another attack. The Turkish defences around Gaza would remain constantly alert. A contemporary observer noted that during the previous six months 'the Turk … had spared no effort to make his line impregnable.'[9]

On the left of the British line, the nearest Turkish trenches were 800 yards away while on their right flank, they were over ten miles away. The distance between the front lines was dictated by the topography and the availability of water. Whereas this great distance presented difficulties for assessing the readiness of the Turkish defences, it would be turned to an advantage by Allenby in the instigation of his deception plan. The Turks during this period performed a series of proactive intelligence gathering exercises looking for the ominous signs of a growing British presence as the prelude to a third, and inevitable, attack.

On 28 June, Murray was replaced by Allenby, fresh from command of the British Third Army on the Western Front. Both the British and the Turks understood the strategic importance of Gaza, the gateway to Jerusalem with its benign coastal climate, readily available supplies of fresh water and the possibility of direct naval support from the Mediterranean. Both sides knew that the British had to attempt a third attack to capture Gaza, but Allenby knew that as the British had already suffered over 10,000 casualties, a third failure could be politically as well as militarily disastrous. Bluett in his 1919 summary concluded that after the second battle the Turks had considerably strengthened their defences, which were 'absolutely up-to-date in every respect [and that from Gaza to Sheria was] one continuous tangle of wire'.[10] The only real opening in the Turkish line was at Beersheba where the Turks were relying on 'exceptionally difficult country' as a major element of their defences.

On his arrival in Palestine and after assessing the situation, Allenby was presented with a plan devised by Lieutenant-General Sir Philip Chetwode (Second-in-Command EEF and GOC, XX Corps) to change the point of attack to Beersheba, 30 miles to the south-east, and encircle Gaza, rather than attack it frontally. Allenby recognised the merits of this plan for unlocking the Gaza defences, which were designed to resist attacks coming from the south-west rather than the south-east. There were significant inherent risks with the plan, primarily concerning the supply of water for troops, horses and camels. There were plentiful sources of fresh water on the Gaza coastal plain but inland Beersheba relied on wells that were easily defended and were susceptible to sabotage, which could inflict losses on the British Army greater than those caused by bullet and shell. Despite these problems, and conscious of the previous two failed attempts, Allenby accepted the plan, although Brigadier-General Guy Dawnay suggested that whereas the fight should still be at Beersheba, the Turks should be convinced that Gaza remained the primary target for a direct assault. Dawnay's plan called for the concealment of the movement of troops eastwards whilst maintaining an apparently growing presence in front of Gaza. Intelligence Officer Major Richard Meinertzhagen persuaded Dawnay that the deception, rather than 'passively' hiding military concentrations, should be 'actively' extended to generate false intelligence. This more complicated plan, which would disguise the point and time of the attack, was accepted by Allenby.

The deception plan would involve real attack preparations being disguised as feint attack preparations and vice versa. From the Turkish perspective, it should look like a frontal attack on Gaza with a feint attack against Beersheba. This plan was plausible and predictable. Falls made the point that the Turks were convinced that Gaza was the sole focus of Allenby's intentions.[11] Allenby appointed Meinertzhagen to develop the details, and it was he who famously conjured up what became known as 'the Haversack Ruse'.

Meinertzhagen was a colourful character who was dismissed from the Army in 1926 for insubordination and whose reputation for honesty and integrity suffered badly after his death in 1967, which called into doubt his claims regarding the ruse. Interestingly, Falls, whilst acknowledging the substance of 'the Haversack Ruse' – the term was coined later – does not refer to Meinertzhagen by name. References in a footnote suggested that the intelligence officer involved requested to remain anonymous! It is difficult to get to the truth of this quixotic character; his *Middle East Diary* for example, includes exaggerated claims regarding his experiences with Lawrence of Arabia.

Although there were doubts regarding Meinertzhagen's authorship of the Haversack Ruse, we can assume he was the originator for convenience, as the substance of the ruse and its effect on the Turks is more interesting than establishing the identity of its creator. Meinertzhagen was no stranger to deception. Allegedly he had previously perpetrated a significant deception when, using a broken German cipher, he ordered a Zeppelin flying from Berlin with supplies to the beleaguered German East Africa forces to return to Germany. The Zeppelin had already reached the North African coast when Meinertzhagen at the British Intercepting Station in Egypt ordered its return.[12] There is no doubt that Meinertzhagen was a complex character. T. E. Lawrence decided that he 'took ... pleasure in deceiving his enemy (or his friend) by some unscrupulous jest'.[13]

The deception plan was arguably the most complex of the war with several integrated threads that combined to satisfy the criteria of plausibility, consistency and predictability. There was the disinformation thread, which focused on the 'Haversack' and subsequent messages and the thread related to EEF troop movements and activities.

Meinertzhagen's first act was to have the head of Turkish espionage, a man able to derail his plans, removed by fabricating evidence of duplicity. Meinertzhagen 'entrusted' a known double agent to deliver a letter of thanks containing money to the head of Turkish espionage. The agent delivered the letter to Turkish intelligence and the spymaster was shot before he was able to prove his innocence.[14] Meinertzhagen now considered that the way was clear to enact the ruse.

Although the general rule of deception was not to present the enemy with a gift of intelligence as this would only arouse suspicions regarding its authenticity, there were occasions, if the situation was managed properly, when intelligence could be 'planted' on the enemy as the result of an apparent error or misjudgement. It was through this means that Meinertzhagen arranged to have a haversack 'delivered' to the Turks. After two colleagues had failed, he undertook the task himself. The plan was feasible because No-Man's-Land was not the same physically imposing barrier as it was on the Western Front. On 10 October, Meinertzhagen and a scout rode out into the desert until confronted by a Turkish patrol. They immediately fled under fire and, apparently wounded, Meinertzhagen dropped a blood-stained (horse's blood) haversack that contained a raft of private and military documents. Within the haversack were personal effects, which included a £20 note, a pair of binoculars and a letter from his 'wife', written by Meinertzhagen's sister Mary, announcing the birth of their baby boy. These were mixed in with a private letter relating to the postponement of the attack on Gaza, backed up by a copy of an agenda from the GHQ meeting confirming the postponement. There was a copy of a British intelligence report that supported an attack against Gaza as there were topographical obstacles around Beersheba, relating to water, transport and supply, which would pose serious problems for an enveloping attack there. There were GHQ instructions for the preparations for an attack on Gaza. A telegram indicated that the GHQ staff was going on patrol to El Girheir, south-east of Gaza to understand the Turkish defences. There were several letters from officers stationed around Beersheba that supported the conclusions of the intelligence report that an attack on Beersheba would be a mistake. Perhaps the most important document in the haversack was a set of notes on an old, redundant cipher, which, together with previous minor security breaches in routine radio traffic, were sufficient to enable the German analysts to break the code.[15, 16]

Once back behind the lines, Meinertzhagen contacted the Desert Mounted Corps (DMC) and informed them of the serious loss and pleaded with them to send out patrols immediately. This they did, as well as sending an angry wireless message to Allenby imploring him not to use such inexperienced officers for reconnaissance, pointing out that Meinertzhagen had seriously compromised the operation.[17] They demanded an immediate court-martial. Meinertzhagen received a message ordering him to report to GHQ for a court of inquiry but it confirmed that he would be returned to duty in time for the attack on 19 November. Instructions were transmitted, in the compromised code, to all brigades and battalions to retrieve the haversack. The units duly sent out patrols into the desert. This certainly put the soldiers at risk, but it leant verisimilitude to the ruse. The need-to-know-principle left the troops in ignorance of the true nature of the haversack. Two captured prisoners actually told the 'truth' about the loss of the haversack.[18] A specially briefed officer wrapped his sandwiches in a copy of the order indicating that the haversack should be returned immediately to GHQ and threw it away whilst on patrol. There was a danger that the British were spoonfeeding too much intelligence to the Turks, although with the vastness and irregular nature of No-Man's-Land this was justified as it was unlikely that *all* parts of the ruse were picked up by the Turks. As there was consistency in its entirety, all of the parts were pieces of the same jigsaw, which should lead the enemy to the same erroneous conclusion.

An attempt was made by the Allies to convince the Turks that as the two previous direct frontal assaults on Gaza had failed, they would try and bypass the coastal strip by an amphibious landing farther north, which would threaten to cut off the Turkish lines of communication with their homeland. Fake amphibious landings were a favourite of the British, suggested on numerous occasions to support Western Front operations. To corroborate the rumours, the British created dummy camps on Cyprus for a landing in Syria at the Gulf of Iskanderon, at Alexandretta, a favoured strategic target for Kitchener, about 400 miles north of Gaza.[19] At the dummy camps, troops were marched around, false wireless traffic was generated, local contractors were contacted about the provision of supplies and docks and wharves were labelled for embarkation. The Turks were unimpressed as aerial reconnaissance showed that the preparations were false. Although this ruse was unsuccessful, it did not compromise the main deception plan as there was no connection between the amphibious landings and Beersheba. The failure of this ruse probably actually enhanced the credibility of the deception plan as it reinforced the notion that Gaza would be the target of the main attack. Considering the consistent success that the Allies had both on the Western Front and south of the Gaza-Beersheba line in terms of *Creation*, this raises the question of whether the exposure of the preparations in Cyprus as fake was a deliberate ploy by the British, a double bluff.

The Commander-in-Chief of the Desert Mounted Corps (DMC) and his staff were invited by GHQ to a race meeting in Cairo on 14 November. Cairo was covered in posters announcing the meeting and the Egyptian Gazette published the race card. Colourful marquees were erected on the racecourse. It appeared that the DMC, a vital unit in any desert attack, was concerned with gambling on nags rather than gambling on its ability to close in on the Turks without sustaining serious casualties! As a final twist, Meinertzhagen, knowing the Turkish penchant for cigarettes, had 120,000 of them manufactured containing opium, which were dropped by the RFC over enemy lines at Beersheba.[20]

The contents of the haversack had created an illusion regarding the point of attack; the compromised code now gave the British the opportunity to mislead the Turks regarding the time. They transmitted a series of messages to their front line units that suggested the major offensive was scheduled for mid-November. These messages reinforced previous indicators – the order for Meinertzhagen to appear before the military tribunal, a message that indicated Allenby was on leave and would not return until 7 November, and the race meeting, scheduled in Egypt for 14 November. The use of as many channels as possible to convey a message was another key principle of deception plans, provided that the intelligence conveyed disparate information that would have to be assembled to reach a conclusion. Real messages indicating that Beersheba would be attacked on 31 October were transmitted to all the relevant units using secure codes. The concealment of the time of the attack would prove critical to the success of the offensive plans and the capture of Gaza.

The key to the deception and a vital element of the actual attack was the provision of water and securing of the water sources. Gaza on the coastal plain had sufficient water to support an army and on this basis alone, logistically and strategically it was a wholly sensible aim to capture it. Beersheba had sufficient water but the sources were seventeen wells that had been mined by the Turks. Logistically, or even on the basis of common sense, an attack on Beersheba was high risk in the extreme and Allenby's recognition of this dictated the details of the deception plan. Over the past 90 years it has been argued by some that Allenby's success was all down to luck. As with any plan, there was of course an element of luck – but the deception activities removed some elements of chance, which is exactly what they were designed to do.

On the coastal strip, the EEF was camped between Rafah and Dier el Belah and between Abasan el Kabir and Gamli. Allenby now instigated the deception plan to conceal the movement of some of the troops and artillery to Beersheba 30 miles away.[21] At the same time, he had to make it appear that the troop numbers in these camps in front of Gaza were increasing.

The real attack against Beersheba had to look like a feint. This meant that the Turks must not notice the movement of large numbers of troops but they had to be given a glimpse of some redeployments, through a planned lapse in security, to create the impression of minor movements consistent with a feint. Concurrently, the illusion had to be created that a large bodies of troops and artillery were building up in front of Gaza, which had to be achieved with fewer and fewer men. Both elements would have satisfied Magruder's Principle as von Kressenstein believed, perfectly reasonably, that the British had to attack Gaza and that any movement against Beersheba would have been too high risk.

On 27 October, before any large British troop movements took place, the Turks attacked El Gerheir. The attack was repulsed but it appeared that the Turks were testing the defences, possibly in response to their reference in the captured haversack. As the front settled down, the troops of the XX Corps consisting of the 10th (Irish), 53rd (Welsh), 60th (2/2nd London) and 74th (Yeomanry) Divisions, together with four brigades of heavy artillery and the DMC (the Imperial Camel Corps Brigade, the Australian and

New Zealand Mounted Division, the Australian Mounted Division), were moved in secret at night towards Beersheba. Prior to this, on 21 October, two brigades of Engineers had moved to Esani to improve the water supplies, while the Camel Brigade moved to Abu Ghalyun, south-east of Esani and then on 22 October to Khelasa to fix wells that had been blown up by the Turks. With the water supplies secured, the major moves from Amr and El Fukhari towards Esani, sixteen miles away, took place between 24 and 28 October with further transfers on the following nights to Khalassa (Khelasa) and final destinations.[22] Great clouds of dust hung over the plain over ten miles in length, in the middle of which were 'thousands of half-suffocated men and horses'. All movement ceased before dawn, as the troops were ordered to 'disappear into the desert' and the dust settled down.[23] During the day the troops and their animals hid, camouflaged in wadis. Any soldiers caught in the open by an approaching enemy plane immediately threw themselves face down in the dust and remained motionless until the danger had passed. Aggressive patrolling by the RFC helped, although one German aircraft managed to photograph the troop concentrations. It was brought down near Khelasa before being able to return to base. The 20th Machine Gun Squadron (GOC, Lieutenant D. Marshall) reported that they were subjected to enemy aircraft bombing at the the camp at Esani.

There were already prepared camps scattered throughout the desert, the locations of which were well known to the Turks. These camps were used to cover the 'gap' in the front lines between Gaza and Beersheba. This gap meant that No-Man's-Land was ill-defined and wide but was too inhospitable for significant attacks. In the desert, water supplies were the key to defences. These camps became the basis for the migration. As one unit moved out another would move in, so that the camps appeared to have steady populations, with any excess formations hidden in the camouflaged areas.

In general the troops would arrive at one of the water stations during the night, remain hidden for one day before moving on the following night to their next destination. An exception was the New Zealand Brigade, which remained at Esani for four days before moving to Asluj on 29 October. Although there is no evidence, it could be that these troops were left in position to ensure that they would be noticed to alert the Turks to the eastward movements.[24] Throughout the region Bedouin Arabs, agents of the Turks, reported the presence of the troops but the Turks concluded that this was still consistent with a feint towards Beersheba. It was questionable whether the Arab agents were able to distinguish between the different units. The *absence* of troops in the region would have raised suspicions amongst the Turkish command. The deception plan resulted in 28,000 mounted men being in place in front of Beersheba ready for the attack.

The movement of the British troops eastwards from their various places of encampment meant that they all passed through Esani, location of the only undefended water supply between Gaza and Beersheba, close to the Gaza-Beersheba line. The other sources at Sheria and Hareira, as well as Beersheba itself, were defended by the Turks.[25] There were other reliable sources of water farther south at Khalasa and Abu Ghalyun that had been reconnoitred before the eastward transfer of troops.[26] The water supply at Esani was used by both British and Turkish patrols to water their horses – although not at the same time![27] The sharing of the water supply at Esani exemplified the nebulous character of No-Man's-Land compared with the Western Front, which permitted Meinertzhagen to 'plant' intelligence on the Turks. The presence of soldiers at Esani was not unusual and the British troops moving eastwards would have been spotted by the Turks at this point. They did become alarmed at the large numbers of British troops but still interpreted their presence as the precursor of a feint attack against Beersheba, although for safety they strengthened their defences on their left flank to secure Gaza. Esani was not only a water source, but it was also one of the few crossing points of the lower Wadi Ghazze, which was characterised along its western reaches by precipitous cliffs. For this reason, the Turks judiciously strengthened their flank opposite Esani in case the British were planning a crossing to outflank the Gaza defences. The pursuit of additional intelligence by von Kressenstein would have revealed that the troops transferred were too numerous for a mere feint attack. Von Kressenstein selectively analysed only the intelligence that supported his belief that Gaza was the direct, main target.

In the previous April, Sir Archibald Murray had built a railway line northwards towards Gaza for the rapid movement of troops from the camps on the coastal strip. Allenby now had another rail line built in September from the camps to Wadi Ghazze, which reinforced the threat against Gaza and possibility of outflanking the defences. See Map 14.

On 27 October 1917 The Royal Navy and the artillery around Gaza all ranged their guns on the Turkish defences in preparation for a joint bombardment. At the same time in front of Gaza, troops of 52nd (Lowland) (GOC, Major-General J. Hill), 54th (East Anglian) (GOC, Major-General S.W. Hare) and 75th (GOC, Major-General P.C. Palin) Divisions from XXI Corps

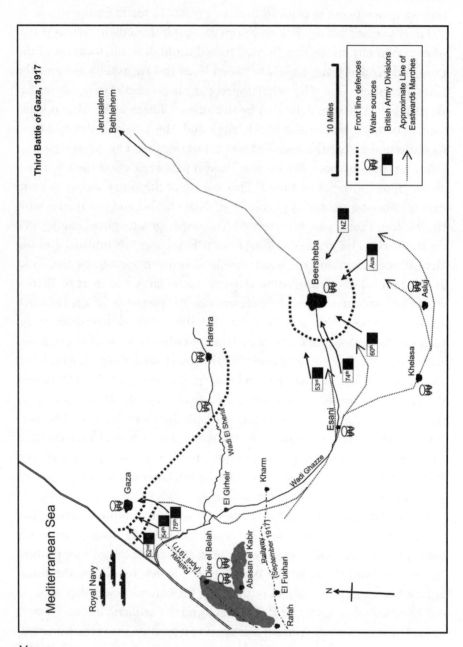

Map 14

(GOC, Lieutenant-General E.S. Bulfin) began the usual preparations for an assault. 30 miles away, by the morning of 31 October, the Australian Light Horse had moved into position five miles north of Beersheba, while the New Zealand Mounted Rifles were east of Beersheba across the Hebron Road, the New Zealand Machine Gun Corps had moved from Asluj to south of Beersheba and the 20th Machine Gun Squadron were now stationed at El Semin, seven miles south of Beersheba.[28] The remaining attacking units from the 53rd (Welsh), 74th (Yeomanry) and 60th (2/2nd London) Divisions were in position west of the town. Their original camps near Gaza were maintained to create the illusion that they were still fully populated. All the tents remained standing while the remaining troops lit large number of fires at night. Throughout the levels of frantic wireless communications emanating from this region were kept up at a high volume. As always the RAF maintained control of the skies so that Turkish aerial reconnaissance could not compromise the plan. Despite the large troop movements eastwards and their 'detection' by the Turks, they only expected a feint attack against Beersheba by a single infantry division and one mounted division.[29]

The British had concealed the point of the attack and the units involved. These were two of the aims of most deception plans but the third, which has often been ignored in post-war analysis of the action – the concealment of the time of the attack – was to have a profound effect on the success of the operation as a whole at Beersheba and even more so at Gaza.

The real operation was planned for 31 October but the deception plan as we have seen indicated through numerous channels that the attack would be towards mid-November, the most likely date being 14 November. As on the Western Front, the state of alertness of defences was commensurate with the threat they perceived. This threat was a combination of the build-up of the attacking forces and intelligence concerning the date of the expected offensive operation. If the enemy was deceived about either of these, then the defences were relaxed, as a high state of alert could not be maintained for prolonged periods. The Turks responded exactly as the deception plan intended. They redeployed their forces from Beersheba to Gaza to strengthen the defences and significantly this transfer took place in a leisurely fashion. This lack of sense of urgency extended to the Turkish attitude to their aerial support. 50 aircraft, packed in crates, were transported by rail to Gaza; because the Turks thought that they had sufficient time, the planes were still in those crates when the EEF attacked and were either destroyed by fire or captured intact.[30]

The attack on Beersheba on 31 October at 05:55 captured the town and crucially captured its water supply intact. The wells in Beersheba were captured undamaged partly because of the rapid advance of the troops, in particular the Australian Light Cavalry, but was also in part because the Turkish officer in charge of blowing the wells was away on leave. This has to be the result of concealment of the time of the attack. None of the other Turkish officers present took responsibility for the destruction of the wells. But why would they? The Turkish defenders had been informed that, despite evidence to the contrary, this was just a feint which could be dealt with easily. Under these circumstances, why would they blow the charges and destroy the wells as they would need the water for themselves later, after repelling the attack?

The securing of these wells meant that the British Army was in a position to outflank Gaza, although water supplies at Hareira and Sheria would first have to be captured. With the attack coming from the east, the Turkish defences were not best aligned to resist, although it was not until 6 November that the positions were captured. Even with these water sources under British control, the move westwards to outflank Gaza was still hard in the heat and the dust.

On the coast, after the naval and artillery bombardment, units from the 52nd (Lowland), 54th (East Anglian) and 75th Divisions advanced towards Gaza on the night of 1/2 November, suffering 2,500 casualties but gradually pushing the Turks back. With the fall of Hareira and Sheria on their left flank, the Turkish positions in Gaza became untenable as the British threatened encirclement. The Turks withdrew and Gaza fell on 7 November. The Turks retreated towards Jerusalem.

General Kress von Kressenstein had not released reinforcements for Beersheba as he still believed it to be a ruse and that Gaza was the main target. Hence the garrison at Hareira, less than five miles away, made no attempt to counter the 'feint' attack at Beersheba. As the EEF came towards Gaza, it found an order from Colonel Ali Fuad, Officer Commanding XX Turkish Army Corps, which relayed the story of the lost haversack, found by a Turkish NCO who had been suitably rewarded. The order indicated that they had determined the date of the attack and that it was now 'time to crush the arrogant English'. He urged the Turks to learn a lesson from the English error and not to carry any military papers whilst on reconnaissance patrols.[31, 32] The plan had been plausible and predictable as it fitted with von Kressenstein's beliefs regarding British intentions.[33] Allenby simply had to ensure consistency.

The haversack ruse was copied with equal success in the Second World War when the Allies deceived the Germans regarding the landing at Sicily in 1943 with a deception codenamed 'Operation Mincemeat', which substituted the haversack with a dead body ('The Man Who Never Was'). Chained to the body was a briefcase containing documents indicating the attack against Sicily was a feint with the real target being Sardinia. The briefcase also contained personal letters, bank statements (overdrawn), a receipt for an engagement ring, love letters and theatre stubs. (For the full extraordinary story, see *The Man Who Never Was – Operation Heartbreak* by Ewen Montagu and Duff Cooper.)

Battle of Megiddo, 19–26 September 1918[34]

As the war drew to a close, Allenby was still focussed on the defeat of the Turks and the liberation of Palestine. Having broken through at Gaza in the previous year and secured Jerusalem, with two weeks to spare with respect to Lloyd George's directive, the EEF moved northwards. Early in 1918, it was massively weakened by the transfer of 60 of its 90 or so battalions from the 52nd (Lowland) and 74th (Yeomanry) Divisions to the Western Front, in response to the German's Spring Offensives. Additionally, Allenby's entire tank force was sent to the Western Front even though Allenby still had to maintain pressure on the retreating Turks. Until 1919, Palestine was the only theatre outside Europe where tanks were deployed and the ones there were more or less viewed as a reserve for the more important Western Front.

In February 1918, General Erich von Falkenhayn was replaced by General Otto Liman von Sanders, who immediately ordered the retreat to cease and for troops to dig in on a line from the Jordan Valley to the coast. This move changed the whole dynamic of the operation and by summer Allenby had been reinforced by two Indian infantry divisions. A series of camps south of the Turkish positions were constructed on the coastal plain to accommodate them. Of the remainder of the Allied forces, the majority were stationed in the Jordan Valley, 60 miles away. With the Turks holding the Arsuf-Jordan Valley line, Allenby found himself facing something approaching a Western Front-style confrontation. He decided that a deception plan needed to be implemented to weaken enemy defences by affecting troop deployments and state of readiness. T.E. Lawrence suggested that after Gaza, 'deceptions ... became for Allenby a main point of strategy'.[35] Allenby's plan called for the secret redeployment of his own troops in order to create a local superiority in numbers against an ill-prepared Turkish defence. The main attack along the Mediterranean coastal strip would capture the communications centres at El-Afuleh and Beisan to trap the Turkish forces west of the Jordan. To achieve this, the British left flank would have to capture the ancient ruined city of Megiddo, 30 miles from their starting positions and six miles south-east of El-Afuleh. Hence British units would have to be transferred westwards but the camps on the coast would have to appear to have a stable population, while those in the Jordan Valley would have to appear to be growing. This deception would maintain the Turkish dispositions whilst creating a superior British force along the coastal strip. For his plan to succeed, Allenby would need to encourage the regular brigade (GOC, Jaafar Pasha) of the Arab Northern Army, the Sharifian Army[36] and Egyptian Camel Corps commanded by T. E. Lawrence, together with some British units, to maintain pressure on the Turks in the Jordan Valley and beyond. See Map 15.

So the Turks had to be convinced that the threat in the west was weaker than it really was, and that from the east was stronger than it was. The deception was orchestrated by Colonel M.V. Nugent (Head of Intelligence, EEF) and temporary Brigadier-General Archibald Wavell, the future Field Marshal and commander of the British Army forces in the Middle East during the Second World War.[37] The plan was developed and implemented and it was fortuitously aided by Turkish memories of beng duped at Gaza a year earlier. Their resolve not to be caught out again was so great that just prior to the attack, when they were given the details of the deception by an Indian NCO deserter, they refused to believe him on the basis of the 'bona fide' intelligence that they had received![38] For the Turks, the deserter was Megiddo's 'haversack'.

The plan was to generate false intelligence that the camps in the Jordan Valley were gradually increasing while the camps in the coastal plain were losing troops as they moved eastwards to bolster the forces there. It was high risk because if the deception was penetrated it would become apparent to the Turks that the Allies were vulnerable along their eastern flank.

There had been initial preparations in anticipation of the implementation of the plan. The camps in the coastal area had been set up during the summer but had been distributed so that additional troops could move in without attracting undue Turkish attention. Although the camps had been established initially as battalion camps they had only been populated with

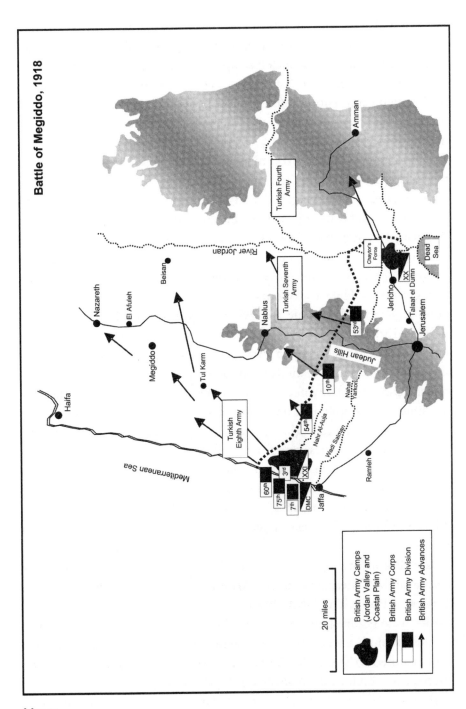

Map 15

half battalions, so that the population of the camps could grow without actual physical expansion. The camps in the coastal plain were classified as either 'open' or 'concealed'. The open camps were those set up during the summer while the concealed camps were new camps required to billet the additional troops that could not be accommodated in the open camps. In the open camps, normal troop movements and activities were allowed provided there was no discernible increase in numbers. The Turks were used to these camps. It was easy with the right level of management and discipline to conceal the extra men and still allow them, at certain times, the freedom of the camp. The additional camps were set secretly in the coastal orange and olive groves and on the shore below the cliffs north of the river Nahr al-Auja where the ground was more open. The 7th (Meerut) Division had previously dug 80 wells for the expected influx of troops. In the concealed camps, all movement and activity was tightly controlled. There was no movement between 04:30 and 18:30, basically daylight hours. The cavalry horses had to be watered, so between 12:00 noon and 14:00 the whole area was aggressively patrolled by the RAF to deter Turkish aircraft. The men cooked on solidified alcohol cookers, rather than the normal open fires. As these camps were completed and subsequently populated, the RAF photographed them to study the camouflage and suggest any necessary improvements.[39] Regardless of the type of camp, new troops could only move in under the cover of darkness. The secret of the camps relied heavily on British air superiority.[40] British aircraft kept Turkish planes away from everything other than that which they were meant to see. The Turks were allowed to see the open camps so that they were reassured by the intelligence gathered.

Stationed in the Jordan Valley were the DMC, the 60th Infantry Division and the 4th Cavalry Division, all of which would have to transfer westwards. The Desert Mounted Corps (GOC, Lieutenant-General Harry Chauvel) consisted of the 4th and 5th Indian Mounted Divisions, the Australian Mounted Division and Armoured Car detachment and the 7th Light Car Patrol. The DMC headquarters was at Talaat el Dumn. These troops were gradually moved out to the camps in the coastal strip north of Jaffa through a series of night marches. A deception plan was initiated which aimed to 'show' the Turks that the camp in the Jordan Valley was growing as a prelude to an attack on the British right.

As the troops moved out of the Jordan Valley, they left behind their tents, which remained standing and old unserviceable tents were added to create the illusion of an increasing force. During the day, West Indian battalions and other troops were marched into the camp and were then transported back to their starting point at night in lorries.[41] This exercise was repeated again the following day and after about four round trips, the troops doubted the sanity of their staff. The EEF followed a strict rule that all troop movements westwards must be made at night, while those apparently going east were to be made during the day.

Extra bivouac fires were lit at night in these camps in the Jordan Valley and during the day mules drew sledges around to create the dust associated with a growing assault force while the appropriate volume of dummy wireless traffic was maintained between the camp and GHQ at Ramleh.[42] As the DMC moved out, on about 5 September, two weeks prior to the attack, the real horses were replaced with 15,000 dummies within the horse lines.[43] Wireless traffic from the DMC HQ at Talaat el Damn continued long after the DMC had left. Agents were also despatched by Lawrence to bargain for large quantities of forage in Amman, which they hinted to the local Arabs was needed for a move into the area by large numbers of British cavalry livestock. To add to the illusion, the British Imperial Camel Corps joined an irregular Arab force in a raid near Amman and scattered tins of corned beef and a variety of documents about as evidence of their presence.

Additionally, rumours were spread of troop concentrations near Jerusalem with new billets being marked out and Fast's Hotel commandeered by GHQ. The hotel, which was a German house before the war, was initially taken over by the British Canteens Board and used as an officers' billet. However, it was suddenly emptied of all other residents and secured with sentries and the rumours began to circulate that the building was to become the advanced HQ of the Commander-in-Chief.[44] With Allenby's headquarters 25 miles from Jerusalem at Ramleh on the road to Jaffa, the acquisition of Fast's Hotel was an unmissable indication that there was a shift in focus towards the east. A race meeting, a deception favourite, was scheduled to take place near Jaffa on 19 September 1918, the date scheduled for zero-day.[45] British newspapers carried reports of this impending race meeting and advertising handbills were circulated throughout the region.

Wavell described his deception as the Gaza plan only in reverse. After the westward movement of the British forces, Allenby's left flank of fifteen miles was occupied by 35,000 infantry, 9,000 cavalry and 383 guns, compared with 8,000 Turkish infantry supported by 130 guns.[46] Over the remainder of the front the British had 22,000 troops, 3,000 cavalry and 157 guns, while the Turks had 24,000 men and 270 guns. The Turks did not respond to the westward troop movements and the attack along the coastal strip by the British XXI Corps (GOC, Lieutenant-General Edward Bulfin), bolstered by the forces from the Jordan Valley, took the Turkish Army by surprise and victory was decisive. Liman von Sanders had deployed his troops inland to meet a threat that was weaker than his intelligence had indicated. An intelligence map captured on 21 September at the Yilderim HQ at Nazareth showed that the Turks believed the DMC was still stationed in the Jordan Valley with their HQ at Talaat el Damn, the 4th Cavalry Division at Jericho, the Australian Mounted Division holding the northern end of the Jordan Valley and the 60th (2/2nd London) Division still east of the Nablus road.[47] On 19 September the Turks still believed that the British troop dispositions were the same as on 4 September.

As the main force attacked along the coastal plain, units from the 10th (Irish) and 53rd (Welsh) Divisions of the XX Corps (GOC, Lieutenant-General Sir Philip Chetwode) launched the subsidiary, but significant, attack along the Nablus road before swinging eastwards to threaten the Turkish Fourth Army. Meanwhile Chaytor's Force (GOC, Major-General Edward Chaytor) consisting of the Anzac Mounted Division, the West Indian Brigade and the Jewish Legion moved towards Amman, reinforcing the threat posed by the Arab Army and Lawrence's irregulars.

With the breakthrough to Megiddo complete, the EEF in the west and the Arab Army and British contingents in the east advanced towards Nazareth and Dera'a and on to Beirut and Damascus. On 30 October 1918, the Ottoman Empire signed an armistice with the Allies and the war in Palestine was over.[48]

9

Deception, GHQ and the Army Commanders

That general is skilful in attack whose opponent does not know what to defend.
Sun Tzu

This book has attempted to show that the First World War generals did try to exhibit the skill Sun Tzu describes. The popular perception has been that they were an unimaginative, arrogant breed with a callous disregard for their men, sending them, largely ill-prepared, in frontal assaults against well armed defenders behind formidable and impenetrable fortifications. This view was not subscribed to in the immediate post-war decade, when despite the publication of anthologies by the war poets, the vast majority of published works supported the pursuit of the war. The contrary view probably began with the publication of David Lloyd-George's *War Memoirs* beginning in 1933, five years after the death of Field Marshal Sir Douglas Haig. This view has been fuelled periodically throughout the intervening years and led to Alan Clark's 'Lions led by Donkeys' charge.[1] However, over the last twenty years research has seriously challenged this notion. There was no doubt that the BEF that left Britain in August 1914 was ill-prepared, more so than French or German forces, for the conflict that was to follow.

The main problem with the BEF, apart from the lack of military technology, was that it was small, but the idea of Britain having a conscripted peacetime army in line with France and Germany was politically unacceptable. It suffered from the lack of a sufficient reserve and a mighty army had to be created from scratch, beginning with Lord Kitchener's proclamation to the British Cabinet on 5 August, one day after war was declared, that a million men would need to take the field for at least three years. With hindsight, this was a serious underestimate even though at the time the popular view was that it was a gross exaggeration and that the war would be 'over by Christmas'. The regular British Army in 1914 consisted of about 247,500 troops scattered across the British Empire to maintain the peace, of which the fully trained professional fighting force that was the BEF comprised about 160,000 men, although only about 100,000 were transported to France at the outbreak. In addition there were about 218,000 reservists and 270,000 members of the Territorial Force. By comparison, the German Army consisted of 700,000 soldiers, which, within a week of the declaration, expanded to 3.8 million men through the mobilisation of previously conscripted reservists, while the French Army had 823,000 regular troops and 2,900,000 reservists who were mobilised within two weeks. The French and German Armies were comparable in terms of numbers of troops and on this basis the BEF would be insignificant!

However what the BEF lacked in quantity it made up for in quality and in the first few weeks demonstrated a fighting capacity in excess of the numbers of troops deployed. But the BEF had to learn the lessons of continental-style, industrial warfare. That meant all aspects of offensive and defensive operations from tactics, weapon systems, all-arms co-operation, logistics and planning. The British Army of 1914 was simply not designed to wage a continental-style war and, unlike France and Germany, had never been engaged in one. The New Armies had to learn how to neutralise enemy defences primarily through artillery firepower, and improving the firepower of the attacking soldiers beyond the culture of the bayonet. In his book examining 1915, Neillands makes the obvious but important point that the nature of the warfare and its scale were unique. As a consequence, the learning curves were steep, complex and without precedent.[2] The British Army travelled along another learning curve as well as that of offensive operations, based on deception. The High Command were not content with the 'standard' military approach of weakening defences through firepower alone, they also sought to weaken them through the less obvious means of deception, something attempted in military conflicts since time immemorial.

From December 1914 Sir John French realised that continuous multiple systems of well defended, well sited trench lines would require novel approaches if they were to be overcome. Neither side possessed sufficient men and materials to attack or defend all along the 450-mile front line. Hence deception was used to create an imbalance between attackers and defenders in specific locations, which meant 'persuading' the Germans to defend sectors distant from the impending attack. It has been estimated that the attackers probably needed three to five times more men that the defenders for success. On those occasions when the Germans went on the offensive, at Verdun 1916 and the Spring Offensives of 1918, they also employed this approach.

The Allies' objectives were simple enough. If the Germans could be convinced through intelligence generated by a variety of deception techniques that a particular sector was under threat of an imminent attack, they would be forced to defend that sector with the appropriate numbers of men and potentially weaken the actual target sector through the transfer of troops; if the Germans could be convinced that a number of different sectors were under threat, even better. If the Allies could then conceal the build-up of troops in the attack sector, this should create an imbalance between the attackers and defenders. Sun Tzu: 'Numerical weakness comes from having to prepare against possible attacks; numerical strength, from compelling our adversary to make these preparations against us.'

Deception alone would never capture an enemy trench. While it might cause a favourable disparity between attackers and defenders, it could never completely denude the trenches of defenders, and as a result the efficiency and aggressiveness of the attack still remained the decisive factor for a successful outcome.

The beginnings of the use of deception can be found as early as December 1915, when Sir John French agreed to a request from Joffre to support a French attack in Champagne with a series of British Corps attacks. These were variously scaled back, in some instances to mere demonstrations but they would still extend the apparent frontage of the attack, while affording the troops a certain level of protection. French ordered that if the opportunity arose, the units were to seize the moment and capture any enemy trenches in front of them. This would ensure that the preparations for the demonstrations were more realistic and more believable to the Germans, as the local British commanders had to take the preparations 'seriously' and be prepared to act on any favourable situation that arose. This type of tactic would become favoured by Haig whenever orders were issued for a demonstration. In December 1914, scaled back operations were ordered simply because of a constraint in men and materials and were not instituted with deception in mind. Though there was one identifiable exception. In the preliminary instructions issued by Lieutenant-General A.J. Murray, Chief of the General Staff on 12 December 1914, he ordered the II and III Corps to attack against defined targets but told the IV Corps simply to carry out local operations 'with a view to containing the enemy now in their front'. Although nowhere near as elaborate as later ruses, this is the earliest example unearthed of deception on the Western Front.

By March 1915 the deception plans had matured considerably and as a result, instead of expecting an attack on a 2,000-yard front near Neuve Chapelle, the Germans seemed to be threatened with multi-unit, multi-sector attacks along a 30-mile front from south of La Bassée to near Ypres.[3] This approach to offensive operations involved French, Haig and Lieutenant-General Sir Henry Rawlinson, as GOC IV Corps, the future commander of the British Fourth Army. The Germans knew that the British did not have sufficient men and materials to target all the 'threatened' sectors, but that did not help them deploy reinforcements and reserves. The defenders became extremely reliant on intelligence gathered by direct observation, aerial reconnaissance, behind-the-lines spies and prisoner interrogation. The British duly targeted these methods and generated false intelligence, which would be gathered and fed into the German OODA Loops. The British Army *concealed* through the use of camouflage, *created* other artefacts, similarly camouflaged, and caused *confusion* in the German decision-making process. Ferris calculated that on the Western Front throughout 1918, if defenders were able to detect operational preparations but were unable to locate reserves, perhaps 10–20 per cent of forces, then they would need to prepare for attacks at *every* point where operational preparations were detected.[4] Ferris concluded that a defender who could locate only 80 per cent of the enemy's divisions was heading for disaster and that if an attacker could double his strength on a ten-mile front for three days, then a breakthrough was possible.

These conclusions had probably already been arrived at by Haig. In his final despatch dated 21 March 1919, Haig indicated that deception was the key to operations because of its potential for misleading the enemy with respect to time, place and units.

... a defensive policy involves the loss of the initiative, with all the consequent disadvantages to the defender. The enemy is able to choose at his own convenience the time and place of his attacks. Not being influenced himself by the threat of attack from his opponent, he can afford to take risks, and by greatly weakening his front in some places can concentrate an overwhelming force elsewhere with which to attack.

The defender, on the other hand, becomes almost entirely ignorant of the dispositions and plans of his opponent, who is thus in a position to effect a surprise. This was clearly exemplified during the fighting of 1918. As long as the enemy was attacking, he obtained fairly full information regarding our dispositions. Captured documents show that, as soon as he was thrown once more on the defensive and the initiative returned to the Allies, he was kept in comparative ignorance of our plans and dispositions. The consequence was that the Allies were able to effect many surprises, both strategic and tactical.

As a further effect of the loss of the initiative and ignorance of his opponent's intentions, the defender finds it difficult to avoid a certain dispersal of his forces. Though for a variety of reasons, including the fact that we had lately been on the offensive, we were by no means entirely ignorant of the enemy's intentions in the spring of 1918, the unavoidable uncertainty resulting from a temporary loss of the initiative did have the effect of preventing a complete concentration of our reserves behind the point of the enemy's attack.[5]

In many respects, Haig in this final despatch was simply reiterating the thoughts of Sun Tzu. But Haig's words were also written to counter any in the government, the population or army who might argue there had been a failure in high command.

At Neuve Chapelle, least than seven months after the start of the war, the British Army command had already understood the limitations posed by No-Man's-Land and had also understood what was needed to turn these limitations into advantages. On 8 March 1915, Brigadier-General H. Butler at Aire issued First Army Operational Order Number 9, on behalf of Haig, which indicated that the attack by the Indian and IV Corps would be supported by simultaneous demonstrations from the Canadian Division from the First Army together with activity by the British Second Army and the French Tenth Army. What the order also contained was the rider that the Canadians must be prepared to take the offensive at any time following the issue of orders directly from First Army Headquarters.[6] To ensure that there were sufficient guns and materials available to the First Army,

Sir John French decided to postpone any action by the Second Army but he instructed that the V Corps, on the left flank, and the II Corps in the centre should conduct minor operations and actions as if a major offensive was about to be launched from the high ground east of Ypres. Further, French ordered that the III Corps, east of Armentières should make an active demonstration towards Pérenchies-Fort Englos, the outer defences of Lille. Although General Sir Hubert Plumer was short of men and materials, as these had been transferred farther south, he still ensured that the V, II and III Corps maintained a credible threat. In his seventh despatch, dated 5 April 1915, to the Secretary of State for War, Sir John French specifically mentioned the efforts of the Second Army, which he insisted were instrumental in tying down the Germans and prevented them transferring reserves south to meet the British First Army. This report and the recognition of these deception activities became public and enemy knowledge when the despatch was published in the London Gazette on 14 April 1915. Haig issued the specific instructions that the attack had to be a surprise to the Germans and that this was to be achieved through the gradual and secret deployment of the guns, unostentatious registration and troop movements at night, amongst other measures.[7] Already through these instructions, Haig and French had both demonstrated that they understood some of the 'finer points' of deceptions plans. They understood, for instance, that they needed to conceal the point of attack by extending the attack front and that all activities needed to be gradual.

The plans of French and Haig were designed to drag the German reserves to other sectors and thereby render them redundant. This immediately established the 'golden rule' of multi-unit, multi-army deception plans regularly practised throughout the remainder of the war.

The First Army attacks throughout the remainder of 1915 followed the same pattern. At Festubert, Lieutenant-General Louis Vaughan, SGSO 2nd Division (S G Staff Officer) issued the specific instruction at 21:30 on 13 May 1915 that the attack at Festubert by the 2nd and Meerut Divisions should come as a surprise and that this was to be achieved through an advance made in complete silence. At Loos, the Commanders of the Armies and GHQ Reserves were informed on 18 September 1915, by Lieutenant-General W.R. Robertson, Chief of the General Staff, GHQ, that in addition to the real attack, there would be subsidiary operations by units of the Second Army and units of the First Army not engaged in the main attack. These actions would also be in conjunction with offensive operations by the French Army towards Douai. By the 19 September, Major-General R. Butler, General Staff, First Army, issued First Army Operation Order No.95 which detailed all of the activities within the First Army area including the main attack and the subsidiary attacks. The Corps commanders, from a quick glimpse at the map, would have understood the significance of the part they were to play.

By December 1914, the British Army had been expanded into the First and Second Armies and regardless of the offensive operation, units from either army not involved would simulate preparations for an attack. This approach was maintained as the Third, Fourth and Fifth Armies were formed. From the initial operations in 1915, British deception plans were supported by units from the French Army, which showed that Joffre had an appreciation of the problem caused by No-Man's-Land and the need to weaken defences through all means possible. The co-operation between the British and the French with regard to deception would continue throughout the entire war: Joffre, Pétain and Foch all appreciated the value of deception.

If we compare the British Army of 1914 with the Army at the end of 1915, we find that deception activities had greatly improved. This period spanned the time during which Sir John French was Commander-in-Chief and hence a great deal of credit should be given to him regarding the use of deception throughout the entire war, even though by January 1916 he was back home commanding the forces on mainland Britain. During 1915, the main uses of deception were practiced by Haig's First Army, but clearly with French's guidance as the plans involved units from the Second Army. However after December 1915, with Haig in charge, the use of deception became standard throughout all of the five armies on the Western Front and with the transfer of generals, spread to other theatres, notably Palestine.

The publication of Lloyd George's *War Memoirs* promoted the notion that the generals within the higher command structure, were un-thinking and incompetent and simply launched attacks in a callous manner against formidable defences. But to launch an attack against a particular sector and instigate demonstrations and feints against geographically distant sectors indicated not only an understanding of the value of deception but also an understanding of the nature of static warfare. A continuous front line without any flanks was unique in military history and would not have been contemplated at any of the pre-war military training establishments.

Yet the generals rapidly appreciated and understood the implications. The generals' appreciation was also seen in the commitment of the precious commodity of men and materials to engage in seemingly – on the need-to-know principle – futile ventures. Troops engaged in feint attacks and demonstrations must have taken a dim view of their commanders as their world would have been limited at most to a few miles of trench and that there would have been no appreciation of actions potentially 100 miles away.

The initial instructions issued at the inception of each major engagement invariably included the phrase 'must come as a complete surprise to the enemy', appearing routinely in the instructions sent from GHQ and from the individual army commanders. The attainment of surprise became the main objective of the deception plan that was always a subset of the operational plan. At a conference held at the Château de Bombon on 24 July 1918, when the assumption was still that the war could not be won until 1919, General Foch, the Supreme Commander of the Allied Armies, stated that the future offensives 'must at all costs achieve surprises [as] recent fighting has shown this to be an indispensable condition of success.'[8]

This was further emphasised on 5 August 1918 by Lieutenant-General Herbert Lawrence, Chief of the General Staff GHQ, in a memorandum issued to all five armies, the Cavalry Corps, the RAF and the Tank Corps. Lawrence, speaking on behalf of Haig, stated that to ensure that the surprise element was present in the 1919 operations, 'the resources for misleading the enemy should be developed now.' Lawrence stated that the way to do this was through camouflage, false wireless transmissions and the dissemination of false information. Lawrence made the point that the targets for the false information were 'our own troops and enemy agents' alike.[9] This was best exemplified at Gaza in 1917 when the Desert Mounted Corps and other units searching for the haversack were not only ignorant of Meinertzhagen's scheme but were actively targeted by the plan so that their sense of genuine outrage would be picked up through Turkish surveillance. With of course Allenby's connivance, Meinertzhagen visited the DMC headquarters after dropping the haversack, sure in the knowledge that the normal rumours, which would spread, would be gathered by the Turkish intelligence organisations. As previously established, it was a dangerous game to overtly feed information into the enemy's OODA Loops, but rumour and gossip were an excellent way of doing this provided that the high command were privy to the ruse and that the rumour was carefully managed. This approach was not confined to Palestine. On the Western Front, it was used at Arras in 1917 in support of the Cambrai offensive. The persistent rumours of amphibious landings on the North Sea coast probably caused as much confusion amongst the Allies as they did amongst the Germans. The practice of leaving front line troops holding a quiet sector in ignorance of the massive build-up behind them of men and materials for an attack, only moving these troops out at the last possible opportunity, was the most utilised example of need-to-know.

Lloyd George considered Haig to lack 'any of the elements of imagination and vision'.[10]

> The Germans were accustomed to the heavy-footed and clattering movements of Joffre and Haig – the long laborious and noisy preparations, whose rumble you could hear for leagues with a favourable wind. They knew that not a shot would be fired until the last shell had been pinnacled in the last dump, and the last duckboard had been nailed in the last line of approach. That always meant that ... the Germans had ample warning and time to make their counter preparations.'[11]

Neither of these criticisms are defensible. The contemptuous reference to 'long laborious and noisy preparations' ignores the deception activities that invariably surrounded the preparations for an offensive.

The issue of noise was always a concern. At Cambrai, the 'Notes on Infantry and Tank Operations' issued by the Third Army on 30 October 1917, made the specific point that tank engines could be heard up to 400 yards away, which was why tanks were moved up with their engines on idle and, for insurance, with their tank commanders walking in front of them. This was a reminder to all commanders that tanks should not be brought nearer than 400 yards to the enemy's front line, codified in the training manual SS135 (published December 1916). The 'noisy preparations' Lloyd George complains of did not prevent 500 tanks concentrating in front of Cambrai undetected although some of the credit for this has to be given to the deception plan instigated by Byng. The noises of tanks and, as a consequence, tanks themselves were often reported from sectors distant from the actual attack sector. The attacking tanks were shrouded in silence while those farther afield were fired up. At Arras in 1917, six 'noisy' tanks were used to simulate the build-up of a large attacking tank force which was entirely believed by the Germans, judging from the number of artillery shells expended to destroy it.

With regard to the 'long laborious' preparations, attacking formations could be moved under darkness in the night prior to the attack. The main build-up of troops and materials was in the back area, which was generally not accessible to enemy aircraft owing to the activities of the RFC/RAF. This area was accessible to spies, although aggressive security limited the intelligence gathered. As early at Neuve Chapelle, Haig as First Army commander had assembled the attacking formations six miles behind the lines and had brought them up at night prior to the attack. The issue of instructions for preparations to begin and the subsequent build-up men and materials in the forward zone were not necessarily related events. As became the custom, the activity in the forward zone often consisted of the creation of camouflaged positions with the main concentration of troops and tanks in the back areas, with no forward movement until the night before the attack. The additional artillery generally moved in to their pre-prepared positions at night and in strict silence and remained in this state once the method of silent registration had been perfected.

The notion that the Germans had 'ample warning' is not true. The biggest perceived disaster of the war from a British perspective was undoubtedly the first day of the Battle of the Somme. But the deception plan, as shown in Maps 5 and 6, was a tremendous example of inter-Army co-operation across 100 miles of front. It was clear throughout that, save for the last ten days, the German Army commanders, Crown Prince Rupprecht, von Below and Albrecht were each persuaded that they were the Allies' prime target. Even after 1 July, Falkenhayn kept the strategic reserve behind the German Sixth Army as he remained convinced that Rawlinson's Fourth Army attack was merely a feint to attract reinforcements. It was not until 4 July that Falkenhayn ordered troops to be sent from the Sixth Army sector to support his Second Army. The failure of the British Army on 1 July cannot be attributed to the fact that the Germans were given 'ample warning'.

Did Haig's sternest critic, Lloyd George, realise that an offensive on the Western Front was not simply the build-up and attack of British forces in the targeted sector? Although Haig had mentioned deception-type activities in his second (29 December 1916), fourth (25 January 1917), fifth (20 February 1918) and eighth, and final (21 March 1919), despatches it seems doubtful whether Lloyd George understood the significance in view of his comments in his *War Memoirs*. He accused Haig of 'continually attacking where the enemy was strongest [whilst] the weakest parts of the enemy's ramparts were neglected.'[12] Lloyd George either failed utterly to appreciate the application of deception or Haig failed to explain it to him.

Lloyd George stated that Haig failed to take preventative steps in January 1918 when it was obvious that the Germans were targeting the Third and Fifth Armies.[13] Bean, the Australian Official Historian, considered that the German deception plan associated with the Spring Offensives completely deceived Haig and Pétain with respect to the point of attack. Both cannot be right. The truth probably lies somewhere in between as Haig became half-convinced that the Germans would target the Third and Fifth Armies at the conjunction with the French but was ever mindful of the threat that was building up against his Second Army. In reality, the Germans targeted all these armies but with offset timings. This type of approach required a real investment in men and materials and was a gamble since if the attack could be held, as all available men and materials had been committed, the attackers were vulnerable to a possibly war-winning counterattack. A deception plan to conceal the time and place of attack should not involve the commitment of men and materials to the same degree as a real attack.

The British generals understood this, continually investing in demonstrations and feint attacks. The Germans generally failed to grasp the true significance of this principle, which could also be seen in their deception plan to support the Battle of Verdun in 1916. In the latter half of 1918, it would have been easy for Haig, Pétain and Foch to have made the same mistake. The British Army's advances from August 1918 until the end of the war were a balanced mixture of real and fake attacks with multi-sector, multi-unit and local deceptions but with a strategic aim. The left flank of the First Army and subsequently the Fifth Army maintained an implied threat against Douai and Lille. This prevented the Germans transferring troops north against the British Second Army and south against the British First, Third and Fourth Armies.

All of Haig's Army Commanders on the Western Front were fully conversant with deception plans. On the Western Front, Generals Sir Julian Byng at Cambrai (1917) and Sir Henry Rawlinson at Amiens (1918) had arguably the most notable successes. But there were fine contributions from General Sir Henry Horne at the Scarpe and Canal du Nord (1918) while Plumer at Hooge in 1915 as well as at The Bluff and Mount Sorrel in 1916, used deception to great effect under difficult circumstances. However, perhaps the best example of the use of deception came from other theatres, as we have seen, notably from Generals Sir Charles Monro and William Birdwood for the extraction of the MEF from the Gallipoli peninsula in 1915 and from General Sir Edmund Allenby for his exploits in Palestine in 1917 and 1918.

Allenby had recognised the merits of deception by the time that he became commander of the Third Army in November 1915 on the Western Front. At the Third Army School, originally set up by Monro, the previous army commander, which became the model for the other army schools, Allenby encouraged the attending officers to share their experiences of the implementation of ruses so that there would a consistency, at least across all Third Army units. On his arrival in Palestine as EEF commander, it was not surprising that Allenby, already a convert to deception, was easily persuaded by Chetwode, Dawnay and Meinertzhagen to implement a deception plan to crack the problem that was Gaza.

Although the deception template was a notional concept rather than a physical document, either through practice or shared experiences, maybe at army schools, the 'template' was applied wherever the British Army pre- pared for the offensive. At the initial planning meetings for every offensive, objectives were set, outline artillery fire programmes and infantry assaults were discussed. Corps, divisional and brigade instructions explicitly ref- erenced 'secret' and 'surprise'. Charles Bean, the Official Historian of the Australian Imperial Force, thought that Haig was convinced that complete surprise was the key to any offensive operation by the end of 1917.[14] Haig had arrived at this conclusion a lot earlier.

Throughout the First World War, on the vast majority of occasions, British generals did not advertise their offensive preparations and tried to divert German attention to other sectors of the front. There were constraints in men and materials that had a deleterious effect on the plau- sibility, consistency and predictability of this effort and the close proximity and observational advantages of the Germans made implementation dif- ficult. However, the generals understood what they were trying to achieve.

10

The Effectiveness of Deception

All warfare is based on deception.
Sun Tzu

With the establishment of a flankless trench system on the Western Front, the Allies quickly surmised that any build-up of troops, ordnance and materials for an attack would be instantly recognised by the Germans. They would then concentrate their artillery registered on No-Man's-Land, Allied gun emplacements and troop concentrations. It would allow them to bolster their front line troops and create a local reinforcement for the counterattack if needed. Faced with these inevitabilities and certain failure, the Allies had three options. They could either destroy or neutralise the built-up German defences in the attack sector through a prolonged artillery programme; they could convince the Germans through deception that the attack was elsewhere and prevent the build-up in the first place; or they could combine both approaches. In all the major operations throughout the war the Allies chose the latter.

This was not simply a matter of the concealment of real preparations whilst openly making false preparations; that would have alerted the enemy. To be credible, both the real and false preparations would need to be concealed, the real deception trick being to ensure that there was a subtle difference ensuring that the false intelligence was more believable. If this was not achievable then the aim was simply to swamp the enemy with so much intelligence that it was difficult for him to quickly separate real and false. Artillery programmes would have to be developed and implemented at all targeted sectors and not just those where the real attack was planned. Hence for effective deception plans, there was a considerable investment in men and materials although in the phony sectors the real investment was offset by the use of fake artefacts. Regardless, all preparations had to appear consistent especially as they would be subjected to direct enemy observation across No–Man's–Land, to aerial observation and information gathered by spies operating behind the Allied lines. Although battle zones could be 'sealed off' to preclude the entry of unauthorised personnel, spies could gather vital intelligence simply by visiting the estaminets frequented by soldiers fresh out of the battle zone. Hence the warnings frequently issued against gossip and the use of the need–to–know principle.

There have been a number of books and studies which have looked at various aspects of deception but perhaps the most comprehensive review, as mentioned earlier, came from the United States Army. Produced during the last twenty years, this document is now declassified. The Military Intelligence branch of the United States Army produced an analysis of deception activities since the First World War and arrived at a number of criteria which needed to be satisfied to develop effective deception plans.[1]

The US Army study concluded that the primary aims of deception plans were to hide troop and weapon redeployments in readiness for an attack through distraction, overloading the enemy's intelligence apparatus, creating illusions of strength and weakness and conditioning the enemy to particular behaviour patterns. Their conclusions were derived mainly from the Second World War and later conflicts, but it is evident that Field Marshals Sir John French and Sir Douglas Haig and their respective army commanders would have wholeheartedly concurred with these findings.

The study concluded that deception plans should confuse the enemy's intelligence organisation with respect to size (strength), activity, location, unit, time and equipment: SALUTE. From Neuve Chapelle through to Hooge and Loos, French and Haig implemented a series of deception plans and ordered demonstrations and feint attacks along distant sectors of the front which satisfied the criteria related to size, activity, location and unit. It mattered little that the Germans had estimated British strength and knew that they could not amount attacks along the entire front which the British were posturing along. To mask the time (T) of the attack, French and Haig typically employed variations in the artillery fire programmes assisted by infantry demonstrations to create the impression that every artillery bombardment was the prelude to an imminent infantry attack. Amidst the noise, smoke, HE and shrapnel, the infantry readied themselves and went through all the last activities prior to the attack. Bayonets were fixed, whistles blew, troops cheered, rifles were fired to provide rapid support cover and cut-out silhouettes were shown above the parapet, but throughout the troops remained within the comparative safety of their trenches. This activity repeated over a period of days left the enemy conditioned to ignore the charade and hopefully 'paralysed' when the real attack came. These actions were repeated along the line of the apparent attacks. Finally, the equipment (E); every effort was make to conceal artillery positions and tank build-ups on the attack front but slightly less effort was made to conceal the build-up of dummy installations, especially tanks, in the sectors targeted by the deception plan. French and latterly Haig and of course the army commanders at the time, did not understand the SALUTE concept despite the fact that they were following it to the letter. By following SALUTE, albeit unknowingly, French and Haig and their generals distracted the enemy's focus, overloaded his intelligence gathering activities and created strength and weakness in all the wrong places from the enemy's perspective.

The US Army's assessment examined how SALUTE and the other aims could be achieved. It concluded that effective deception plans needed to obey a number of maxims or principles, arguably the most important of which was Magruder's Principle: that deception plans should aim to 'maintain a pre-existing belief rather than present notional evidence to change that belief.' Throughout the war this was probably the most utilised maxim and there were numerous examples of its use by the British including targeting Liman von Sanders at Gallipoli (1915), Erich von Falkenhayn on the Somme (1916) and Kress von Kressenstein at Gaza (1917).

The second maxim known as *Susceptibility to Conditioning* reasoned that the enemy was unable to detect small changes over a period of time even if the final change was massive. This maxim was at the heart of GHQ and army commanders' instructions to assemble the additional artillery required for an offensive in a gradual manner, usually under the cover of darkness into concealed positions. Interestingly this maxim did not extend to tanks as even the presence of a small number would cause panic within the enemy ranks and would be interpreted as the sign of an impending attack. Throughout 1917 and 1918, the British used this as part of the deception template to convince the Germans that an attack was building in a particular sector. This actually chimed with the next maxim, the *Law of Small Numbers*. Provided that the intelligence was particularly sensitive, only a small sample was needed to deceive. The intelligence that related to the presence of tanks on the Western Front, fitted this principle perfectly. The British used low numbers of tanks, both dummies and real models to mislead German defenders. This was done effectively at Cambrai (1917) and throughout the Final Hundred Days. As the Canadians stated 'the British did not hesitate whenever possible to deploy fakes.'[2] The slightest indication of the presence of tanks, both real and imaginary, led the Germans to exaggerate the size of the threat they faced.[3]

The *Cry-Wolf* maxim challenges Magruder's Principle as the most important to the British Army in the First World War. Throughout this document, it has been referred to as *Behaviour Modification*. The US Army described how 'repeated false alarms ... have historically contributed to surprise [by] de-sensitizing an enemy before an attack.'

Jones' Dilemma, the next maxim, holds that the greater the number of conduits for disinformation the more likely that the deception would be effective. Provided that the plausibility, consistency and predictability criteria were maintained, the enemy's OODA Loops would arrive at the desired conclusion. This was perfectly demonstrated at Gaza (1917) with the 'Haversack Ruse' where Allenby and Meinertzhagen used every possible means of generating intelligence to fool the Turks. There is however a risk in this approach in that the more channels that are used the greater the level of discipline required. Haig and the army commanders on the Western Front imposed this discipline top–down and of course employed a strict need–to–know principle (the *Monkey's Paw* maxim) so that the lower units actually generated 'real' intelligence even when they were unknowingly part of the deception plan.

'*A Choice Among Types of Deception*' was the term given to the maxim that it was good to reduce uncertainty in an enemy's mind, by making him not 'less certain of the truth but more certain of a particular falsehood'. This maxim works strongly in conjunction with Magruder's Principle but to be effective the target of the deception must be identified from the start. The best example is probably the targeting of von Falkenhayn rather than the individual German army commanders on the Somme in 1916.

The *Sequencing Rule* was used to maintain the deception for as long as possible by initiating activities over a period of time. There were examples of this during the landings at Suvla Bay in 1915 and at Loos (1915) where deceptions were co-ordinated to maintain the deception for a period of time on day zero. Further, Haig maintained pressure on the Germans from July to November 1916 by ordering the Third, First and Second Armies to initiate large numbers of demonstrations and feint attacks to prevent German reinforcements being transferred to oppose the British Fourth Army.

To Haig and his generals, the MI study would have been a document that was stating the obvious! The approach of the British Army in the First World War is summed up in the thinking of the modern British Army. When discussing offensive operations, 'An active deception plan should be implemented … considerable effort will be needed to distract and fix the enemy so that when he does realise genuine intentions, he cannot respond effectively.'[4] The document quotes from a paper by Whaley: 'The ultimate goal of stratagem is to make the enemy quite certain, very decisive and wrong.'[5]

The British Army's higher command understood that camouflage was not the answer to the problems, particularly on the Western Front. This was summed up in the army manual SS206, 'The Principle and Practice of Camouflage', published in March 1918: 'Deception, not concealment, is the object of camouflage.' The concealment of military artefacts was not an end in itself but a means to an end and that the outlay in men and manpower could not simply be justified in the act of concealment but it could be justified in the act of deception. This was had been understood by Baden-Powell at Mafeking in 1900 and by the Japanese Army fighting against the Russians (1904–05).

The critical question still remains, were deception plans as practised during the First World War effective and did they make a difference? There were some operations where without deception, the outcome would have certainly been less favourable for the British. At Gallipoli (1915), Gaza (1917), Amiens (1918) and Megiddo (1918), the deception plan was the key to the operational plan.

Apart from the four well-known examples, did deception make an effective contribution elsewhere? The answer in 1915 and 1916 is that it did but did not necessarily affect the outcome of the overall battle. There were examples of local deception plans, particularly based on Behaviour

Modification, being effective, for example at The Bluff and Mount Sorrel in 1916, where German defences were taken by surprise. At Hooge in August 1915, deception confused the defences, which meant that the 9 August attack was successful. But in the remainder of instances, deception managed to confuse German defences and tie down troops to particular sectors but with the inevitable exposure of the deceit after a number of hours and the inability of the attacking troops to consolidate positions and resist counterattacks, the Germans were able to transfer reinforcements to repel attackers. On the Somme throughout 1916, the Third, First and Second Armies did maintain threats within their sectors to prevent the Germans transferring troops to the Fourth Army front. Although these measures were largely successful, any weakening in the German defences was not really decisively exploited.

However in 1918, after Amiens, Haig was able to change tactics and employ the Fourth, Third, First, Fifth and Second Armies in real concurrent offensive operations, which prevented the transference of German reinforcements up and down the line. Army commanders now employed deception on their own fronts, with Horne of the First Army probably leading the way. Because the whole dynamic between attackers and defenders had changed during the Final Hundred Days, any advantage generated by deception could now actually be used by the offensive operations. The individual army commanders persisted with the implementation of deception plans as each would now be the direct beneficiaries of their own plans. It is hoped that this book has shown the direct relevance of Sun Tzu's advice to British deception planning in the First World War and I leave the last word to the mysterious strategist:

> When we are near, we must make the enemy believe we are far away. When far away, we must make him believe we are near …
> Numerical weakness comes from having to prepare against possible attacks; numerical strength, from compelling our adversary to make these preparations against us …
> Thus one who is skilful at keeping the enemy on the move, maintains deceitful appearances, according to which the enemy will act …

And remember,

> All warfare is based on deception.

End Notes

Throughout this book the army units are named thus – First Army, I Corps, 1st Division and 1 Brigade

Introduction

1. Boyd never wrote a book and only described his theory in a short essay and a multitude of slide presentations, the majority of which are freely available on the Internet. For instance, www.d-n-i.net carries the original documents as well as newly created versions.
2. Battlefield Deception (FM 90-2, Headquarters Department of Army, Washington DC, 3 October 1988). The document is available on the Federation of American Scientists web site (www.fas.org)
3. The relevance of Magruder's Principle is discussed in detail in Chapter 10. It states that all deception plans should reinforce an enemy's existing belief rather than trying to change that belief and create a new one.
4. French, D., *Failures of Intelligence in Strategy and Intelligence. British Policy During the First World War.* Dockrill, M. and French, D. (eds.), (London: The Hambledon Press, 1994) p.67
5. Latimer, J., *Deception in War*, pp.31-35
6. Centre for First World War Studies (www.firstworldwar.bham.ac.uk)
7. Jukes, G., *The Russo-Japanese War 1904-1905*, p.91
8. Jukes, G., *The Russo-Japanese War 1904-1905*, pp.32-33
9. Bluett, A., *With Our Army in Palestine*, p.67
10. Barrett, A.W., 'Lessons to be Learnt by Regimental Officers from the Russo-Japanese War,' *Journal of the Royal United Services Institute* 52 (part 2), 1907, pp.797-823

11. Estler, E.D., 'Tactical Deception in Today's Army', *Military Intelligence,* 9 (Oct-Dec 1983), pp.24-27

12. Fuller, J.F.C., 'The Tactics of Penetration. A Counterblast to German Numerical Superiority', *Journal of the Royal United Services Institute,* 59 (2) 1914, pp. 378-89

13. Haldane, R.B., *Before the War,* pp.177-224

14. Handel, M.I., *Masters of War: Classical Strategic Thought,* p.161

15. Godson, R. and James J. Wirtz. *Strategic Denial and Deception,* p.98

16. Charters, D. and Tugnell, M., *Deception Operations: Studies in the East West Context,* p.197

17. Occleshaw, M., *Armour Against Fate,* pp.125-27

18. Downham, P. (ed.), *Diary of an Old Contemptible,* pp.132-33

19. War Diary 6/East Lancashire Regiment (13th Division) from 1.12.15 to 31.12.15 (WO/95/4302)

Chapter 1. The No-Man's-Land Conundrum

1. Addison, G.H., *Work of R.E. in the European War, 1914-19. Camouflage Service* (1926) (reprinted by Naval & Military Press, 2006)

2. War Office, *Manual of Field Works (All Arms)* 1921 (Provisional) (London: HMSO, 1921)

3. Edmonds, J.E., *History of the Great War 1915 Vol. II,* p.187

4. Addison, G.H., *Work of the R.E. in the European War,* p.126

5. War Office, *Manual of Field Works (All Arms) Chapter IX Camouflage* (London: HMSO, 1921), pp.93-103 (reprinted by The Naval and Military Press, 2003)

6. War Office, *Manual of Field Works,* p.95

7. Edmonds, J.E., *History of the Great War 1918 Vol. IV,* pp.431-32

Chapter 2. Tools of the Trade

1. Nicholson, G.W.L., *Official History of the Canadian Army in the First World War,* pp.363-65

2. General Sir Alexander John Godley was appointed GOC ANZAC Corps, 25 November 1915.

3. Aspinall-Oglander, C.F., *History of the Great War. Gallipoli Vol. II,* pp.440-60

4. Edmonds, J.E. *History of the Great War 1915 Vol. II,* p.173

5. Bailey, J., 'British Artillery in the Great War', in P. Griffith, ed., *British Fighting Methods in the Great War* (London: Frank Cass, 1998), pp.23-49

6. Edmonds, J.E., *History of the Great War 1915 Vol. II,* p.167

7. Wavell, A.P., *The Good Soldier* (London, Macmillan and Colt., 1948), p.157

8. Daniel, D.C. and. Herbig, K.L (eds.), *Strategic Military Deception* (Oxford, Pergamon, 1982), pp.5-7

Chapter 3. The Western Front 1914: Local Necessities

1. Haldane, R.B., *Before the War,* pp.177-224

2. The use of the ruse based on the command, 'retire!' by the Germans was a specific problem for the British throughout the war. This was so serious that it was dealt with in the manual SS135 which indicated that the British would use the command 'Withdraw!' together with the name of the officer giving the order.

3. Edmonds J.E., *History of the Great War 1914 Vol. II*, pp.456-57.

4. The British Army which had gone to France starting on 12 August 1914 had consisted of two corps (I and II Corps). It was joined by the III Corps (31 August) and the IV Corps (throughout October).

5. Occleshaw, M., *Armour Against Fate*, pp.115-17

Chapter 4. The Western Front 1915: Laying the Foundations

1. Demonstrations were simulated infantry attacks whereby the infantry engaged in all the normal pre-attack activities but they usually remained in their trenches. At 'zero hour', there would be a great deal of commotion in the trenches, bayonets would be fixed and there was cheering and whistle blowing and rapid rifle fire, all of which were designed to distract the Germans from the real attack in an adjacent sector. The demonstrations would usually be accompanied by a machine gun barrage and an artillery bombardment which would include smoke shells, to simulate gas, and cause general uncertainty across No-Man's-Land where visibility would be significantly reduced. In some instances the troops were issued with head-and-shoulder silhouettes which would be raised and lowered to make it appear that troops were climbing over the parapet. Depending on the officers involved, there were instances when the troops did momentarily leave their trenches to add another level of authenticity to the demonstrations before crawling back to the own lines. If the demonstration was successful, the troops could expect to attract the attention of the German artillery.

2. The use of feigned retreats, which lured enemies from their strong defensive positions, and the employment of dummies on horseback to deceive enemies regarding numbers, were favourite tactics used by Genghis Khan in the thirteenth century. It has been speculated that the use of these tactics could be the origin of the phrase 'Chinese Attack', a term used extensively throughout the First World War to describe a fake attack, something that consistently featured in British Army operations. There are other suggestions for the origin of this term.

3. In the normal quiet periods within the trenches, bayonets remained sheathed as the exposed weapons would have been dangerous in the confines of the cramped trenches. However, immediately prior to any infantry attack, the soldiers were ordered to fix bayonets. As the soldiers readied themselves to go 'over the top', their bayoneted rifles were, for safety reasons, held vertically. At this point, the bayonets became clearly visible above the level of the trench. Hence as a deception measure, simply fixing bayonets would alert the enemy sentries to a forthcoming attack and the alarm would be sounded for the troops to emerge from their dugout to man their fire-steps. At this point, they would be targeted by machine gun and artillery shrapnel barrages. This simple

ruse was a favourite of the British and was used to support a large number of demonstrations, feint attacks and Chinese Attacks.

4. Edmonds, J., *History of the Great War 1915 Vol. II*, pp.30-32

5. The British Third Army had been formed on 13 July 1915 and was commanded initially by General Sir Charles Monro. On 25 October 1915, Monro took over as Commander-in-Chief of the Egyptian Expeditionary Force on the Gallipoli peninsula. The Third Army was taken by General Sir Edmund Allenby.

6. Barrett, A.W., 'Lessons to be Learnt by Regimental Officers from the Russo-Japanese War,' *Journal of the Royal United Services Institute* 52 (part 2) 1907 pp.797-823

Chapter 5. The Western Front 1916: The Reality of Deception

1. *United States Army Military Intelligence Battlefield Deception* (FM 90-2) 1988 Chapter 1.

2. Tethered balloons were anchored behind the lines and were raised as observational platforms, from where observers would relay messages back to the ground crew. The observers would map enemy trenches and spy on the back areas for any military activity, particularly the build-up of troops and materials. As a consequence, the balloons attracted machine gun and rifle fire and the attentions of enemy aircraft. Through the 'excessive' use of these balloons in the targeted sectors, the Germans created concern amongst the British and French Armies that their defences were being analysed as the prelude to a major attack.

3. Nicholson, G.W.L., *Official History of the Canadian Army*, pp.144-5

4. Edmonds, J.E., *History of the Great War 1916 Vol. I*, pp.309-10

5. Edmonds, J.E., *History of the Great War. 1916 Vol. I* pp.459-60

6. Hills, J. D., *The Fifth Leicestershire*, p.53

7. Occleshaw, M., *Armour Against Fate*, pp.125-27

8. Haig, D., *Sir Douglas Haig's 2nd Despatch (Somme), 23 December 1916*. It appeared in the *London Gazette* Supplement 29 December 1916

9. Haig's view on the subsidiary nature of these attacks is at odds with that of the Official History, which indicated that these attacks were expected to capture significant German objectives and not simply distract the enemy. Edmonds, J.E., *History of the Great War 1916 Vol. I*, pp.425-6

10. These dummy figures were head and shoulder silhouettes which the infantry, from the relative safety of their trenches, raised over the parapets to simulate infantry leaving their trenches. Amidst smoke, dust and machine gun and artillery barrages, these silhouettes would have appeared to be fairly realistic given that the time to observe them would have been minimal. How convinced the Germans would have been by such a display could be measured by the level of artillery bombardment that was attracted.

11. Duffy, C., *Through German Eyes*, p.58

12. Marden, Thomas Owen, *A Short History of the 6th Division*, pp.14-17

13. Occleshaw, M., *Armour Against Fate*, p.128

14. Duffy, C., *Through German Eyes*, p.253

15. Miles, W., *History of the Great War. 1916 Vol. II*, pp.551-79

Chapter 6. The Western Front 1917:
Reaping the Rewards

1. Williams J., *Byng of Vimy*, p.144

2. Williams J., *Byng of Vimy*, p.154

3. The High Explosive (HE) bombardment was designed to destroy enemy defences through sheer explosive power. The HE shells which burst after burial in the ground created a lethal 360 degree effect around the point of impact together with a large shell hole. This meant that the German defender behind the front line and British soldier in front of the German line were equally at risk unless under cover. However, the shrapnel shell used in the barrage to support infantry attacks was completely different. The shrapnel shell was designed to burst immediately on contact with ground, which became more of a regular occurrence with the introduction of the 106 fuse. The shrapnel shell was available for a variety of guns and, for instance, the 3" field gun fired a shell containing 270 half-inch metal balls through the air that were destructive to intact barbed wire (to some extent) and human bodies alike! However, unlike the HE shell, the majority of the blast was forward in the same direction as the travel of the shell. This meant that British soldiers could follow the barrage closely ('lean on the barrage') and, provided that they remained behind the fall of the shell, they were relatively 'safe'.

4. Williams J., *Byng of Vimy*, p.156

5. Haig, D., *Sir Douglas Haig's 4th Despatch (1917 Campaigns), 25 December 1917*

6. Hills, J.D., *The Fifth Leicestershire*, p.72

7. Addision, G.H., *Work of R.E. in the European War*, p.127

8. Miles, W., *History of the Great War 1917*, p.36

9. Mitchell, F., *Tank Warfare*, pp.138-9

10. Marden, T.O. *A Short History of the 6th Division*, pp.22-25

11. Miles, W., *History of the Great War. 1917 Vol. III*, pp.306-09

12. A fougasse is an improvised weapon buried in the ground and loaded with explosive, spent shell cases and other metal debris. It is detonated remotely and sends the shrapnel upwards. It is ideal for concealing in positions that are likely to become occupied by the enemy. At Cambrai it was used as an improvised device to distract the German defenders. The Bangalore Torpedo, a conventional weapon, consisted of a number of threaded pipes joined together, the end one of which contained explosive. The tubes were pushed forward from concealed positions and through barbed wire defences where once detonated a path would be cleared. This type of action at Cambrai would have created the impression that paths were being cleared through the German barbed wire as the prelude to an infantry attack.

13. Brosnan, M.J., *The Tactical Development of the 56th (London) Division on the Western Front, 1916-18*. Thesis September 2005, Centre for First world War Studies, University of Birmingham (Thesis available online at www.firstworldwar.bham.ac.uk)

14. The German Second Army (GOC, von der Marwitz) was part of Crown Prince Rupprecht's Group of Armies.

Chapter 7. The Western Front 1918: The Learning Curves Coincide

1. Hartcup, G., *Camouflage. A History of Concealment and Deception in War,* p.31

2. Nicholson, G.W.L., *Official History of the Canadian Army in the First World War,* p.341.

3. Bean, C.E.W., Official History of Australia in the War of 1914-1918. Vol. V, p. 108

4. Hartcup, G. *Camouflage. A History of Concealment and Deception in War,* p.23

5. The British Fifth Army had been destroyed as an effective fighting unit by the German Spring Offensives and General Sir Hubert Gough was relieved of his command on 27 March 1918. He was replaced by General Sir Henry Rawlinson who brought his staff with him and the command was renamed the Fourth Army. The 18th (Eastern) and 58th (2/1st London) Divisions, remnants of the decimated Fifth Army, were reinforced with fresh troops, while the 47th (2nd London) Division was transferred to the Fourth Army together with the four divisions of the Australian Corps. Before Amiens they would be joined by the Canadian Corps. On 13 November 1917, General Sir Herbert Plumer had transferred to the Italian theatre together with five divisions and the original Second Army and front had been taken over by Rawlinson and the force was renamed the Fourth Army. On 17 March 1918, Plumer's force had returned from Italy and after resuming their original positions around Ypres, had been renamed the British Second Army. As a consequence, Rawlinson was given a variety of posts including the British Permanent Military Representative to the Supreme War Council before taking command of the new Fourth Army. A new Fifth Army was reconstituted on 23 May 1918 under the command of General Sir William Birdwood and took over the front north of Arras.

6. The attack involved two companies of 131st and 132nd Infantry Regiments of the 33rd American Division. Despite Pershing's objections, the local American commanders took the decision to engage their troops in combat.

7. Lynch, E.P.F., (Davies, W. ed.) *Somme Mud,* pp.242

8. Bean, C.E.W., *Official History of Australia in the War of 1914-1918. Vol. VI,* p.274

9. Nicholson, G.W.L., *The Official History of the Canadian Army,* p.363-6

10. Bean, C.E.W., *Official History of Australia in the War of 1914-1918. Vol. V,* p.480

11. Blaxland, G., *Amiens 1918* (London: Frederick Muller, 1968), pp.160-2

12. Edmonds, J.E., *History of the Great War 1918* Vol. IV, p.32

13. Edmonds, J.E., *History of the Great War 1918* Vol. VI, p. 21

14. Edmonds, J.E., *History of the Great War 1918* Vol. IV, p.20

15. Pitt, B. *1918. The Last Act* (Barnsley: Pen & Sword Military Classics, 2003), pp.195-6

16. Terraine, J., 'Passchendaele and Amiens', *Journal of the the Royal United Service Institute,* 104 (1959), pp.331-340

17. Mitchell, F., *Tank Warfare,* p.226

18. Mitchell, F., *Tank Warfare,* p.226

19. Nicholson, G.W.L., *The Official History of the Canadian Army,* pp.363-5

20. Mitchell, F., *Tank Warfare,* pp.215-8

21. Mitchell, F., *Tank Warfare,* pp.218

22. Nicholson, G.W.L., *Official History of the Canadian Army,* pp.363-5

23. Edmonds, J.E., *History of the Great War 1918* Vol. IV, p.17

24. Mitchell, F., *Tank Warfare*, p.227

25. Blaxland, G., *Amiens 1918* (London: Frederick Muller, 1968), pp.160-62

26. Edmonds, J.E., *History of the Great War 1918 Vol. IV*, p.21

27. The German front line troops opposite Amiens had heard the tank noises and reported this to their commanders. However their reports were not accepted and Ludendorff attributed them to 'phantoms of the imagination or nervousness.' ('Die Katastrophe des 8 August 1918,' Die Schlachten des Weltkreiges, Vol 36, pp.17-20)

28. Edmonds, J.E., *History of the Great War 1918* Vol. IV, p. 37

29. Edmonds, J.E., *History of the Great War 1918* Vol. IV, p.514

30. Edmonds, J.E., *History of the Great War 1918* Vol. IV, p.19

31. Nicholson, G.W.L., *Official History of the Canadian Army*, pp.363-5

32. Fletcher, D., *The British Tank 1915-19* (Marlborough: The Crowood Press, 2001), p.154

33. *Bulletin for Field Officers*. No.6, 9 November 1918. (The documents are available online from Army Command & General Staff College, Combined Arms Research Library, Fort Leavenworth.)

34. www.cmhg.gc.ca/cmh/en/page_734.asp (Government of Canada website)

35. Oldham, P., *Battleground Europe. The Hindenburg Line* (Barnsley: Leo Cooper, 2000), p.85

36. Farr, D., The Silent General, pp.209-210

37. Sheffield, G., *Forgotten Victory. The First World War Myths and Realities* (London: Headline Book Publishing, 2001), p.206

38. Edmonds, J.E., *History of the Great War 1918* Vol. IV, p.513

39. Edmonds, J.E., *History of the Great War 1918* Vol. V, p.129

40. Priestley, R.E., *Breaking the Hindenburg Line. The Story of the 46th (North Midland) Division* (London: Fisher Unwin, 1919), p.42

41. Weetman, W.C.C., *The Sherwood Foresters in the Great War 1914-1919. History of the 1/8th Battalion*. (Nottingham: Thomas Forman & Sons, 1920) (Available from The Project Gutenberg, 2007), p.127

42. Edmonds, J.E., *History of the Great War 1918* Vol. V, p.313

43. Priestley, R.E., *Breaking the Hindenburg Line. The Story of the 46th (North Midland) Division* (London: Fisher Unwin, 1919), p.135

44. Mitchell, F., *Tank Warfare*, pp.266-70

45. Mitchell, F., *Tank Warfare*, pp.269-70

46. This is supported by German documentation which was captured, translated and published by the American Expeditionary Force (AEF). The documents are available from Army Command & General Staff College, Combined Arms Research Library, Fort Leavenworth. *Bulletin for Field Officers*. No.6, 9 November 1918

Chapter 8. 1915-1918: Other Theatres, Similar Stories

1. Downham, P., (ed.), *Diary of an Old Contemptible*, p.210

2. Anderson, R., *The Forgotten Front. The East Africa Campaign* (Stroud: Tempus Publishing Ltd., 2004), p.76

3. Hamilton, I., (General Sir), *Gallipoli Diary Volume I* (New York: George H Doran, 1920), p.40 (available from The Project Gutenberg)

4. Moorhead, A., *Gallipoli* (Ware: Wordsworth Military Library, 1997), p. 109

5. Downham, P. (ed.), *Diary of an Old Contemptible*, pp.132-33

6. War Diary 6/East Lancashire Regiment (13th Division) from 1.12.15 to 31.12.15 (WO/95/4302)

7. Bluett, A., *With Our Army in Palestine*, p.56

8. Morrison, F. L., *The Fifth Battalion Highland Light Infantry in the War 1914-1918*, p. 75

9. Luxford, J.H., *With the Machine Gunners in France and Palestine*, p. 205

10. Bluett, A., *With Our Army in Palestine*, p.68

11. Falls, C., *History of the Great War. Egypt and Palestine Vol. II*, p.32

12. Occleshaw, M., *Armour Against Fate*, pp.115-17

13. Lawrence, T. E., *Seven Pillars of Wisdom*, p. 384

14. Lloyd, *The Art of Military Deception*, pp.15-17

15. Falls, C., *History of the Great War. Egypt and Palestine Vol. II*, p.31-32

16. Latimer, J., *Deception in War*, pp.92-94

17. Occleshaw, *Armour Against Fate*, pp.129-31

18. Lloyd, *The Art of Military Deception*, pp.15-17

19. Falls, C. *History of the Great War. Egypt and Palestine Vol. II*, p.30

20. Cave Brown, A., *Bodyguard of Lies* (New York: Harper & Row, 1975), pp.280-82

21. Different sources often differ in the spelling of place names throughout Palestine, as do the modern names. Some places have 'disappeared' – for instance the town of Jaffa is now a suburb of Tel Aviv, having been merged with it in 1950.

22. Luxford, J.H., *With the Machine Gunners in France and Palestine*, p. 205

23. Bluett, A., *With Our Army in Palestine*, p.70

24. Powles, C.G., *The History of the Canterbury Mounted Rifles 1914-1919*, p.168

25. Gullett, H.S., *The Official History of Australia in the War of 1914-1918 Vol. VII*, p.348

26. Powles, C.G., *The History of the Canterbury Mounted Rifles 1914-1919*, p.166

27. Anon, *Through Palestine with the 20th Machine Gun Squadron*, p.12

28. Anon. *Through Palestine with the 20th Machine Gun Squadron*, p.14

29. Wavell, A.P., *The Palestine Campaigns*, pp.124-25

30. Occleshaw, M., *Armour Against Fate*, pp.129-31

31. Occleshaw, *Armour Against Fate*, pp.129-31.

32. Lawrence, T. E., *Seven Pillars of Wisdom*, p. 385

33. Raugh, H.E., 'The Haversack Ruse', *Military Intelligence*, 10 (Jan-Mar 1984), pp.11-14

34. Known by the British as the Battle of Megiddo, it has also been referred to as the Battle of Armageddon or the Battle of Nablus Plain.

35. Lawrence, T. E., *Seven Pillars of Wisdom*, p.537

36. The Sherifian Army was originally the officers and soldiers from within the Turkish Army who supported the revolt by the Arabs lead by Sherif Hussein ibn Ali, beginning at Mecca in June 1916.

37. Colonel Richard Meinertzhagen had left Palestine and he first moved to the War Office in London followed by a period in the intelligence branch at GHQ on the Western Front where his attempt to get close to battle left him severely

wounded. He subsequently attended the Paris Peace Conference at Versailles in 1919.

38. Occleshaw, M., *Armour Against Fate*, p.133
39. Falls, C., *History of the Great War. Egypt and Palestine* Vol. II, pp. 461-7
40. Dewar, M., *The Art of Deception in Warfare*, pp.41-2
41. Hartcup, G., *Camouflage. A History of Concealment and Deception in War*, p.33
42. Occleshaw, M., *Armour Against Fate*, p.133
43. Lloyd, *The Art of Military Deception*, p.17
44. Gullett, H.S., *Official History of Australia in the War of 1914-1918,* Vol. VII, p.686
45. Falls, C., *History of the Great War. Egypt and Palestine* Vol. II, pp. 461-7
46. Wavell, A.P., *The Palestine Campaigns,* pp. 200-10
47. Falls, C., *History of the Great War. Egypt and Palestine* Vol. II, pp. 461-7
48. After the war, General Sir Edmund Allenby took the title First Viscount Allenby of Megiddo in honour of this battle.

Chapter 9. Deception, GHQ and the Army Commanders

1. The phrase was used as the title for Alan Clark's book *The Donkeys*. Clark attributed the phrase to a conversion between General Erich von Ludendorff and General Max Hoffman in which Ludendorff comments that the English soldiers fight like lions. To which Hoffman is said to have agreed and added that by common knowledge that they were lions led by donkeys.
2. Neillands, R., *The Death of Glory. The Western Front 1915* (London: John Murray, 2006), pp.268-69
3. If the frontage at Neuve Chapelle is analysed further it shows that the actual attack front was 2,000 yards while the apparent attack front was 52,950 yards (30 miles). Although the British were not signalling attacks across the whole of the 30 miles, they were signalling a number of discrete operations over that distance. This would be more plausible as the Germans knew that in 1915 especially the British could not have mounted such an operation. However this still posed a problem for the Germans with respect to the deployment of reserves and artillery as the apparent front was 26 times greater than the actual front. This becomes an intelligence game and the deception plan needs to be as perfect as possible to prevent the enemy being able to eliminate certain sectors.
4. Ferris, John (ed.) *The British Army and Signal Intelligence during the First World War,* p.18
5. Haig, D., Final Despatch dated 21 March 1919, printed in the Supplement to the *London Gazette,* 8 April 1919
6. Edmonds, J.E. and Wynne, C.G., *History of the War. France and Belgium 1915* Vol. I, pp.382-3
7. Edmonds, J.E., and Wynne, C.G., *History of the War. France and Belgium 1915* Vol. I, p.77
8. Edmonds, J. E., *History of the Great War. Military Operations France and Belgium, 1918* Vol. III Appendix XX Memorandum by General Foch Read at the Conference held by the Commanders-in-Chief of the Allied Armies 24 July 1918. pp.367-70
9. Ferris, John (ed.), *The British Army and Signal Intelligence during the First World War,* p.173

10. Lloyd George, D., *War Memoirs,* p.2014
11. Lloyd George, D., *War Memoirs,* p.890
12. Lloyd George, D., *War Memoirs,* p.1302
13. Lloyd George, D., *War Memoirs,* pp.1704-05
14. Bean, C.E.W., *Official History of Australia in the War of 1914-1918. Vol. VI,* p.480

Chapter 10. The Effectiveness of Deception

1. Battlefield Deception (FM 90-2) Chapter 1
2. www.cmhg.gc.ca/cmh/en/page_734.asp (Government of Canada website)
3. Edmonds, J.E., *History of the Great War 1918* Vol. IV, p.513
4. *Army Doctrine Publication Volume 1 Operations* (DGD&D/18/34/46) June 1994, p.88
5. *Army Doctrine Publication Volume 1 Operations* (DGD&D/18/34/46) June 1994 p.95. The document quotes from a paper by Barton Whaley 'Stratagem: Deception and Surprise in War' from the Center for International Studies, Massachusetts Institute of Technology, 1969

Bibliography

Addison, G.H. *Work of R.E. in the European War, 1914-19. Camouflage Service* (1926) (reprinted by Naval & Military Press, 2006)

Anderson, R. *The Forgotten Front. The East Africa Campaign* (Stroud: Tempus Publishing Ltd., 2004)

Anon. *Through Palestine with the 20th Machine Gun Squadron*, (London: Baxter, 1920) (available from The Project Gutenberg, www.gutenberg.org, 2005)

Aspinall-Oglander, C.F. *History of the Great War. Military Operations Gallipoli Vol. II May 1915 to the Evacuation* (London: William Hienemann, 1932)

Battlefield Deception (FM 90-2) United States Army, Military Intelligence, October 1988. (available on-line at Federation of American Scientists, www.fas.org)

Bean, C.E.W. *Official History of Australia in the War of 1914-1918. Vol. V. The Australian Imperial Force in France during the Main German Offensive, 1918 (Eighth Edition, 1941)* (Sydney: Angus & Robertson, 1941), (Available at the Australian War Memorial website, www.awm.gov.au)

Bean, C.E.W. *Official History of Australia in the War of 1914-1918. Vol. VI. The Australian Imperial Force in France during the Allied Offensive, 1918 (First Edition, 1942)* (Sydney: Angus & Robertson, 1942), (Available at the Australian War Memorial website, www.awm.gov.au)

Bluett, Anthony, *With Our Army in Palestine* (London: Andrew Melrose, 1919) (available from The Project Gutenberg, www.gutenberg.org, 2006)

Bulletin for Field Officers. No.6, 9 November 1918. (The documents are available on-line from Army Command & General Staff College, Combined Arms Research Library, Fort Leavenworth, www.cgsc.leavenworth.army.mil/carl/contentdm/home.htm).

Cave Brown, A. *Bodyguard of Lies* (New York: Harper & Row, 1975)

Charters, D. and Tugnell, M. *Deception Operations: Studies in the East West Context.* (London: Brassey's, 1990)

Clausewitz von, C. *On War [Vom Kriege]* Translated by Colonel J.J. Graham (London: N. Trüber, 1873) (available on-line at The Clausewitz Homepage, www.clausewitz.com/CWZHOME/VomKriege2/ONWARTOC2.HTML)

Downham, Peter (ed.) *Diary of an Old Contemptible. From Mons to Baghdad 1914-1919* (Barnsley: Pen & Sword, 2004). [Diary of Private Edward Roe, 1/East Lancashire Regiment]

Dewar, M. *The Art of Deception in Warfare* (Newton Abbot: David and Charles, 1989)

Duffy, C. *Through German Eyes. The British and the Somme 1916* (London: Orion Books, 2006)

Edmonds, J.E. *History of the Great War. Military Operations France and Belgium, 1914 Vol. II. Antwerp, La Bassée, Armentières, Messine, and Ypres, October-November 1914* (London: Macmillan & Co., 1925)

Edmonds, J.E. and Wynne, C.G. *History of the War. France and Belgium 1915* Vol. I (London: Macmillan & Co. Ltd., 1927)

Edmonds, J.E. *History of the Great War Military Operations France and Belgium, 1915 Vol. II. Battle of Aubers Ridge, Festubert and Loos* (London: Macmillan & Co., 1928)

Edmonds, J. E. *History of the War. Military Operations France and Belgium 1916* Vol. I (London: Macmillan & Co. Ltd., 1932)

Edmonds, J. E. *History of the Great War. Military Operations France and Belgium, 1918* Vol. III. *May-July: the German Diversion Offensives and the First Allied Counter-offensive* (London: Macmillan & Co., 1939)

Edmonds, J.E., *History of the Great War. Military Operations France and Belgium, 1918* Vol. IV. *August 8-September 26. Franco-English Offensive* (London: Macmillan & Co., 1947)

Edmonds, J.E. *History of the Great War. Military Operations France and Belgium 1918* Vol. V. *September 26-November 11: The Advance to Victory* (London HMSO, 1949)

Falls, C. *History of the Great War. Egypt and Palestine Vol. II. From June 1917 to the end of the war* (London: HMSO, 1930)

Farr, D. *The Silent General. Horne of the First Army. A Biography of Haig's Trusted Great War Comrade-in-Arms* (Sollihull: Helion, 2007)

Ferris, John (ed.) *The British Army and Signal Intelligence during the First World War* (Stroud: Alan Sutton, 1992) (Printed for the Army Records Society)

Godson, R. and Wirtz, James J. *Strategic Denial and Deception: The Twenty-First Century Challenge* (Piscataway: Transaction Publishers, 2002)

Gullett, H.S. *Official History of Australia in the War of 1914-1918, Volume VII The Australian Imperial Force in Sinai and Palestine* (Sydney, Angus and Robertson, 1941) (Available at The Australian War memorial website, www.awm.gov.au)

Haldane, R.B. *Before the War* (London: Funk and Wagnalls, 1920)

Handel, M.I. *Masters of War: Classical Strategic Thought* (London & New York: Routledge, 2001)

Hartcup, G. *Camouflage. A History of Concealment and Deception in War* (Newton Abbot: David and Charles, 1979)

Hills, J. D. *The Fifth Leicestershire. A Record of the 1/5th Battalion, the Leicestershire Regiment, T. F. During the War 1914-1918* (Loughborough: Echo Press, 1919) (Available from The Project Gutenberg, www.gutenberg.org, 2005)

Hughes, M. *Allenby and British Strategy in the Middle East 1917-1919* (London: Frank Cass, 1999)

Jukes, G. *The Russo-Japanese War 1904-1905* (Oxford: Osprey Publishing, 2002)

Latimer, J. *Deception in War* (London: John Murray, 2001)

Lawrence, T. E. *Seven Pillars of Wisdom* (Jonathan Cape: London, 1935)

Lloyd, M. *The Art of Military Deception* (London: Leo Cooper, 1997)

Lloyd George, D. *War Memoirs* (London: Oldhams Press, 1938)

Luxford, J.H. *With the Machine Gunners in France and Palestine. The Official History of the New Zealand Machine Gun Corps in the Great War 1914-1918* (Auckland: Whitcombe and Tombs, 1923) (Available on-line from the New Zealand Electronic Text Centre, www.nzetc.org).

Lynch, E.P.F. *Somme Mud. The Experiences of an Infantryman in France, 1916-1919* (Davies W. ed.) (Sydney: Doubleday, 2008)

Marden, Thomas Owen, *A Short History of the 6th Division* (London: Hugh Rees, 1920) (Available from The Project Gutenberg, www.gutenberg.org, 2006)

Miles, W. *History of the Great War. Military Operations France and Belgium, 1916 Vol. II. 2nd July to the End of the Battles of the Somme* (London: His Majesty's Stationery Office, 1938)

Miles, W. *History of the Great War. Military Operations France and Belgium 1917 Vol. III. The Battle of Cambrai* (London: His Majesty's Stationery Office, 1948)

Mitchell, F. *Tank Warfare. The Story of the Tanks in the Great War* (London: Thomas Nelson & Sons, 1933) (reprinted by Naval & Military Press)

Montagu, Ewen and Cooper, Duff *The Man Who Never Was – Operation Heartbreak* (Stroud: Spellmount, 2006)

Morrison, F. L. *The Fifth Battalion Highland Light Infantry in the War 1914-1918* (Glasgow: MacLehose, Jackson & Co., 1921) (available from The Project Gutenberg, www.gutenberg.org, 2007)

Neillands, R. *The Death of Glory. The Western Front 1915* (London: John Murray, 2006)

Nicholson, G.W.L. *Official History of the Canadian Army in the First World War – Canadian Expeditionary Force, 1914-1919* (Ottawa: Ministry of National Defence, 1964)

Occleshaw, M. *Armour Against Fate. British Military Intelligence in the First World War and the Secret Rescue from Russia of the Grand Duchess Tatiana.* (London: Columbus Books, 1989)

Powles, C.G. *The History of the Canterbury Mounted Rifles 1914-1919* (Auckland: Whitcombe and Tombs, 1928) (Available on-line from the New Zealand Electronic Text Centre, www.nzetc.org).

Priestley, R.E. *Breaking the Hindenburg Line. The Story of the 46th (North Midland) Division* (London: Fisher Unwin, 1919)

Ramsay, D. *'Blinker' Hall: The Man who Brought America into World War I* (Stroud: The History Press, 2008)

Sun Tzu *The Art Of War* (available online through The University of Glasgow website, www.gla.ac.uk/~dc4w/laibach/artofwar.html)

Wavell, A.P. *The Palestine Campaigns* (London: Constable & Co., 1928)

Williams, J. *Byng of Vimy. General and Governor-General* (London: Leo Cooper, 1983)

Index